THIS IS NOT FLORIDA

THIS IS NOT FLORIDA

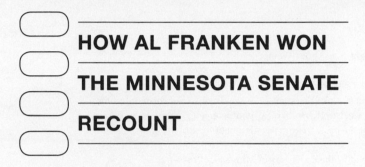

HOW AL FRANKEN WON

THE MINNESOTA SENATE

RECOUNT

JAY WEINER

University of Minnesota Press
Minneapolis
London

Published by the University of Minnesota Press
111 Third Avenue South, Suite 290
Minneapolis, MN 55401-2520
http://www.upress.umn.edu

Library of Congress Cataloging-in-Publication Data

Weiner, Jay, 1954–
  This is not Florida : how Al Franken won the Minnesota Senate recount / Jay Weiner.
     p. cm.
  Includes bibliographical references and index.
  ISBN 978-0-8166-7038-3 (hc : alk. paper)
  1. United States Congress. Senate—Elections, 2008.   2. Elections—Minnesota.   3. Franken, Al.   I. Title.
  JK19682008   S73   2010
  324.9776′054—dc22   2010021772

Printed in the United States of America on acid-free paper

The University of Minnesota is an equal-opportunity educator and employer.

16 15 14 13 12 11 10   10 9 8 7 6 5 4 3 2 1

For Ann

Such a close contest could easily provoke chaos in a less settled society.

—The Washington Post

CONTENTS

HOW I GOT HERE

A few weeks after returning from Beijing, where I covered my seventh Summer Olympic Games, the editors at MinnPost.com, a news Web site in Minneapolis–St. Paul, asked me if I would ever consider covering politics. I had been around Minnesota's political scene off and on for about fifteen years, but it was the strangest of politics—the politics of sports. That encompasses an odd merging of team owners, mayors, governors, legislators, civic boosters, high-priced sports marketing consultants, right-wing "no new taxes" nuts, and left-wing "I hate billionaires" wackos.

My personal brand in the Twin Cities (and a little bit nationally) was as a "smart sportswriter." I specialized in the Olympics, college sports issues, sports business, and stadium finance battles. I hadn't covered traditional games or written stories that most sports fans care about for twenty years, but I was a sportswriter and couldn't deny it. After nearly three decades of doing that, change was the new normal. My cushy, union-protected life at the Minneapolis *Star Tribune,* where I worked for twenty-eight years, was over. In June 2007, I took one of those new-fangled twenty-first-century buyouts, trading years of service for a decent severance package, and joined the growing diaspora of middle-aged journalists jettisoned from the world of crumbling newspapers.

Like a bunch of my former *Star Tribune* colleagues, and some from the equally disintegrating St. Paul *Pioneer Press,* I began working for Minn-Post.com, a "new model" of news on the Internet, a nonprofit enterprise that brought to the online space the relatively high standards of daily local journalism, performed by experienced professionals. MinnPost.com was old school on a new platform.

Preface

By the fall of 2008, MinnPost's writing "staff" of regular freelancers could fit comfortably into a Honda Civic. During the 2008 general election campaign, and especially during the national political conventions, MinnPost showed that it could compete with the local newspapers and other Twin Cities outlets with thoughtful reporting. As Al Franken and Norm Coleman duked it out for the U.S. Senate, I was immersed in preparing to cover the Beijing Olympics for a group of news organizations. I did not follow the campaign at all, not one bit. Not as a voter and not as a reporter. The U.S. Senate campaign was over now, and there was a recount on the horizon.

I had covered Coleman from time to time when he was the mayor of St. Paul. Our relationship was professional but a bit chilly, mostly because I often wrote about the problems with the funding of arenas and my belief that bringing a National Hockey League team back into the Twin Cities and building yet another arena would clutter the sports market and stress other publicly funded facilities. Coleman touted the return of hockey to Minnesota as one of his great achievements.

The last time I saw Coleman was at a fancy downtown Minneapolis restaurant with my family a few years before the 2008 campaign. "Hey," I said to my teenage sons after we had finished dinner, "would you like to meet a U.S. senator?"

"Not really," they said in unison. But, to score points with a man who could, potentially, bail these same sons out of a foreign jail one day, I proactively brought my wife, Ann, and sons, Henry and Nate, over to Coleman to say hello. It was a warm and friendly exchange. I must disclose that for all the times he ran for office in St. Paul and Minnesota, I never voted for Coleman.

As for Franken, I had met him once, months before the 2008 recount, at a meal hosted by an acquaintance of mine to break a Ramadan fast. I didn't know Franken would be there, but it turned into a campaign stop for him. We shook hands. That was that. I was never a *Saturday Night Live* viewer, so I wasn't familiar with his comedy until 1998. He and my wife happened to have been in the same college class, Harvard 1973, but they didn't know each other. I attended their twenty-fifth reunion as an alumna spouse; Franken emceed the class talent show and was fall-down, stomach-aching, nose-running hysterical with his jokes and comments.

That's all I knew about Franken until the night of June 14, 2006, when I attended a banquet of the Society of Professional Journalists in St. Paul, and he was the keynote speaker. He was in the embryonic stages of running for office. That morning the *Pioneer Press* published a wire-service feature about right-wing author Ann Coulter, her latest book, and her use of "outrageousness as a marketing tool." The writer of the piece (not a *Pioneer Press* staffer but someone from Newhouse News Service) listed Franken as someone with the same marketing shtick and described him as, among other things, an "omnipresent blabbermouth." With a couple hundred local journalists, journalism professors, and guests all poised to be entertained, Franken proceeded to take repeated umbrage, in a surprisingly surly way, at the *Pioneer Press* for calling him an "omnipresent blabbermouth." With such thin skin, it didn't seem to me that this famous TV star was ready for political prime time.

Soon after Election Day 2008, MinnPost editors Roger Buoen and Don Effenberger asked that fateful question: "Would you like to help out with the recount?" I figured, "Sure, whatever. Sounds like fun." I had no dog in the fight and, like everyone else who knew absolutely nothing about the process, I thought it would last a few weeks, and then I would move on to something more familiar, like another stadium debate, for which Minnesota was always ripe.

The recount lasted eight months, and I was there for just about every day of it. That's how this book happened.

SOURCES

I began covering the recount on November 12, 2008, and then became immersed in the process until July 7, 2009, when Al Franken was sworn in as U.S. senator. I missed only a few days of the state Canvassing Board's meetings and one day of the election contest trial. I attended almost every media briefing conducted by the two campaigns, their lawyers, and the secretary of state's office during the recount and trial.

During the recount and afterward, I conducted interviews with more than forty key participants, including Franken. Through two intermediaries on four different occasions and in one lengthy letter delivered to his home, I attempted to interview Norm Coleman. He never responded.

Almost all of my interviews occurred face-to-face in Washington, D.C., Seattle, or the Twin Cities. Some were by telephone, and just one was conducted in writing at the request of one of Coleman's lawyers. Most of the interviews were on the record, some of them off the record.

Preface

As part of my arrangements with some of my sources (including Franken's lawyers, who had concerns about his attorney–client privilege), I agreed to review with them direct quotations from our interviews before including them in this book.

The reporting of the Associated Press, Minnesota Public Radio, *Pioneer Press, Star Tribune,* the UpTake, the Minnesota Independent, Talking Points Memo, Daily Kos, and Power Line was invaluable, as were the archived videos at the Web sites of the Minnesota House of Representatives Television Services and Senate Media Services departments.

Of course, any mistakes and omissions are my own.

CAST OF CHARACTERS

NORM COLEMAN Republican U.S. senator from Minnesota, 2003–2009

AL FRANKEN Democratic candidate for senator, winner by 312 votes over Coleman

MARC ELIAS Washington, D.C.–based lawyer and quarterback of Al Franken's recount legal team

KEVIN HAMILTON Seattle-based lawyer and lead trial lawyer for Franken

DAVID LILLEHAUG former Minnesota U.S. attorney, Franken's lead Twin Cities–based lawyer

CHRIS SAUTTER Democratic recount expert and lawyer

STEPHANIE SCHRIOCK Franken's Senate campaign manager and overall "CEO" of recount effort

CULLEN SHEEHAN Norm Coleman's campaign manager

FRITZ KNAAK former Minnesota state senator, lawyer, and spokesman for Coleman during recount

TONY TRIMBLE Minnesota Republican Party lawyer, Coleman recount and trial attorney

JOE FRIEDBERG Twin Cities criminal defense lawyer, Coleman pal, and lead trial attorney

Cast of Characters

JAMES LANGDON   partner in Dorsey & Whitney law firm and member of Coleman's trial team

ROGER MAGNUSON   partner in Dorsey & Whitney law firm, represented Coleman before the Minnesota Supreme Court

BEN GINSBERG   Washington, D.C.–based chief legal spokesman for Coleman during election contest trial

CHARLIE NAUEN   Minneapolis lawyer who represented Franken voters

STATE CANVASSING BOARD   composed of Supreme Court Chief Justice Eric Magnuson, Supreme Court Associate Justice G. Barry Anderson, district court judges Kathleen Gearin and Edward Cleary, and Secretary of State Mark Ritchie

ELECTION CONTEST TRIAL PANEL   district court judges Elizabeth Hayden, Kurt Marben, and Denise Reilly

MINNESOTA SUPREME COURT   associate justices Paul Anderson, Christopher Dietzen, Lorie Gildea, and Helen Meyer and acting Chief Justice Alan Page

PROLOGUE

"Counsel, this is not Florida!"

Roger Magnuson had been here before: attempting to influence the outcome of an election as the entire nation watched. As always, he was confident. One of Minnesota's most sought-after lawyers, with ultra-conservative politics and Stanford, Harvard, and Oxford degrees on his office wall, Magnuson was not used to getting jabbed in the gut or cuffed on the chin. But on December 17, 2008, staggered he would be. The legal punch that nailed Magnuson radiated to his client, incumbent U.S. Senator Norm Coleman. It was a verbal whack from a Minnesota Supreme Court justice, a slap that helped to define and shape the contours of the 2008 U.S. Senate recount between Republican Coleman and challenger Al Franken of Minnesota's uniquely named Democratic-Farmer-Labor Party, or DFL.

Eight years earlier, almost to the day, Magnuson plied his trade during an election recount even more historic than this one. It came to be known simply as *Bush v. Gore*. On December 12, 2000, Magnuson was working in Tallahassee, Florida, representing the Republican Party. He told the Florida Senate that day of its responsibilities to appoint twenty-five electors to join the Electoral College in Washington, D.C. His advice was intended to ensure that a recount was swiftly concluded—shut down, really—so that George W. Bush, and not Al Gore, would become the forty-third president of the United States. Magnuson and his pals won that round.

Now, in St. Paul, with Barack Obama the newly minted president-elect, the stakes were almost as high. Minnesota's U.S. Senate seat, fought for during a nasty, forty-million-dollar campaign by Coleman, the incumbent senator, and Franken was in the balance. So, too, was control of the U.S. Senate. A Franken victory could push the Democrats to a sixty-member, filibuster-proof majority. A teetering economy, the future of two wars, the fate of national health care, and the makeup of the U.S. Supreme Court were on an agenda that either Coleman or Franken would influence. They stood firmly on opposite sides of just about every issue.

When results trickled in from Minnesota's 4,130 precincts after Election Day, November 4, 2008, Coleman led by a razor-thin 215 votes out of nearly three million cast. By state law, a mandatory hand recount was now required. Franken's operatives, organized and prepared for the recount phase, were cautiously optimistic. Based on data and history, they felt the margin would change. By how much, no one knew, but Democrats are simply sloppier voters than Republicans: in 2008, they were especially younger, possibly first-time, and, perhaps, non–English speaking voters. Coleman's team, relying on hubris and the lessons and legal theories of Florida 2000, presumed their candidate would prevail, a level of complacency that invited errors in strategic judgment.

With the Obama campaign promoting a full-fledged absentee-ballot effort, Minnesota's absentee voters more than doubled from the 2006 election and increased by more than 25 percent over the 2004 presidential election. About 294,000 citizens opted to vote via absentee ballots. The demographics of that spike—young, motivated, Obama-leaning— boded well for Franken.

Franken's lawyers wanted to include in the recount more than one thousand absentee ballots that appeared to have been wrongly rejected by local election judges, ballots that seemed to be legal, that looked as if they should have been counted, but for various reasons were not. The Franken lawyers took their case to include those ballots in the recount to the state Canvassing Board, a five-person body that normally rubber stamps results and usually gets as much public scrutiny as the meetings of the state board of barber examiners. In most years, it takes minutes— not months—for the Canvassing Board to complete its duty to approve Minnesota's election results.

As with Bush's lawyers in Florida in 2000, the attorneys working for Coleman sought to halt the counting of any additional votes. When your candidate is ahead, you fight to put an end to newfound votes. Why expand the vote universe when victory is in hand? When your candidate is behind, as was Franken (and Gore), you search under every rock and you slither through every loophole looking for another ballot. "Put points on the board — that's the most important thing in a recount," said one Franken lawyer. A combination of that sort of aggressive lawyering, meticulous data collecting, and constant media messaging by Franken's lawyers and communications staff bombarded the board and the public. After weeks of consideration and some flip-flopping, the Canvassing Board sided with Franken and determined that some absentee ballots that were rejected in the hinterlands should get another look. If a voter followed the law, which clearly defined a legal absentee ballot, then why shouldn't the vote count?

In response, Coleman's side ran to the Minnesota Supreme Court to block the Canvassing Board's decision. This is when Roger Magnuson, of national repute, of the *Bush v. Gore* chops and aristocratic air, arrived on the scene. Oddly, Magnuson was a partner at Minneapolis's Dorsey & Whitney law firm, where former U.S. vice president Walter Mondale, an icon for Minnesota Democrats and opponent to Coleman in the 2002 U.S. Senate race, was a longtime partner and still was senior counsel. Magnuson, however, gladly represented Coleman, the one-time DFL mayor of St. Paul who flipped to the GOP in 1996, became a consistent George W. Bush backer, and was considered a pariah-for-life among Minnesota liberals.

On this cold December day, Magnuson approached the lectern in the middle of courtroom 300 in the Minnesota Judicial Center. His swagger suggested he felt he was on his home court. The five robed Supreme Court justices moved up in their seats, awaiting his well-known turns of phrase and his thoughtful persuasion. Magnuson was a respected personality, and there was real anticipation to hear what he would say. It was as if an entire state leaned forward impatiently waiting for a decision on its second U.S. senator. Five weeks had passed since Election Day, and no one knew if Coleman had retained his seat or if Franken had taken it. No one knew who would control the U.S. Senate in 2009. Five weeks seemed a long time to wait for an election result.

"May it please the Court," Magnuson said crisply, authoritatively. "On December twelfth, the state Canvassing Board, with the best of intentions, accepted an invitation, we believe, to go to Florida . . . And as tempting as that invitation is, given the weather outside the courtroom today . . ."

Before he could attempt another syllable, before he could utter another learned peep, Justice Paul H. Anderson, appointed fourteen years earlier by a Republican governor, barked disdainfully at Magnuson. As much as the gentlemanliness of the courts allowed, Anderson was in Magnuson's face. More than the typical appeals court interruption, Anderson's was a show-stopping, judicial eruption.

"Counsel . . . I know you've been to Florida," Anderson said, his words so loud and emotional that they were distorted by the microphone amplification. The fingers on Anderson's right hand stabbed at the hard wood of his judge's bench. "This is not Florida, and I'm just not terribly receptive to you telling us that we're going to Florida and we're comparing to that. This is Minnesota, we've got a case in Minnesota, argue the case in Minnesota."

Right there, in that tense nutshell, is the most succinct way to explain how the Franken–Coleman recount played itself out in a state noted for its clean politics, its pride in fairness, its need to be liked, and its desire to completely differentiate itself from any *Bush v. Gore* link. Justice Anderson wanted to make sure of that. But there were no "hanging chads" of the 2000 *Bush v. Gore* saga, no attempts by election officials to halt a statewide recount, no partisan judiciary. Every step along the way was televised live, mostly via streamed video on the Internet. Anyone who wanted to watch, anywhere in the world, could. This was Minnesotan to the hilt.

It surely was not a rushed event. The 2000 presidential recount, from Election Day to the U.S. Supreme Court's awarding the office to George W. Bush, took thirty-six days, with an Electoral College deadline pushing the process. The Franken–Coleman recount and legal episodes, from Election Day to Franken's swearing in, took thirty-five *weeks*. If there were any nexus to Florida (besides the reappearance of some *Bush v. Gore* lawyers), it was that Democrats had vowed after their defeat in 2000 to never again stumble on a recount playing field. Gore was altogether too polite in Florida, preferring to stay above the fray. Franken's legal team was not polite. Fray was what they did, making sure that this 2008 recount bore no resemblance to Florida's, not by a long shot.

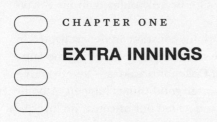

CHAPTER ONE

EXTRA INNINGS

"It's going to be really, really close."

Countless Web sites and CNN were streaming election results on side-by-side screens on his desk. Marc Elias talked rapid-fire with operatives from New Hampshire to Alaska. A tiny Blackberry phone filled his right ear. His six-foot-five frame was hunched over like an elongated question mark as he paced in the Democratic Senatorial Campaign Committee war room in Washington, D.C., a short walk from the U.S. Capitol. A Democratic Party operative shouldn't have been nervous on this Election Night, November 4, 2008, but Elias is just that way.

The Republicans were about to get crushed. For Democrats, it was blossoming into a joyous night across America. Seven hundred miles and a time zone away in Chicago, Barack Obama was poised to emerge as the nation's savior. Elias's partner and mentor, Bob Bauer, one of the pioneers of election law in Washington, D.C., was in Chicago with his client, the next president of the United States. People were clinking champagne glasses, holding hands, and sniffling back tears in living rooms from Aliquippa to Yakima as news spread that Obama was the nation's forty-fourth president. But Elias was in his own zone, pacing, that cell phone an appendage to his ear, CNN's talking heads pontificating and the Web sites flickering with numbers that he constantly refreshed in his obsessive-compulsive way.

Elias is brilliant and well-off, commanding more than five hundred dollars an hour for his time and advice. He simultaneously earned a master's degree in political science and a law degree from Duke. He is happily married to another Duke-trained lawyer with whom he has two

1

children. He has been a political and legal wunderkind, representing high-powered politicians since he was twenty-five years old. He is marginally good looking, although he appeared significantly older than his thirty-nine years on that historic night.

For all of that, he is the insecure sort, his constant anxiety reflected in his childish superstitions: wearing the same clothes, consuming the same foods — chili, hash browns, and a Diet Coke for breakfast — and drinking the same beverages for days on end after good things happen. A bombastic lawyer in court who is never undecided out of court, he loves to schmooze with political journalists on and (mostly) off the record. He is your classic ants-in-your-pants kind of guy, who jiggles change in his pockets and bounces his legs under the table, even as poker-faced judges determine the outcome of his case.

So on Election Night, he wandered back and forth in his small office on the second floor of the Mott House. This war room was one of his two Washington law offices, but this one was his own private heaven. With relatively unadorned white walls, it appeared temporary, which it was not. Its shelves were furnished with dusty three-ring binders filled with scintillating advisory opinions from the Federal Election Commission. A George W. Bush anxiety doll sat on his desk for squeezing. Staring down at Elias was a New York Giants football jersey with the number 20 on it. Atop the number is the name ELIAS, for Keith Elias, a not-very-good running back — a Princeton grad, for gosh sakes — but an Elias who was a Giant nonetheless. Besides the Democratic Party, Marc Elias's other fervency is his beloved Giants, a team for which he commutes a few times a year to New Jersey from his suburban Great Falls, Virginia, home, using the season ticket that his father bought in 1959. In courtrooms Elias uses recesses to jabber about NFL free agency and off-field player crime as much as he does his high-profile case at hand.

Once the mansion of maverick, liberal philanthropist Stewart Mott, the Mott House is on the National Register of Historic Places. It is home to the Democratic Senatorial Campaign Committee (DSCC), the fund-raising and attack-dog arm for the Democrats. On this Election Night, Elias — jittery, concerned, in touch nationwide to campaign managers — was the lawyer for nearly all of the fifty-one sitting Democratic U.S. senators and every Democratic candidate in competitive races nationwide.

Of all the candidates seeking to grab seats from Republicans in 2008, Franken was the most unorthodox and most targeted by the GOP. Once TV's satirical *Saturday Night Live* self-help nerd Stuart Smalley, Alan

Stuart Franken was a flashpoint for conservative talk radio and cable TV attackers. He wrote smart, satirical, and laugh-out-loud books against liars and big fat idiots aligned with the Republican Party. Franken didn't have a voting record, but he had a trail of written material, televised skits, radio tapes, and a documentary film, *God Spoke,* that made no mistake about where he stood on issues. It all provided the Republicans with an abundance of ammunition.

In 2004, to counter the power of right-wing-oriented talk radio, Franken helped launch the left-of-center talk-radio network Air America, where he also hosted a show. By 2007, he decided to run for U.S. Senate in his home state of Minnesota, seeking the seat once held by liberal champion Paul Wellstone, who had become his friend. Wellstone was the principled firebrand whose death eleven days before the 2002 election made it possible for Coleman to win that election. After Wellstone's death, the 2002 U.S. Senate race disintegrated into tragedy and controversy. It triggered a genuine statewide numbness. Coleman won because the other guy died.

In this 2008 attempt to inherit Wellstone's mantle, Franken wanted badly to take on Coleman, who was considered a political chameleon for jumping parties and for backing George W. Bush's legislative agenda 86 percent of the time. It made for the nation's dirtiest and most expensive U.S Senate campaign of 2008, with nearly forty million dollars spent leading up to Election Day,[1] and, incredibly, another twenty million dollars in recount costs afterwards. The eyes of the Democratic leadership in Washington were also on the race. A Franken victory, plus a handful of other victories in other states, could strengthen the Democrats' hold on the Senate. There was even a possibility—depending on the outcomes in Alaska and Georgia—that Franken would become the sixtieth Democratic senator, making the chamber filibuster-proof.

All of those circumstances got Elias's juices flowing. Franken was his favorite candidate this cycle, mostly because of their first encounter on March 7, 2008, after a training session for senator wannabes and their campaign managers. At the Phoenix Park Hotel, in the shadow of the U.S. Capitol, Elias, known for his theatrical presentations, warned candidates about what sorts of donations could get them into trouble; which sorts of solicitations could lead them to perp walks; what kinds of gifts they should never, ever receive; and, generally, how to approach a campaign. He paced, his big hands and arms flailing, his declarations crystal clear, his voice rising, often repeating himself.

This particular presentation included a David Letterman–like top-ten list, with the final piece of advice being, "You're running a multimillion dollar business. Act like it." Another item on his list: "Recount."

When Elias's show for the 2008 class of candidates and their handlers ended, Franken approached Elias. Franken made millions as a writer and performer on TV and from his best sellers, such as *Rush Limbaugh Is a Big Fat Idiot* and *Lies and the Lying Liars Who Tell Them.* He was a big-time joke writer. Franken waited for the other new candidates to leave the conference room, sidled up to Elias, and said, "You know, you're a very funny guy."

Elias replied, "That's the nicest thing anyone's ever said to me."

For weeks, anyone Elias bumped into heard about his exchange with Franken and Franken's praise for his sense of humor. As he tends to do, Elias fixated on the comment. "This is one of the great comedians of our time and he thinks I'm funny," Elias told anyone who would listen. Four months later, at a fundraiser in Martha's Vineyard for the DSCC, the two saw each other again. Of course, Elias reminded Franken that he'd called him funny a few months back and added, "That is the most significant thing anyone has ever told me at any political briefing ever. So, anything you need, you let me know."

Franken looked at him quizzically, but apparently kept that promise in the back of his mind. "I think I won him over," Franken said, with his wry, dry delivery. "I won his eternal loyalty."

Another important actor arrived on the scene weeks after Elias impressed Franken with his wit. As his campaign teetered, Franken hired Stephanie Schriock as his campaign manager in May 2008. She brought a pleasant but laser-like management style and maturity to a Franken campaign that was struggling amid scandal and disorganization as he sought the endorsement of the Minnesota DFL Party. A veteran of Howard Dean's presidential campaign in 2004 and a handful of other House and Senate races, Schriock was the stable force Franken's effort needed.

Weeks after Schriock took control of Team Franken, Elias was in Chicago to conduct a session with campaign managers of all Democratic senate candidates. Schriock was there now. They knew each other through earlier DSCC work. The topic of the session was recounts, and the takeaway message was, "Congratulations, you are about to have a series of conference calls with this fellow named Elias to make sure you will be prepared in the event of a recount." First task, find local lawyers.

Schriock returned to Minnesota and eventually hired a well-known, prematurely white-haired, extremely serious, fifty-four-year-old former U.S. attorney named David Lillehaug.

On Election Night, while the eyes of the world were on Chicago and a newly elected and historic president, Elias was stationed firmly inside the little office inside the Beltway, his stomping grounds. As if an electoral bowling alley, Elias's clients were speckled balls mowing down GOP pins. His silver laptop's screen was digitally flashing the Democratic senatorial gains. Virginia: no contest, Mark Warner whipped Jim Gilmore. In New Hampshire, Jeanne Shaheen was unseating John Sununu. North Carolina's Kay Hagen was trouncing incumbent Elizabeth Dole. Big wins. The map was turning blue. Elias was high-fiving himself. Life was good. But three other races fed Elias's fidgety nature, Mississippi, Alaska, and Franken's Minnesota contest with Coleman, the one in which each candidate had raised and spent twenty million dollars. In spite of such record spending, Franken and Coleman and their venomous campaigns were so off-putting to the state of Hubert Humphrey and Walter Mondale that neither could attract more than 42 percent of the vote. Independence Party candidate Dean Barkley looked as if he might gain as much as 15 percent. Barkley was a former aide to Minnesota's wrestler-turned-governor, Jesse Ventura. He was Ventura's appointee to replace Wellstone after the awful late–October 2002 plane crash and had served as Minnesota's senator for two months. A comedian-turned-senator may not have been much stranger than a wrestler-turned-governor, but Barkley had the potential to be a real spoiler. Franken and Coleman were neck and neck, with neither of them set to get a majority of the votes. "None of the above" was the most attractive candidate for many voters.

Elias hoped that maybe, just maybe, when this election cycle was over he wouldn't have to pack up and head to some godforsaken location to help a Democrat win a recount. He had been working on recounts for years, but always in a lawyer's role, not as the big fish of any operation. His first recount was a congressional race in Connecticut in 1994; his second, in 1996, was the lengthy recount victory and legal battle to seat Mary Landrieu of Louisiana in the Senate; and then, still only twenty-nine years old, he was part of the legal team in the early stages of the 1998 recount for Senator Harry Reid as he won reelection in Nevada.

This is the very same Harry Reid who was now the Senate majority leader and, in some ways, Elias's ultimate boss at the DSCC. The Reid case is where Elias and the Democrats' leading recount expert, Chris Sautter, first crossed paths.

In 2000, Elias helped Maria Cantwell win her Senate recount in Washington State. His legal teammate then was Seattle's most prominent trial lawyer, Kevin Hamilton, a master of complex, document-heavy litigation who walked both sides of the legal street. Some days he represented Starbucks or Boeing in Seattle. Other days he represented the Democratic Party and candidates in distress. Hamilton was the lawyer for Washington's governor, Christine Gregoire, in 2005 when she trailed in her election, but flipped the result during a lengthy recount, complete with an election contest trial in which wrongly rejected absentee ballots were a key issue.

On Election Night 2008, with his fortieth birthday three months away, Elias was ready to settle down, to spend more time with the kids. "You pace yourself to be done on Election Day," Elias said of the biorhythms that pulsate through a political junkie. "You structure your whole life [so] that things are going to be relatively easy for you after the first week of November. On Election Night, I was ready to be done."

Even as he digested the returns from Mississippi, Alaska, and Minnesota on this November night in 2008, Elias couldn't avoid thinking back one election cycle earlier, to 2004. Then, Elias was the general counsel for Democratic presidential candidate John Kerry's campaign committee, a committee that faced all the ammunition the Republicans could muster, including the Swift Boat allegations that Kerry wasn't truly a Vietnam War hero. That smear was orchestrated by a Republican lawyer and political consultant named Ben Ginsberg. On Election Day, the early exit polls claimed Kerry was to be the next president of the United States and George W. Bush a one-term president. Elias's ticket was getting punched. Lawyer to the president of the United States was a good gig. As the day and night wore on, Elias commuted a mile between the Kerry war room and this very same Mott House as he saw the election slip away. In the morning and the afternoon, when Kerry seemed ahead, a victory speech was being prepared, the Mott House was buoyant—until the late-night results barged in and defeat punched Elias in his belly. It was an empty feeling he'd never had before. He told friends he went through "a period of mourning," but he did so without missing a day of work. The Wednesday after Kerry's defeat, Elias returned to his law office and began to sketch out what his world would look like next. Not much would change, except he knew this: losing was no fun.

Four years later, as the lawyer for most of the Democrats running for the U.S. Senate, Elias hoped Obama's stylish coattails were long. Perhaps even Alaska, Mississippi, and Minnesota would go the Democrats' way. Put Georgia in the mix and that magic, powerful number of sixty blue senators might just emerge.

In late October, with Hamilton attending meetings at Georgetown Law School, his alma mater, Elias and Hamilton pondered responsibilities in the coming weeks. If the opportunities arose, where should Hamilton go to defend Democratic turf? Elias wondered, teasing Hamilton, "Alaska or Minnesota?"

"Alaska or Minnesota?" Hamilton squealed. "You've got to be kiddin' me."

"Don't worry," Elias said. "These recounts will only take a few weeks."

In Minnesota, thanks to Schriock's foresight, a Franken recount plan was in place. In late October, Elias and Hamilton met in Washington, D.C., at their law firm's offices near the White House. The firm, Perkins Coie (pronounced "coo-ee"), has long made its money representing large corporations. Everyone in D.C. thought Perkins Coie was a Washington firm, and it was, but a Seattle, Washington, firm, which is where Hamilton was based. Bob Bauer, Elias's mentor, set up shop in that other, power-centric, Washington in the 1970s in the wake of the passage of the Federal Election Campaign Act and the formation of the Federal Election Commission. He helped to build Perkins Coie into one of the nation's first election-law shops. The firm owned that niche on the Democrats' side. It became more than a boutique operation as members of Congress kept stumbling into scandal and House Speaker Newt Gingrich kept whacking the Democrats in the mid-1990s. Then, *Bush v. Gore* wrapped itself around the nation's political and legal psyche in 2000. Bauer was a member of Gore's team. Soon after, election law grew just as investigative reporting did after Watergate. It was trendy. It was lucrative. Bauer became the Democratic godfather of election law. Before long, Elias was the heir to that business at Perkins Coie.

The recount plan, developed by Lillehaug, lived in a desk drawer in Schriock's St. Paul campaign headquarters. Minnesota law said any outcome with a margin of less than one-half of 1 percent triggered an automatic hand recount. Assuming that as many as three million Minnesotans voted, that would mean a gap of fewer than fifteen thousand votes.

Schriock knew she would need to train a strike force of volunteers. She knew she would need a SWAT team of experienced lawyers. She knew she would need a boatload of money. She and Franken would need millions, mostly to feed the energy, creativity, and billable hours of Elias, Hamilton, Lillehaug, and their coterie of Ivy League–educated legal minds.

As the clock in Washington, D.C., ticked toward midnight on Election Night, it was clear that Mississippi wasn't going to be in play. Republican Roger Wicker was handily defeating Democrat Ronnie Musgrove. Alaska remained undecided, but Senator Ted Stevens, under indictment, appeared to be in real trouble. Georgia was headed for a runoff. Elias had been in touch with Schriock throughout the day. At about midnight, Minnesota time, with Obama's victory speech completed, Elias, back in his Virginia home, had Schriock on the other end of his cell phone. It looked as if Coleman was ahead by 700 votes, she said. Minnesota was guaranteed a recount.

Earlier on Election Night, Hamilton, in Seattle working as general counsel to Washington's Obama campaign, had e-mailed Elias, "If this goes, just say the word, I'm on a plane." Hamilton was on board as the chief of litigation. Conference calls needed to be scheduled. An elite gang of recount pros had to be instantly recruited. Elias told Perkins Coie associate Ezra Reese to catch the first airplane to Minneapolis Wednesday morning. E-mails were pinging from coast to coast. He needed one other key operative, and that was Chris Sautter. Sautter, a lawyer, law school teacher, and media expert, was a recount expert extraordinaire, someone who really knew how to count ballots. Elias first met Sautter during the Harry Reid recount a decade earlier.

Sautter is a sort of carny of recount gurus. It's not the kindest way to describe his peripatetic recount role, but it's the most accurate. He is the Democrats' Ferris wheel operator at these recount county fairs. He builds the foundation of the field operation for recounts and the on-the-ground rules of engagement. He frames the structure. He trains volunteers. He tells campaigns how to collect data. Sautter started working on recounts as a college student in 1985 in what, among recountistas, has come to be called Indiana's Bloody Eighth. There, incumbent Democratic Representative Frank McCloskey led by seventy-two votes on Election Night. After the recount, challenger and Republican Richard McIntyre forged ahead by 418 votes. But a host of flaws in the election, including some double counting of votes and a too-quick certification by Indiana's Republican secretary of state, led to the Democrat-controlled House of Representatives refusing to seat McIntyre. Instead, the House ordered the General Accounting Office to conduct its own recount. Democrat McCloskey won by four votes.

The significance of Sautter's maiden voyage into recount land was that no recount before or since has been considered as bitter. As legal scholar Jeffrey Toobin wrote about the McIntyre–McCloskey recount in his book on the 2000 presidential recount, *Too Close to Call*, "It was as close to an outright theft as had occurred in modern American political history." And, guess what? The recount leader on the McIntyre side of this warped Indiana election equation was a recent law school grad, a Democrat-turned-Republican named Ben Ginsberg. It was his first recount too, and a theft that stuck with Ginsberg, placing a giant chip on his shoulder for years to come, or, as Toobin wrote, the "Bloody Eighth" triggered in young Republicans like Ginsberg "a sustained pitch of perpetual rage."

By 1994, Sautter had participated in another handful of recounts and coauthored a thin document with two other recount specialists, Tim Downs and Jack Young. *The Recount Primer* foreshadowed all that Elias, Schriock, and others were to execute over the next eight months. By 2008, Sautter had worked on more than twenty-five different recounts: from Indiana to New York to Florida (including for Al Gore in 2000, where he had once again faced off against Ginsberg). To Sautter, election law is "the new rock and roll," and recounts a rush. "I love the tension of close elections and recounts," he said. "I find it amazingly exhilarating when your candidate comes from behind and turns it around . . . It is like climbing a mountain or running a marathon, both of which I have done. Or perhaps a better analogy would be winning a tough chess match after you get behind. And, there is nothing more disheartening than losing a recount narrowly, especially as in Bush–Gore, when the votes were actually there to turn it around."

That was Elias's new venture, to find the votes to turn this undecided Coleman–Franken election around. Elias and Franken were about to get to know each other a whole lot better than they ever could have expected. This relationship between two funny men was about to turn extremely serious.

On Election Night in Minnesota, it was getting dicey and dreary. In the Minneapolis suburb of Bloomington, in a Sheraton hotel the Republicans had used for years to celebrate victories of President George W. Bush and Governor Tim Pawlenty, the party wasn't heating up at all. Everyone knew that Obama was going to win large in Minnesota and, as the night wore on, across the country. Even in enemy territory there was a legitimate sense of historic excitement that an African-American was about to become the nation's president. As much as the slowly assembling Republicans feared his policies, they'd gained a level of respect for Obama during the campaign and, at least on this decisive night, they all wanted to inhale the significance of this national moment of transition. But the close Senate race was distracting them.

As Election Day had neared, Coleman's campaign manager, Cullen Sheehan, thought his incumbent candidate was going to win by, perhaps, a percentage point, maybe two. A bunch of outside interest groups had flooded the Twin Cities market with TV commercials showing Franken to be an angry, irrational, sexist, overly partisan jerk. Despite the economy's tailspin and Obama's clear path to victory, Franken's poll numbers were actually dipping as November 4 approached. A TV spot—one of thousands that ran during the bitter campaign—linking Coleman's wife to an alleged scandal involving payments for work she hadn't performed seemed to have backlashed. Sheehan was cautiously optimistic as results began to stream in. His own rise had been somewhat fairy tale–ish. When Coleman ran for governor in Minnesota in 1998, Sheehan was his driver, his caddie. He'd made an impression on Coleman. Now, for this reelection campaign, he was driving Coleman's entire organization.

That cautious optimism was helped by the day's turnout. It wasn't what the Democrats had wanted. The Democrats figured an 80 percent turnout at the polls would ensure victory for Franken. Turnout reached slightly less than 78 percent, still the nation's best, but not good enough for Franken. Sheehan had calculated that Coleman had to rely on the gap between Obama votes and Franken votes. If Obama could sweep Minnesota over John McCain by 15 percentage points, then Coleman was toast. But if Coleman could win over some Obama voters—even a percentage point or two—that could be the difference, especially with third-party candidate Barkley skimming votes from Franken.

About two weeks before Election Day, Sheehan contacted Coleman's Washington law firm, Patton Boggs, anticipating a potential recount and preparing for so-called election protection; that is, making sure votes were counted and preserved securely by election officials, particularly in Democrat-friendly precincts. Sheehan was worried, too, about one key element of any post–Election Day process, especially if absentee ballots came into play. The McCain national campaign hadn't developed the sort of database of voters and potential voters that the Bush organization had so ably done in 2000 and 2004. It was a nationwide shortcoming of McCain's. In Minnesota, the situation was even worse; Coleman's database was, as one insider put it, "for shit." List development, as the political insiders call it, simply hadn't occurred.

In Washington, no one knew better that McCain's campaign had failed miserably than Ben Ginsberg, Coleman's lawyer at Patton Boggs, the competitor law firm and philosophical opponent to Elias's Perkins Coie. Ginsberg wore his GOP sentiments on his sleeve as noisily as Elias wore his Democrat stripes on his. Ginsberg and Coleman had been pals for the six years Coleman had been a senator. Like Elias, Ginsberg was an expert on election law. But Ginsberg was known to the Democrats as more of an evildoer than a lawyer. Some Democrats believed he had singlehandedly blocked Elias and Kerry from that White House path they believed they were on. He was for a while the chief counsel to George W. Bush's reelection campaign and the lawyer for the Swift Boat Veterans for Truth officers who attacked John Kerry as a Vietnam War fraud during the 2004 election. Once it was revealed he worked for both, Ginsberg had to resign from the Bush reelection team. Still, Ginsberg owned a deftly creative way of spinning talking points into downright political poetry. He was good at being the voice of the bad guys. He relished the role.

Ginsberg earned his all-star status in 2000 as the quarterbacking lawyer for Bush against Gore. Recount chief executive James Baker, the former secretary of state of the United States, ran the show, but Ginsberg was George Bush's lead attorney in the Florida recount. He was such a rock star that he was highlighted in a made-for-HBO film, *Recount*. Actor Bob Balaban, looking just like Ginsberg, played the one-time newspaper reporter in the film. Ginsberg was proud of that cinematic star turn.

But Election Night 2008 was no red-carpet event for Ginsberg. He actually spent most of November 4 playing mournful pundit on the *Washington Post*'s online video stream. No cocktails or hors d'oeuvres for him.

He'd been loosely monitoring Coleman's situation in Minnesota, but figured Norm was going to pull it out. As the polls closed in Minnesota, the results showed Coleman ahead. Tony Sutton, the Minnesota Republican Party's secretary–treasurer, told staffers, "We're going to win, but it's going to be close."

The Republicans weren't taking any chances on protecting that lead. A half-hour drive from Coleman headquarters, not very far from Franken's downtown St. Paul suite, an odd confrontation occurred. Election officials completed their counting of machine-inserted ballots and absentee ballots at St. Paul's elections warehouse. About 11:30 p.m., as Ramsey County elections manager Joe Mansky, one of the state's most experienced voting officials, was closing up shop for the day, a woman entered the building. The mysterious woman told Mansky she had recently flown in to Minnesota from Washington, D.C., and said, "I'm here to guard the ballots."

"That's great," Mansky replied. "What are you talking about? Our ballots are locked in here. It's a secure facility and no one can go in here."

She told him she was sent to the St. Paul warehouse by the Coleman campaign. Mansky's coat was on. He was about to lock up the facility. "You're welcome to stay in the parking lot," Mansky told her. Two men in a dark car waited outside for the woman from Washington. That night, and two more, the men remained in the lot just off Plato Boulevard. As far as Mansky could tell, the men slept in the car for three nights, until Friday morning when the canvassing process began. Similar election-protection pods of Republican operatives arrived at ballot warehouses across the metro area, and even at Secretary of State Mark Ritchie's office at the State Office Building in downtown St. Paul, where there were no ballots to monitor. Months later, when the voting phase morphed into the litigation phase, Franken lawyer David Lillehaug used these GOP stakeouts against Coleman, suggesting it was his campaign that might have been the cause of mysteriously missing ballots. But on Election Night, the Republicans thought victory was at hand, and no one was going to fiddle with it in the dark of night.

The Franken suite at the St. Paul Crowne Plaza, a stone's throw or window leap from the Mississippi River, looked like a scene from a 1920s bootleggers' orgy. Champagne filled a bathtub. Boxes of other sorts of alcohol lined the floors. Plates of cold cuts, cheeses, and rolls, wrapped in plastic, sat on coffee tables. Celebration was anticipated. A half-dozen TV sets had been brought in, most showing different local Twin Cities channels; the others, cable channels. Laptops were strewn around the suite, with key numbers crunchers, media relations types, and local campaign attorney David Lillehaug monitoring results from the secretary of state's office and county auditors. During the day, campaign manager Schriock had been receiving exit polls that showed her candidate up by as much as 8 percentage points. She didn't believe them. She told Franken not to believe them. Still, there was an emotional texture to such numbers. Hopes were buoyed. She knew not to rely on them, but even she, level-headed CEO of the campaign, couldn't help herself. As the night wore on, and the ice in the bathtub began to melt, it became clear to Schriock and Lillehaug that her Election Day morning assessment to her staff—"It's going to be really, really close"—would halt any champagne guzzling.

At about 10:30 p.m., Franken's political and field director Dan Cramer, who had been analyzing the results with a numbers-crunching colleague in Washington, D.C., briefed the candidate and his wife, Franni.

"How we doin'?" Franken asked Cramer.

"It's gonna be close," Cramer answered.

"How close?" Franken probed.

Cramer looked at his spreadsheet with the precinct results still to flow in, knowing he should supply a sophisticated answer to the man. All he could muster was, "Real close."

Franken grew irritated. "Dan, what do you mean 'real close'?"

"Al, it's going to be really, really close." In his mind, Cramer was thinking about 200 votes, either way.

About that time, a handful of Franken staffers received a rude message. They had all assembled in a basement banquet room of the Crowne Plaza. Their goal was to stuff their faces with free pizza and vodka—until word came down from on high, from Schriock's suite, "No more drinking. There's going to be a recount." A meeting was set for Wednesday morning. Everyone had to be sober.

About 5 a.m., Schriock and Lillehaug together walked slowly from their twentieth-floor nerve center to the tense room two flights below. There, on his first Election Night ever as a candidate, sat Franken, Franni, their two children, and Franni's mother. The results were pretty much in, Schriock and Lillehaug reported. Coleman was ahead. A recount was certain.

There was talk of missing ballots in Duluth, on Minnesota's traditionally Democratic Iron Range in the northeastern part of the state. There was talk of Somali voters in Minneapolis's inner city being denied access. There was an error rate within the voting machines too, a very small one, to be sure. Yes, Lillehaug and Schriock advised Franken, it was hard to flip the results of an election, but there was some reason to be hopeful. Schriock had been speaking with Elias, and another call was planned soon. A legal team, including Lillehaug, was being assembled. Elias, a fellow from Seattle named Hamilton, and other recount consultants would be in Minnesota within days. Franken sat there in silence, in sadness. With Obama doing so well in Minnesota, Franken had thought he was going to win. Now, he was hanging on for dear life.

Lillehaug went back to the twentieth floor and, with Franken's deputy campaign manager and communications chief, Eric Schultz, began tapping out a statement to be released when the sun rose over Minnesota. Lillehaug's goal was to express two key points: First, the recount was automatic and required by Minnesota law, so this was not a Franken ploy. Second, they had to emphasize how close it was. The message had to come from Franken and he had to communicate it effectively, as if he were to be the next senator.

At 6:32 a.m., the Associated Press called the election in Coleman's favor. The wire service told the world Coleman was ahead by 762 votes, and, by the estimates of AP's political editors locally and nationally, he had been reelected. The cell phones of Franken campaign spokespeople Andy Barr and Jess McIntosh rang, and they rushed to finish up copies of their candidate's statement. Franken and Lillehaug raced downstairs to the Crowne Plaza's ballroom where journalists had camped out all night. Franken had to explain what was next.

"The secretary of state's office reports that all but nine of Minnesota's 4,130 precincts have reported in," he told the reporters and the cameras. "And this race is too close to call, with a margin of just about 1,100 votes out of 2.9 million cast. That's four one-hundredths of one percent of the vote. And we expect that when those final nine precincts are counted this morning, that 1,100-vote margin will shrink into the hundreds."

He continued, "Under Minnesota state law, we will now enter into an automatic statewide canvass and recount. It will be the first one since 1962, when I was 11 years old. I remember that year very clearly for two reasons. The recount between Elmer L. Andersen and Karl Rolvaag. And the Gophers were in the Rose Bowl that year."

Franken, with Lillehaug and Schultz's help, allowed a little joke and a Minnesota-ism to sneak in.

"Let me be clear: Our goal is to ensure that every vote is properly counted. The process, dictated by our laws, will be orderly, fair, and will take place within a matter of days. We won't know for a little while who won this race, but at the end of the day, we will know that the voice of the electorate was clearly heard."

The statement went on, and here's where Lillehaug's lawyerly voice was inserted: "There is reason to believe that the recount could change the vote tallies significantly. Our office and the Obama campaign have received reports of irregularities at various precincts around the state. For instance, some polling places in Minneapolis ran out of registration materials. Our team has been working on those issues for several hours already, and they will continue to do so this morning as the recount process begins . . . This has been a long campaign, and it's going to be a little longer before we have a winner."

Soon after, the Associated Press wire service "uncalled" the election. AP said its determination that Coleman was the winner was premature.

Less than four hours later, around 10:30 a.m., at his campaign headquarters midway between Minneapolis and St. Paul, with a blue dress shirt opened at the collar, Norm Coleman approached the lectern. His wife, Laurie, the center of an emotional last-day campaign TV commercial, stood at his side. A small group of supporters applauded. A tired Minnesota media corps waited to hear Coleman's side of the story. Despite the slimmest of margins, Coleman declared he had won. In his own mind, he had been reelected to a second term.

"Where we are today, after a pretty long night, is me being humbled and grateful for the victory that the voters gave us last night . . . I have great confidence in the Minnesota system. I've run a lot of races. I've never questioned the way in which our election system works . . . I don't believe there'd be any reason to believe there will be any significant change, particularly when the margin in this case is 725 votes."

Curt Brown, a veteran reporter for the Minneapolis *Star Tribune*, the state's largest newspaper and most read Web site, called out a question. Not only had Brown covered Coleman since his mayoral days, but they were neighbors in the Crocus Hill section of St. Paul. "Senator, if you were down by 725, would you say forget it and save the taxpayers' money?"

The implication, the quest of the question, was this: If Coleman were Franken, would he give up? Would he concede in the face of a 725-vote deficit barely fifteen hours after the polls closed and less than twelve hours after most county election headquarters locked up for the night and even as that 725-vote margin was dipping into the two hundreds as he spoke?

Coleman: "Curt, to be honest, I'd step back. My friend John Thune was down in 2002 when he ran . . . now the senator from South Dakota — I believe he was down by five hundred–something votes, and he said, 'We need to heal,' and he stepped back. I can only speak for me. If you ask me, 'What I would do?' I would, I would step back. I just think the need for the healing process is so important, the possibility of any change of this magnitude in the voting system we have is so remote, but that would be my judgment. I'm not . . . again, Mr. Franken will decide what Mr. Franken will do. But do I think under these circumstances it is important to come together? I do."

Coleman seemed earnest, but his comment was one he would regret. Minutes before the news conference, some of his closest media relations staffers specifically told him to not discuss the details of the recount, to not go where he had gone. "Act as if you've won," he was told, taking a page from the Bush 2000 script, and stick to that theme. But, short on sleep, still reeling from an insanely controversial final week of the campaign, he went one step further, giving advice to Franken, to the last man on earth who would take it from him. As time moved on, as Election Day morphed into a recount and the recount moved to the state Canvassing Board, and as the Minnesota Supreme Court became a way station en route to a full-blown, eight-week-long election contest trial, Coleman's words became more than presumptuous. They were bitterly ironic because, as the months wore on, he became the man who would not step back.

His campaign's assertion that the changing numbers were "statistically dubious" was just wrong. Minnesota history shows that vote tallies jiggle around for quite a while and change, often dramatically, from the day after an election to the moment the canvassing begins in precincts and counties. In typical elections, where the margin is a bit wider than a few hundred votes, no one notices or cares. The Franken campaign quickly prepared a chart to show how counts go up and down, no matter what the party. For instance, in Democrat Amy Klobuchar's landslide Senate victory over Republican Mark Kennedy in 2006, both candidates saw reductions in total votes, she by 666 and he by 3,520 between the time of Election Day totals and the canvass. In 2004, President George

Bush saw his vote total increase by 713 votes over John Kerry, even though Kerry carried the state. In 1998, Coleman himself saw a jump of 10,409 votes during the count following the governor's race, but Jesse Ventura, the eventual winner, captured 12,431 more votes. The point: numbers change when election officials get down to the nitty-gritty of proofreading machine printouts and checking voter rolls and finding previously uncounted or misplaced ballots.

It was Wednesday now, and a free-falling imagery about Election Day resonated among members of Franken's exhausted staff, who were living on 5-Hour Energy drinks and Franni Franken's brownies. Had they heard it, it would have made sense to Coleman's loyalists too. "On Election Day you jump off a ledge, and you hope the voters catch you," Schriock said. This time, Coleman and Franken were in suspended animation. When all the precincts had reported, Coleman's margin was 215 votes out of more than 2.9 million cast. Not only might there be errors in the counting, not only might ballots be discovered in county officials' desks, or in the bottom of drawers, but some might be lost, some might be counted twice, and a hand count might reveal small errors in voting machines. Not to mention the matter of absentee ballots.

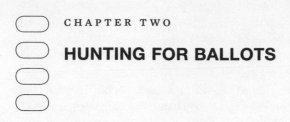

CHAPTER TWO

HUNTING FOR BALLOTS

"Trust me, they screwed it up."

At Secretary of State Mark Ritchie's office, the recount came as no surprise. The Barkley–Coleman–Franken election was bound to be tight.
In August, director of elections Gary Poser warned Ritchie of potential recounts during this cycle. Training of elections officials across the
state was activated. A statewide primary election recount to determine
a Minnesota Supreme Court justice candidate had gone off without a
hitch in September, but that involved fewer than 112,000 ballots. This
recount process would be the first statewide general-election recount
since 1962 when, after more than four months, Governor Elmer Andersen lost to challenger Karl Rolvaag by 91 out of 1.25 million votes in what,
until then, was the largest and longest recount in Minnesota history.
When it finally ended, the Franken–Coleman recount reexamination of
more than 2.9 million ballots became the largest hand recount of votes
in any statewide election in the history of the United States, topping
the 2004 Washington State gubernatorial recount by more than 100,000
votes.[1]

As Ritchie's staff and election officials at 106 locations in the state's
eighty-seven counties prepared for the recount to begin on November
19, the effort to pull Franken into the lead raced immediately down two
distinct tracks. First, Franken's legal team focused on training volunteers
for a fundamental task: carefully tracking the tally of the paper ballots
that were soon to be recounted at tables from Grand Marais to Pipestone
by local election officials. Second, the Franken force also entered into a
more speculative mission: gathering data on absentee votes and voters.

For Coleman, it was all about playing defense. He was ahead. There was no reason to pad the lead. There was every reason to block any newly discovered or previously uncounted votes from being counted.

Even before he landed in Minnesota, Chris Sautter, the recount guru retained by Elias in the hours after Election Night, e-mailed a memo to Schriock and others, a derivative of the 1994 primer he had coauthored. The memo was part recount 101, part crystal ball. Sautter wrote:

> A recount is an audit. It is a thorough examination of all technical elements of an election. A recount is also discovery. Factual evidence discovered in the course of a recount is the basis of a subsequent contest. The two defining elements of a good recount are the ability of all parties to OBSERVE and PRESERVE. Parties should be able to observe the materials examined and decisions made by the election officials, and they should be able to make exhibits or otherwise preserve the materials supporting particular decisions . . . The key to preparing for a recount is information. Information assures that strategic decisions are made properly.

There was another matter to consider, Sautter wrote:

> A certain number of Absentee Voter (AV) envelopes are always rejected by election workers and not opened. Most are rejected for valid reasons, e.g., the envelope is post-marked after the election or there is no voter signature. However, sometimes AV ballots are rejected for reasons that are not valid . . . We need to determine how many AV envelopes have been rejected because of such defects and why.

There was also a presumption in the Franken camp that Coleman would engage in the same sort of absentee-ballot pursuit. In years past, absentee voters, often older, many away at warmer-weather winter homes, many wanting to avoid waiting in lines, tilted toward the Republicans. That was the conventional wisdom: absentees skew toward the GOP.

Sautter estimated the Franken side needed more than two thousand trained volunteers and four hundred volunteer lawyers to monitor all the locations, some with multiple counting tables, across the state. The Democratic Senatorial Campaign Committee, at the urging of its chairman, Senator Charles Schumer of New York, recruited a handful of Washington-based lawyers to fly in to help Schriock and Elias. Lillehaug gathered Minnesota attorneys for the cause.

On the Republican side, a similar recruitment of volunteers and lawyers to staff the recount stations was underway. The Coleman volunteer-training regimen was different from Franken's, but a robust effort was launched by campaign manager Cullen Sheehan, Republican Party general counsel Matt Haapoja, and Minnesota GOP executive director Darren Bearson. For both campaigns, the new phase was painful. From volunteers dropping literature on doorknobs in the final hours to the wandering candidates themselves, Election Day was the presumed finish line to stagger across before collapsing. Now, they all had to instantly pick themselves up and organize an equally massive effort in a compact period of time, raise more money, and quickly study the recount process. Rules of engagement for the recount were still to be finalized by Ritchie, his staff, and the two sides. No one knew when the recount and its related legal proceedings would end.

About the time Sautter's memo landed in Schriock's e-mail inbox, David Lillehaug's phone rang in his fortieth-floor office at the Fredrikson & Byron law firm in Minneapolis. It was Wednesday, November 5, and a groggy Lillehaug answered to hear Angela Bohmann, a former colleague at another high-priced Twin Cities firm, on the line. Bohmann's daughter, Claire, a student at the University of Washington in Seattle but a registered Minnesota voter, had cast her absentee ballot for Franken, Angela Bohmann reported. But that absentee ballot had been rejected by Minneapolis election judges. The claim was that Claire wasn't registered, but, her mother told Lillehaug, Claire indeed was and retained the documentation to prove it. Lillehaug made note of the conversation and began to wonder.

The next day, a DFL observer in northern Lake of the Woods County told Franken headquarters that mailed absentee ballots had been wrongly rejected there too, for alleged voter registration issues. That night, the absentee-ballot universe was raised in a conference call of the still-forming Franken legal team. Kevin Hamilton recalled how absentee ballots helped Christine Gregoire, Washington's governor, in her 2004 recount and election contest. The absentees flipped Gregoire's results. With Hamilton as her trial attorney, Gregoire won her case and her reelection over Republican Dino Rossi.

"Go for the absentees," Hamilton told his colleagues on the call, his high-pitched voice squealing in excitement. "Trust me, they screwed it up. People's signatures change. They get strokes." Stuff happens. Voters mess up. So do election officials.

After the call, Lillehaug returned to his computer to read a growing list of e-mails. One came from an election judge in the Minneapolis suburb of Richfield, who wrote that he was "appalled at the subjectivity of the determinations leading to rejection of absentee ballots." Lillehaug instantly tapped out an e-mail to his teammates on the earlier conference call. "Colleagues—A lot of emails have come across the transom, but this one suggests that our conversation this evening about rejected absentee ballots was on point."

The next morning, Lillehaug and his colleagues at Fredrikson & Byron developed an affidavit form for rejected absentee voters, a document to be used by voters to petition local election officials to reconsider their wrongly rejected ballots. Hours later, Elias's colleague Ezra Reese, the first Perkins Coie lawyer on site in Minnesota, proposed in an e-mail "an absentee ballot chase program." Later, Republicans would suggest Franken "fabricated" votes. No, when you're down by two hundred votes, you hunt, you harvest, you chase.

Voting in Minnesota is easy. Voting in Minnesota is also complicated. It all depends how a citizen chooses to cast the vote. The different voting methods, and then how those ballots were accepted and counted, were critical to the outcome of the election and the Franken–Coleman battle.

Ninety percent of the ballots in Minnesota for the 2008 election were cast in person. The sacred right of participatory democracy is pretty darned easy in the state. If citizens haven't previously registered, they can do so right there at the voting place on Election Day. With that ease of access, Minnesota led all states in 2008 voter turnout, with 77.8 percent of citizens eighteen years old and older exercising their civic duty, the seventh straight general election, back to 1996, for which Minnesota topped all 50 states in turnout. Among registered voters in the state, more than 90 percent voted, a breathtaking embrace of democracy.

The typical 2008 voter arrived at his or her polling place already registered, signed near his or her name on the precinct roll, and was handed an 8½- by 14-inch heavy-stock sheet of paper that read State General Election Ballot. Three distinct columns on the front of the ballot read: Federal Offices, State Offices, and County Offices. Presidential candidates were listed on the upper left-hand module of the ballot. The U.S. Senate candidates' names sat directly beneath the presidential options, with Barkley, Coleman, and Franken stacked in that order.

This method of voting was simple. Voters filled in a blank oval to the left of the candidate of their choice. Scanning the ballot from top to bottom and left to right, the voter darkened ovals for president, U.S. senator, U.S. representative, Minnesota legislative races, a statewide constitutional amendment, county board members, and judges, the latter offices bleeding over to the flip side of the ballot. In all cases, neatly and completely filling in the oval indicated the clear intent of the voter's choice. In 33 of the state's 4,130 precincts, rather than filling in an oval, voters were asked to connect two portions of an arrow. On those ballots, an arrowhead and an arrow tail were separated by a half-inch or so of open space. That space in the broken arrow had to be connected by the voter. No matter which method was used, the voter then inserted the ballot into an optical scanner, which quietly sucked the legal-sized paper into its jaws and, with a very high rate of accuracy, recorded the vote. For the 2008 general election, out of more than 2.9 million votes, about 2.6 million were cast in that routine, but powerful, manner.

The rest were the 293,830 votes submitted by absentee ballot, a state record by total number and percentage of all votes cast. Compared with the 2004 presidential election, absentee voters increased in the 2008 election by more than 62,000, a spike of nearly 27 percent. Much of this was attributable to Barack Obama's presidential campaign in Minnesota: With a concern that Election Day lines might be long and some voters would grow impatient, the Obama organizers had encouraged supporters to go the absentee route. Obama volunteers were also urged to vote absentee so they would be freed up for Election Day tasks, such as driving elderly voters to the polls and telephoning others to get out and vote. Most absentee ballots were placed in U.S. Postal Service mailboxes for delivery to the correct election office on or before Election Day, but some were cast in person at county buildings or city halls.

The absentee-voting process is significantly more complicated than walking into a polling place, filling in a few ovals as if taking a college entrance exam, getting the red I Voted sticker, and returning to a plain-old November Tuesday. One of the reasons is that in 1975, the Minnesota Supreme Court ruled that absentee voting is a privilege, not a right. If voting in person on Election Day in Minnesota is about as easy as it gets, then absentee voting is downright tricky. A voter has to get it just right.

An election official must evaluate the ballot properly. Ballots take unpredictable twists and turns. As Deputy Secretary of State Jim Gelbmann said during the recount, "Every ballot tells a story." Before it was over, hundreds of ballot told tales.

The tales all begin more or less the same way, and all travel lengthy paths. First, a voter must request an absentee-ballot application from his or her city or county elections department. The voter is permitted five different reasons to vote absentee, from being out of the precinct for any reason to disability to service as an election judge. Once the local elections office receives the application, it is evaluated for completeness and for whether the applicant is a registered voter.

The next step has the local elections official delivering absentee-voting materials to the voter. If the voter isn't registered, an enhanced absentee-ballot packet that includes registration materials is sent. A registration form must be completed as a witness watches. As many as eleven forms of identification can be used to prove residence in a precinct.

That done, voters can proceed to mark their ballots by filling in the ovals. All absentee voters need a registered voter—or an elections official or a notary—to witness their act of filling in the ballot. The voter must then fold the ballot and place it in a business-sized manila envelope labeled Envelope A, the so-called secrecy envelope. If he is registering as part of the process, the voter must place his registration form and the secrecy envelope into a white Absentee Ballot Return Envelope, known as Envelope B. The voter is required to sign that envelope and have the witness sign it too. When all of that is completed, the voter must place Envelope B into the larger Envelope C, which is the mailing envelope. Finally, the voter must place his finger on the top of his head, twirl around three times, and say, "Abracadabra." Or so it seems.

For typical Minnesota elections, in which the margin between the first and second voter-getters is larger than the one-half of 1 percent recount trigger, no one knows or cares about strange marks on a ballot or crossed out ovals or silly write-in candidates who are athletes or action figures. An aggrieved loser doesn't get the chance to challenge ballots that are difficult to decipher or to determine the voter's intent. All of this matters only when that one-half of 1 percent differential occurs and a recount becomes mandatory. Then, local election officials and canvassing board members must decipher voter's intent. With absentee ballots, election judges must determine if an absentee ballot has been legally cast.

At the local level, an election official's determination of the voter's intent is known as "the call at the table." If that call, during a recount, is challenged by one of the candidates' representatives, it is then kicked over to the canvassing board for final determination.

As for absentee ballots, their rejection is rarely an issue in a typical election. Until the Franken–Coleman recount, rejected absentee ballots in Minnesota never got a second look by the state Canvassing Board. It has always been presumed that election officials around the state accepted ballots that complied with the law and rejected those ballots that didn't. Some counties or cities have absentee-ballot boards that examine the ballots when they arrive at city halls and county courthouses and before sending them on to the voters' home precincts. In those cases, if a ballot has been cast illegally, the voter is notified and, if there's time, given a second chance to submit a ballot. The rules for absentee-ballot acceptance are spelled out in Minnesota's statutes, but voters must navigate a series of hoops.

A voter must be registered at the address listed on the absentee ballot. Her name, address, and signature on the absentee-ballot return envelope must match the same on the absentee-ballot application. The witness to her absentee ballot must be registered to vote in the state of Minnesota, or be a notary public or other individual authorized to administer oaths. The voter cannot have shown up and voted in person on Election Day. The voter cannot have died between the time she mails her absentee ballot and Election Day. (Don't laugh. This morbid technicality became a part of this improbable recount.) The voter must put her ballot in the secrecy envelope and place it in the outer envelope. The absentee ballot must get to the county courthouse or city hall by the last mail delivery on Election Day, or it can be delivered in person to the elections office by someone else by 3 p.m. on Election Day. Add it all up and then, according to Minnesota law, her absentee ballot should be accepted and counted.

"There is no other reason for rejecting an absentee ballot," the state law reads, but as Kevin Hamilton pointed out, people screw up. In this election, absentee ballots were rejected for a host of inexplicable reasons. Why? Absentee ballots were among the last counted at precincts statewide. Election judges, who had been dealing with long lines during twelve-hour shifts, were tired and eager to get home. In some counties, election clerks knew voters and casually opened absentee envelopes without question. In other counties, election officials closely examined signatures to make sure they matched ballot applications. If they didn't, the ballot was sometimes rejected, even if voters had suffered strokes, were aged and shaky, or simply wrote sloppily. In some counties, election officials wondered about the legitimacy of witnesses. In others, the witnesses' registrations were never checked. Voters regularly messed up that complicated envelope dance, with some placing their voter registration forms inside the secrecy envelope; it made it impossible for election officials to know if in fact the voter was registered. There was one standard state law, one set of rules, but there were many ways that election officials from Ada to Zumbrota executed that standard. In the immediate days after the election, no one knew the extent of the absentee-ballot rejections, but with the phone calls and e-mails they were receiving, Franken's side had a good feeling about the possibilities.

On the other hand, Sautter saw danger in the absentee-ballot chase. Based on the traditional sloppiness of Democratic voters and the closeness of this election, there was a chance that Franken could overcome his deficit in the recount independent of the absentees. What if that happened? Why go scrambling for the absentees if victory is in hand with the machine votes? But no one knew for certain. The two-track strategy went forward.

The recount of "real" ballots cast in person via voting machines was the first order of business, the first path to garnering more votes. Elias liked to say, "There is the count, and then there is everything other than the count." For the Coleman team, the prevailing principle was to preserve victory, and little else. Lawyers Trimble and Knaak, campaign manager Sheehan, and Senator Coleman himself believed they were going to eke out a victory by using the George Bush–Ben Ginsberg Florida strategy: play defense, block any expansion of the ballot universe, and even rely, perhaps, on a Republican-leaning state Supreme Court, if it came to that. Usually, the candidate ahead on Election Day wins when the recount ends. Chris Sautter, a de facto recount historian, remembered only two major recounts in the last quarter century that saw Election Night results reversed: that McCloskey–McIntyre congressional battle in Indiana in which he and Ginsberg squared off in 1984 and Hamilton's Gregoire–Rossi gubernatorial tussle in Washington State in 2004–5, in which absentee ballots played a role. The odds were with Coleman, it seemed. But later a Coleman insider would say, "We thought it was Florida, but it turned out to be Washington State."

Coleman's campaign manager, Sheehan, thought he was prepared for a recount. In mid-October, Republican Party lawyers Trimble and Haapoja wrote a memo to Sheehan and party insiders outlining the legal scenarios of a recount. Tracking polls a week before Election Day indicated the closeness of the election and the recount possibility. But, from the beginning, creativity wasn't the Coleman legal team's forte. To ready himself for the Coleman–Franken case, Trimble said he "dusted off all of our old materials" from the Minnesota Second Congressional District recount in 2000 between incumbent Democrat David Minge and Republican challenger Mark Kennedy. That was the only recount Trimble had overseen. It lasted two weeks and Minge quickly conceded. It involved fewer than three hundred thousand votes, or about one-tenth of the universe of Franken–Coleman voters. The legal maneuvers for that state house recount were different from a U.S. Senate recount. There was no state Canvassing Board stop along the way. One Minnesota district court judge determined all matters. Absentee votes weren't at issue. Legal assistance from the national parties and media glare were nonexistent. The other pesky recount that year, *Bush v. Gore,* had stolen everyone's attention. Kennedy–Minge was a border skirmish compared with the all-out war that the Franken–Coleman recount was to become. But, as generals often do, Trimble seemed from the get-go to be fighting his old battle and not the new, more complex, one. As for Knaak, he had a bit more recount experience, but mostly at the state legislative level. Combined, Franken's lawyers—Elias, Hamilton, and Sautter—had about three dozen major recounts under their belts.

This is not to suggest that Knaak, a former Minnesota state senator, and Trimble, a feisty GOP lawyer and torchbearer, were shrinking violets. Not at all. It may not have been immediately clear to them that they were out of their league in any legal street fight with Team Franken, because Trimble and Knaak had plenty of punches to throw and the deep desire to throw them. As the Duke, Georgetown, and Harvard law school grads representing Franken brainstormed on the phone Friday night about how to chase absentee ballots, those Minnesota-nice fellows Knaak, of White Bear Lake, and Trimble, of Leech Lake, were preparing the recount's first attack, a sneak attack at that.

Votes—absentee ballots, no less—had gone missing in Minneapolis, a Franken hotbed. They were hidden in a car trunk, thirty-two of them.

They were about to be quickly, even surreptitiously, counted on the Saturday morning four days after the polls closed. Egads! The Senate election was spinning toward skullduggery. That's what Knaak and Trimble believed.

Friday evening, November 7, the Coleman campaign received a phone call from the Minneapolis city elections director, Cindy Reichert. She said that thirty-two ballots previously uncounted were about to be opened on Saturday. After all, come Tuesday, a week after the election, every county had to report its final tally—its canvass—to the secretary of state's office. As Knaak was told by someone at Coleman's headquarters who took Reichert's first call, ballots had been "suddenly found" in Reichert's car. At least that's what Knaak believed he heard. Knaak thought this required more investigation and the vote counting should be delayed. Trimble responded by calling back Reichert at 8:30 that night. He demanded that Minneapolis hold off on the counting. No, Reichert said, they needed to be counted as soon as possible. Something smelled fishy to Trimble and Knaak, who quickly dialed the home of Ramsey County Chief Judge Kathleen Gearin. She was in the midst of hosting a party, and thought it was a crank caller. No, it was the real thing. Knaak wanted a temporary restraining order (TRO) to halt the count of those Minneapolis votes. Knaak sought a hearing before the judge, as soon as possible. Franken won 70 percent of the votes in Minneapolis on Election Day with Coleman garnering less than 20 percent. If there were thirty-two votes to be blocked, these would be good ones for Coleman to snuff. Gearin agreed to meet the next morning, Saturday, at 9:30.

But no one bothered to tell the Franken side of the legal proceeding until after 8 a.m. Saturday when Lillehaug was at a veterinarian's office with his sick dog and received a surprise phone call from Knaak. "Just wanted to let you know we're going to have a hearing in Ramsey County District Court," Knaak announced. "Minneapolis wants to count some ballots that shouldn't be counted." To that point, Knaak hadn't sent any legal papers to Lillehaug or to Gearin. A lawsuit hadn't been filed. But in an affidavit submitted that day by Trimble, which Lillehaug also never received, Coleman's lawyer stated that Reichert told him on Friday night that "she was in the personal possession" of the ballots, that she planned to transport them to the City of Minneapolis ballot warehouse, and that the ballots would be opened Saturday at 10 a.m. "I asserted to Ms. Reichert that the integrity of the ballots was seriously in question," Trimble wrote in the affidavit.

But a careful reading of Knaak's "Motion for Emergency Temporary Injunctive Relief and Memorandum in Support Thereof" revealed that the Coleman campaign, in seeking the injunction, wanted to block not only the counting by Reichert of the thirty-two votes in Minneapolis but the counting of votes anywhere else by "any other election officials in the State of Minnesota" that weren't counted on Election Day. The assertion in his memorandum to Gearin was that votes counted after November 4 could only be included when the entire election was challenged in a full-blown election contest, or trial, which could be weeks or months down the road.

Lillehaug left his yellow lab at the vet's South Minneapolis office, received Knaak's TRO petition on his Blackberry, forwarded it to Perkins Coie lawyer Ezra Reese, picked up Reese in downtown Minneapolis, had Reese read it aloud in the car, and arrived at the Ramsey County Courthouse in downtown St. Paul before Knaak. Gearin was there, but after Knaak and a few other Coleman lawyers arrived, everyone waited for Reichert to get there along with Minneapolis City Attorney Susan Segal.

When the hearing began, Gearin was instantly concerned about her jurisdiction over the matter. The thirty-two ballots were cast in Hennepin County, not Ramsey County. Plus, any legal matters related to the election were the stuff of an election contest overseen by three judges appointed by the Minnesota Supreme Court. Gearin obviously wasn't a three-judge panel. Still, she heard from Knaak, Lillehaug, and Segal, and, for a Saturday morning, things got pretty heated. On the one hand, Knaak said, "We're not alleging that the [thirty-two] ballots were tainted . . . What we're looking for right now is some determination, however, that, in fact, there was a procedure filed that indicates that these were secure ballots. It appears to us that that's not the case . . ."

Segal, speaking for the city of Minneapolis, got her chance and declared unequivocally to Gearin that the ballots had been in the custody of election officials the entire time. "There is absolutely no evidence here of any irregularity," she said.

Then it was Lillehaug's turn. If he was going to abandon his sick dog on a Saturday morning, he was going to make the most of it. With his white hair and his round face, his pressed shirts and his exacting notes, Lillehaug is exceedingly formal. In court, against Coleman's forces, then and later, he displayed a constant slow burn and a bit of snideness directed at what he viewed as the Coleman legal team's incompetence. It shined through on this Saturday sneak attack.

"What is the irreparable harm that the Coleman campaign is claiming here?" Lillehaug asked Gearin. "The Coleman campaign's irreparable harm is [that] absentee ballots duly cast, apparently, are going to be opened and we're going to have information. We're actually going to know who people voted for and we're actually going to have the totals changed as a result of that. That's not irreparable harm. That's democracy."

Later, Lillehaug called "outrageous" the sweeping nature of Knaak's request that all election officials statewide be enjoined from counting votes that had not been counted Tuesday night. He pointed out a series of technical flaws in Knaak's motion, which, Lillehaug said, was intended to simply "disrupt" his work and his day. So, Lillehaug asked that Gearin fine Knaak and award Lillehaug his attorney's fees for three-and-a-half hours of work, or in Fredrikson & Byron terms, about $1,460, based on Lillehaug's $418 per hour rate.

Gearin denied everything, telling Knaak she had no jurisdiction over the matter and Lillehaug to forget about extracting legal fees from Knaak. Reichert returned to Minneapolis and counted the votes.

This early legal skirmish completed, a myth was about to be born. A couple of hours after the hearing, Knaak and Trimble conducted a news conference at Coleman's campaign headquarters. Misinformation was served. Knaak told a small group of reporters that the ballots in question "had been riding around in [Reichert's] car for several days, which raised all kinds of integrity questions." That incorrect assertion—that Reichert kept ballots in her car unguarded for days—was soon posted on the right-wing Web site Minnesota Democrats Exposed. A couple of commenters on the site kicked it up a notch by claiming the ballots were in a car "trunk."

But, the car, the trunk, the riding around—none of that was true, Reichert told David Brauer of the Twin Cities Web site MinnPost.com in an e-mail a few days later, and she would reiterate her stance under oath during a pretrial deposition and then later at the Coleman–Franken election contest trial. The truth was that some absentee ballots, which first were delivered to City Hall, didn't get to voters' precincts by the time the polls closed on Election Night. They were returned promptly Tuesday night to City Hall. The delay in counting them was caused by Reichert needing to obtain the voting rosters from the precincts in question. She wanted to make sure that the absentee voters hadn't also voted in person. She was protecting the integrity of the election, not threatening it. Months later, Knaak, in an interview, acknowledged that what once seemed like a big deal was really nothing at all.

In this initial scuffle between Knaak and Lillehaug, foundations were laid for what was to come. For instance, Coleman's team was frisky, if not totally competent. Coleman's lawyers were going to be aggressive in their attempts to keep any new votes out of the count. Franken's team would be masters at the rapid response. Something else came into focus. The Twin Cities' traditional news media and the ravenous and partisan blogosphere, goosed by the speed and national access of the Internet, were going to be all over any little tidbit that dribbled out of the mouths of both sides. The twenty-four-hour news cycle, filled with the aftermath of Obama's victory, was happy to feed off of this contentious recount involving a former comedian who was the bane of the right's existence. As the normal adjustments in tallies statewide began to make the election closer and Franken's deficit smaller, Republican partisans, beginning with Minnesota Governor Tim Pawlenty, attempted to toss doubt on the results. Pawlenty, who was beginning to explore a 2012 presidential bid and who would have to sign an election certificate for the winner of the recount, went on the Fox News Channel on November 11, days after Knaak and Trimble calmed down about the thirty-two ballots, and reignited the controversy. "Finding thirty-two ballots in the trunk of the car and supposedly forgetting they're there, that's a problem," the governor said, adding that it was one of the "strange things" that were a "cause for concern" in the election.

A day later, the *Wall Street Journal,* in an editorial headlined "Mischief in Minnesota," launched its campaign to discredit the election, an effort that continued for eight months.

You'd think Democrats would be content with last week's electoral rout. But judging from the odd doings in Minnesota, some in their party wouldn't mind adding to their jackpot by stealing a Senate seat for left-wing joker Al Franken.

When Minnesotans woke up last Wednesday, Republican Senator Norm Coleman led Mr. Franken by 725 votes. By that evening, he was ahead by only 477. As of yesterday, Mr. Coleman's margin stood at 206. This lopsided bleeding of Republican votes is passing strange considering that the official recount hasn't even begun . . .

[N]early every "fix" has gone for Mr. Franken, in some cases under strange circumstances.

For example, there was Friday night's announcement by Minneapolis's director of elections that she'd forgotten to count 32 absentee ballots in her car...

The myth of the thirty-two allegedly well-traveled ballots included a hint of what was to come with absentee ballots. When they were counted, Franken received eighteen votes, or 56 percent. These were a mixture of regular absentees and so-called UOCAVA ballots; that acronym stands for the Uniformed and Overseas Citizens Absentee Voting Act of 1986. It allows military personnel and citizens living out of the country to vote. Coleman received just seven of those votes, or 22 percent. It was an indication that absentee votes were never going to go Coleman's way.

The Saturday sneak attack also forced the Coleman squad to examine just who its lead spokesman would be. The calculation was that a local voice, someone familiar to the Twin Cities media, was the right fit. Adviser Ben Ginsberg was known far and wide in national media circles but, the Coleman forces thought, he would appear as an interloper in a Minnesota race. He evoked, too, the whiff of the *Bush v. Gore* recount. Sometimes blustery Erich Mische, a longtime Coleman confidante and former chief of staff to the senator, had moved on to a lobbying business and preferred to stay in the background. It fell on Knaak, the cordial fellow with the shaved head, the sly smile, and some experience as a pundit on the opinion-making Twin Cities Public Television public affairs show *Almanac* to fill the mouthpiece role for Coleman. Thus began his appearances at countless news briefings with, "Good afternoon, my name is Fritz Ka-Nock—k-n-a-a-k," a bow to his Minnesota roots that might have felt folksy and comfortable to the local media. Knaak was about to be elbowed out of the national news picture, however, by the arrival on the scene of Marc Elias, who was a regular source to key insider outlets, such as *Politico*, the *Hill*, and Talking Points Memo. Elias was a big hitter about to parachute in to the biggest case of his career.

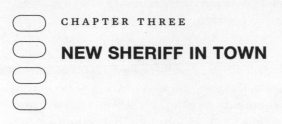

CHAPTER THREE

NEW SHERIFF IN TOWN

"An eighty-four-year-old stroke victim"

Looking a bit gawky, Marc Elias hunched over and firmly placed both of his hands on the wood lectern that stood in front of and beneath him. It was not meant for a six-foot-five fellow. A blue and gold "Al Franken Democrat for U.S. Senate" banner covered the wall behind him, and a U.S. flag stood at attention to his right. Photogenics and messaging were always on Elias's mind and on those of others in this campaign that would not die.

Elias, thirty-nine, wore his dress shirt open at the collar. He was without a sports jacket. He wore khaki pants. He could have been a sheriff offering the details of a local crime from the night before, or a union leader announcing a contract settlement, or maybe an NFL executive explaining the upside of a recently drafted defensive back. Elias was not the picture of a $538-an-hour lawyer with a direct line to the power brokers of the U.S. Senate and even the White House.

The start of a statewide hand recount was six days away, but it looked like a casual Thursday for Elias, a purposely dressed-down introduction to the Minnesota media corps and, through them, to the citizens and decision makers of the state. Five short rows of note-scribbling reporters sat on folding chairs facing him. TV cameras on tripods recorded his bluster. A collection of microphones reached out toward his strong words.

Elias had clout and marching orders from DSCC boss Charles Schumer and Senate Majority Leader Harry Reid to do what it took to lift Franken to victory. Elias also had bubbling confidence. An hour after debarking at Minneapolis–St. Paul International Airport two nights earlier, on November 11, he had made his first visit to Franken headquarters near the University of Minnesota campus and told the assembled staff, "We're going to win." This was his show. Elias struck a deal with Stephanie Schriock, the campaign manager, that he would own complete control over legal strategies. Al Franken was the client, but would remain deeply in the background during the recount. Schriock was Franken's proxy client and the CEO of this soon-to-be $11.3 million recount operation. Elias was the COO, general counsel, quarterback, and chief of mission and vision control. Franken would delegate to Schriock, Schriock to Elias, who would delegate key legal tasks to Hamilton, who would then split responsibilities with Lillehaug. Hamilton would come to be known as the legal team's air traffic controller as more lawyers jumped on board. Lanes were being established. The team members were not allowed to swerve.

Despite his bulging résumé, there was some internal trepidation about Elias acting as the primary spokesman for the Franken recount effort. How would Minnesotans accept this fast-talking, arm-flailing, no-nonsense New Yorker? Wouldn't well-connected Minnesota lawyer Lillehaug, the cautious Lutheran from Sioux Falls, South Dakota, the former prosecutor with ties to Walter Mondale and Paul Wellstone, better bring instant credibility and familiarity to the recount information dissemination? Elias made it clear, however, that if the decisions were his, the explanation of them also had to belong to him. In the course of gathering his pre-arrival intelligence, Elias had learned that the Franken campaign's communications shop had sour relations with some local news outlets, especially with some reporters and editors at the Minneapolis *Star Tribune*. It went back to skirmishes during the campaign and, most recently, the newspaper's gushing editorial endorsement of Coleman's candidacy and its dismissive treatment of Franken. Now, Elias would take over the key media events when actions were to be launched, conclusions announced, legal maneuvers clarified, and Coleman tactics critiqued. No one else would be allowed to speak extemporaneously and on the record to journalists from the Franken camp. All verbiage, save for formal statements issued by press spokespeople Barr and McIntosh, would come from Elias.

Messaging in a recount is different from messaging during a campaign. The audience Elias sought to reach was no longer the mass of voters that Franken, his staff, and his paid advertising tried to woo just nine days earlier. The appeal at this stage needed to be directed to that segment of voters whose absentee ballots may have been wrongly rejected. Franken loyalists also had to know their guy was fighting hard. Members of the state Canvassing Board, who would rule on the intent of challenged recounted ballots, were a niche audience. They needed to hear Elias and, maybe, like him. State judges, who might hear this case in the months to come, were targets. Election officials statewide, who needed to know their work might not yet be complete and that their work would be appreciated by the Franken team, were specific message receivers. Then there were the local journalists who, Elias hoped, would begin to find aggrieved citizens whose rejected absentee votes might help Franken catch up to Coleman.

Just as important, Elias's pals in the national media mattered. Eager for another *Bush v. Gore*–like saga to munch on, their published stories and Web posts would buoy the hopes of Democrats nationally, particularly Democrats with money to continue the funding for Franken's cause. As recount specialist Sautter's *Recount Primer* made clear, "Recounts make good copy because they provide new and often unusual insight into the electoral process. The perception that the recount can be won is critical for maintaining partisan support and for fund raising." Elias took that maxim to heart.

As he found votes for Franken, this political scientist–lawyer–funny man was going to control the narrative, no matter how un-Minnesotan he might appear. When he got to Minneapolis, there were internal campaign conversations about what he would wear when meeting the media and being photographed. Plaid shirt? Jeans? Nah. Did that open collar satisfy the taste of this market better than his Washington, D.C., dark suit? The initial sartorial decision was open collar.

No matter how he dressed, Elias's style bordered on frumpy, but his motor ran high. That was his way, and had been for the past fifteen years, since he had graduated from Duke Law School and became an unusual right-off-the-campus hire by the powerful Perkins Coie firm's political unit, where he instantly became a sensation in Democratic Party election law. When Elias interviewed for the job, Bob Bauer, the Democrats' godfather of campaign finance, congressional ethics, and election law, and his partner Judith Corley saw something special in Elias's natural theatrics, his passion, and his innate ability to see the merger of law and politics. Like a top-flight college football star, Elias was drafted onto this Perkins Coie team, and, like a young quarterback who sits the bench for a few seasons before getting a chance to play, he was groomed for this day, this scenario of 2008, to run a nationally important U.S. Senate recount.

Born to a Wall Street trader who lost much of his wealth in the stock market crash of 1973 and 1974, Marc Erik Elias was born February 1, 1969, and raised in the Rockland County suburb of Suffern, just outside of New York City. The grandson of Russian and Polish immigrants, he was embedded in a post–New Deal Jewish household. His torso allowed him to play high school basketball, but his mind led him toward political science at upstate New York's Hamilton College and then Duke, where in three compact years he earned his law degree and his master's in political science, met his wife (another Duke law school grad), and wowed the Perkins Coie hiring committee.

Upon moving to Washington, he was placed in the Perkins Coie white-collar-criminal defense unit. Within a week of his hiring he was sent to New Jersey to help on what would become a six-week-long government contract fraud case. He argued motions. He cross-examined witnesses; his first ever was an FBI agent. The client he helped was acquitted. Elias was thrilled. He was twenty-five years old.

A few months later, in the fall of 1994, the Republicans gained control of the U.S. House of Representatives and Newt Gingrich became House Speaker. Thanks to Gingrich's venomous partisan attacks, the field of political law broadened and became nicely lucrative. Gingrich used House ethics rules and Federal Election Commission (FEC) guidelines as swords to attack House Democrats. The Senate, also controlled by the Republicans, investigated the campaign finance practices of President Bill Clinton and the Democratic National Committee. Lots of guys in silk ties, dark suits, and black wing tips needed aggressive, politically savvy legal representation. Many went to Bauer, the best in the biz, for help. Before long, Bauer tapped Elias to be at his side.

In that same 1996–97 period, Bauer introduced Elias to his first U.S. Senate election contest, a real doozy in Louisiana between Democrat Mary Landrieu and Republican Woody Jenkins. It taught Elias that the U.S. Senate itself—even more than state courts—is one of the places where decisions can be made about who becomes a U.S. Senator. Right there in the U.S. Constitution, Article I, Section IV, it says, "Each House shall be the Judge of the Elections, Returns and Qualifications of its own Members." In the Landrieu case, she won by nearly six thousand votes, which was a landslide compared with the gap in the Coleman–Franken tussle. Jenkins claimed widespread irregularities in the election. For ten months, the Republican-controlled U.S. Senate investigated Landrieu's alleged involvement in alleged shenanigans. Elias worked on that matter

to ensure Landrieu kept her Senate seat.[1] By 1998 Elias moved on to helping Nevada Senator Harry Reid in the early stages of surviving a recount.
Then he helped Maria Cantwell of Washington State in her 2000 U.S.
Senate recount. Still, until this Franken case, Elias had never fully supervised a recount and had never actually got his hands dirty handling the
complexities of ballots.

Elias's day-to-day practice focused on advising candidates (and donors)
on campaign finance laws, the content of political commercials, minding
lobbying restrictions, and the art of preparing reports for the FEC. As his
client base grew, his career in courtrooms faded. Cross-examinations
weren't his thing. The halls of the U.S. Capitol were his venue of choice.
With Perkins Coie representing the Democratic Senatorial Campaign
Committee, Elias oversaw that account, representing from time to time
pretty much every Democrat in that chamber, including Minnesota's Paul
Wellstone, Mark Dayton, and Amy Klobuchar. He worked closely with
South Dakota Senator Tom Daschle, first the Senate minority leader and
then its majority leader. Daschle became a mentor. Elias was Kerry's general counsel during the 2004 presidential campaign. He consulted with
Stephanie Schriock when she managed the hotly contested 2006 Senate
campaign of Montana's Jon Tester. A recount almost occurred there. He
represented one of Hillary Clinton's New York campaign committees
when she ran for Senate and waded into some hot water with the FEC.

Bauer, who became President Obama's White House counsel in 2009,
remembers the first time he saw his young colleague, then twenty-eight
years old, in full jittery, passionate, vocal mode during the Landrieu Senate battle. "Nobody worked harder than Marc, nobody cared about the
result more, nobody had a greater will to live even after early defeat,"
Bauer said. "There is never a moment when Marc says, 'We'll hang it
up now.' He fights to the last." Bauer knew that Elias was a street fighter
with a law degree, but no one in Minnesota did—not yet.

Before Elias spoke his first words to the assembled media in Franken's
campaign offices on November 13, Lillehaug had already attempted to
get rejected absentee ballots included in the count. On Monday, November 10, while Elias was packing for Minnesota, the Hennepin County
Canvassing Board met to certify the count of ballots cast on Election Day.
Lillehaug focused on convincing the panel in the state's largest county

to examine as many as 461 rejected absentee ballots. But the assistant county attorney resisted, telling Lillehaug that the issue of rejected absentee ballots was for the state Canvassing Board, or an eventual election contest trial, not local canvassing boards. That was the first strikeout for the Franken campaign. Two days later, Secretary of State Mark Ritchie told reporters that absentee ballots that had been rejected — rightly or wrongly — were not to be considered by the state Canvassing Board when it began its business, and he would know because he was the chairman of the board. "The recount is done on ballots that have been accepted," Ritchie said. "There could be a contest. A citizen could go to court and say, 'My ballot wasn't included,' and ask a judge to make a ruling on that decision. But again it's not in our area, it's in the contest area." Take that, Mr. Franken, Ritchie, a progressive Democrat, seemed to say. His comments annoyed the Franken legal team. Elias, especially, was a political animal. He couldn't figure out why a Democrat would assert something that wouldn't be friendly to Franken. That same day, November 12, Ritchie named his teammates on the state Canvassing Board. This further angered the Franken side.

Supreme Court Chief Justice Eric Magnuson, appointed earlier in the year by pal and Republican Governor Tim Pawlenty, and Associate Justice G. Barry Anderson, former counsel to the state Republican Party, were named to be on the panel empowered to evaluate challenged ballots in the recount, determine the fate of absentee ballots, and ultimately decide which candidate received the most legal votes and deserved the coveted election certificate. The Franken lawyers met specially to determine how to react to the makeup of the board. They grumbled that Republicans never do this; they back their own. Democrats tend to bend over backward to demonstrate their fairness. Elias thought Ritchie was going to sell Franken down the Mississippi River in a display of nonpartisanship. So he lashed out at Ritchie via a statement from Andy Barr, Franken's youthful communications director and verbal sniper, a shot to let Ritchie know the Democratic candidate wasn't going to politely accept such imbalance.

The Coleman campaign and its political allies have been trying to claim that Minnesota's Secretary of State is just a left-wing partisan. I think we can all now see that their claims were just political posturing. Today, Mark Ritchie has named two partisan Republican Supreme Court justices to the state canvassing board. Chief Justice Magnuson was Governor Pawlenty's law partner. Justice Anderson spent a decade representing the Minnesota GOP. And both were named to the Supreme Court by Governor Pawlenty, who has been an active surrogate for the Coleman campaign, going on television to spread false claims of foul play in an effort to besmirch our state's good reputation and cast doubt on our electoral process.

Nevertheless, there are clear laws laying out how this recount should proceed. And we will continue to hope that, despite the partisan affiliations of these two justices, they are capable of interpreting those laws correctly and ruling fairly on matters related to this recount.

The real question is: Will the Coleman campaign continue its shameful effort to prevent every vote from being counted fairly, or will they stop spreading baseless claims?

Not to be outdone, Sheehan, Coleman's campaign manager, also blasted Ritchie. This was for something Ritchie had said on the MSNBC cable TV channel when he was asked about Coleman's early criticism of how the vote totals were changing in the days after an election, as they always do. Coleman's minions were claiming the reduction in Coleman's lead as the days wore on seemed fishy. Ritchie's reaction on the left-of-center cable news network was to say, "Their goal is to win at any price. They've invested millions and millions of dollars. We consider this part of the normal political rhetoric . . . We're used to the political rhetoric being amped up."

Sheehan was shocked, just shocked. Of Ritchie, he said, "His accusation today that our campaign intends to win 'at any price' is offensive, demands an apology, and simply underscores our concerns about his ability to act as an unbiased official in this recount. His statement is not reflective of the objective, nonpartisan standards Minnesotans expect and deserve, and which Mr. Ritchie as secretary of state is sworn to uphold. And we are concerned about the pattern we are seeing."

Ritchie's Canvassing Board selections were, in fact, innocent, nonpartisan, and completely by the book. In fact, Ritchie, perhaps the state's most liberal elected official, didn't personally select the members at all. Chief Justice Magnuson, Associate Justice Anderson, and the two other members, Ramsey County District Court judges Kathleen Gearin and Edward Cleary, pretty much self-selected, choosing roles they at first didn't know would be so critical, scrutinized, or time-consuming. "The

State Canvassing Board shall consist of the secretary of state, two judges of the supreme court, and two judges of the district court selected by the secretary of state," Minnesota election law reads. "None of the judges shall be a candidate at the election."

Sometime in late August or early September, an e-mail had gone out from Ritchie's office to the chambers of Magnuson and Gearin, the latter because, in most cases, the state Canvassing Board's duties are perfunctory and the Ramsey County Courthouse is a short stroll from the secretary of state's office. Convenience, nothing more. Magnuson was appointed by Pawlenty in March 2008 and not sworn in until June to lead the high court. While he was still settling into his role, Magnuson received the e-mail seeking the two volunteers from the Supreme Court. His administrative assistant told him such board duties usually took "ten minutes," so, he figured, he would try something new. Because associate justices Paul Anderson and Lorie Gildea were up for reelection, their participation was prohibited. After one round of e-mails triggered no takers from the remaining four justices, Magnuson sent out a second e-mail and "G. Barry," who had practiced election law for the state GOP, raised his hand.

Gearin and Cleary's decisions to become Canvassing Board members were only slightly more complicated. She had performed the task about a half dozen times before, and generally viewed it as "a pain in the butt," but she was the chief judge and such duties seemed to fall in her job description. She agreed to help Ritchie, assuming it wouldn't take more than the twenty minutes or so as it had in the past. She quickly recruited another judge to volunteer. Time passed, Election Day came, and, the day after, Ritchie's top aide, Jim Gelbmann, telephoned Gearin to give her the heads up that a recount was coming. Her Canvassing Board commitment might "take a little longer— quote, unquote —that's what he told me," Gearin said months later. "A little longer, hah!" Understanding the scrutiny the board was to face, Gearin went to chat with Cleary, who was appointed by Independence Party Governor Jesse Ventura and had before that been the director of the nonpartisan Minnesota Office of Lawyers Professional Responsibility and Client Security Board. Cleary was the assistant chief judge of Ramsey County. Gearin told him she thought he should take the second district court slot on the Canvassing Board. Like police killings and other high-profile cases, Gearin believed this Senate recount responsibility should fall on the most responsible jurists, the chief and the assistant chief. (By the way, Gearin wasn't appointed by a governor at all; she ran for an open seat in 1986.) When Magnuson and Gearin got back to Ritchie, he simply accepted their recommendations, no questions asked.[2]

On paper, Ritchie was a natural Franken ally, had appeared at pro-Franken campaign events, and so was an easy target of Republicans. He had succeeded a Republican secretary of state named Mary Kiffmeyer just two years earlier. Kiffmeyer was not unlike Katherine Harris, the partisan, swayable Florida secretary of state who helped shut down the Bush–Gore recount in 2000. Although Minnesota's voter turnout continued to lead the nation while Kiffmeyer was secretary of state, her eight years in office were marked by some questionable office expenditures and episodes of denying the vote to American Indians and University of Minnesota students, people who might tend to be Democrats. Ritchie's own election campaign against her in 2006 accused her of using her office for partisan reasons. Ritchie was a former agricultural policy organizer and an activist for a group called National Voice, which worked to register voters nationwide. The most aggressive of Minnesota's right-wing bloggers, Michael Brodkorb—a local one-man Republican hit squad via his well-read and wickedly entertaining Minnesota Democrats Exposed Web site—regularly attacked Ritchie during his first two years in office, linking him tenuously to a newspaper long ago affiliated with the Communist Party USA and posting a photo of Ritchie at a Franken and Obama fundraiser. Ritchie also received a campaign endorsement from ACORN, the controversial grassroots organization known for registering otherwise disenfranchised voters, most of whom tend toward the Democratic ilk. Ritchie couldn't help but be smack-dab in the middle of this barroom brawl. Republicans were forever suspicious of him. The Democrats thought Ritchie was trying too hard to appear fair to Coleman, and were also concerned about Magnuson, the Pawlenty confidante, and Anderson, the full-fledged GOP lawyer.

The Franken team wanted to establish that it was fighting for the voters, that their guy could stage a comeback, and that the election wasn't over. The Coleman team's message was, we won, those bad guys want to steal it, don't let them. It was as if this were a championship basketball game, with both sides working the Canvassing Board "refs," which is surely what Elias had in mind that first day when he stood behind the lectern in the open-collared shirt and khakis and offered his opening performance on Minnesota soil with hopes of charming the Midwesterners.

In his inimitable, bomb-throwing style, Barr introduced Elias. Barr was a loyal Frankenista, having met Al at Harvard when the comedian–politician taught a course there and his students became researchers for his best-selling book *Lies and the Lying Liars Who Tell Them*. Barr had been one of Franken's top students. He went on to work as a researcher at Air America when Franken hosted his radio talk show, and then followed Franken to Minnesota to help build the campaign. Barr's news conferences sometimes sounded more Al Qaeda than Al Franken. The negativity was exactly what had brought the state to this recount.

"I'd like to discuss a pattern of misdirection and misinformation from the Coleman campaign and its surrogates and allies designed to undermine this process and keep votes from getting counted," Barr said before making way for Elias's debut. "The Coleman campaign isn't lying for sport . . . It's part of a political strategy to discredit the process."

That was a tough act to follow, but Elias tried his best, speaking softly, slowly, and politely. "Thank you. Good morning everyone. I'm Marc Elias, and it is my honor to be here today to talk to you as the lead recount attorney for the Franken campaign." Good start, sort of like the beginning of a boring appeals court oral argument. Elias issued his first talking point, explaining that Franken's goal was to assure that "every person who cast a lawful ballot has that ballot counted," and pointed out that, in some counties, lawful absentee ballots had not been counted.

"I'll give you one example," Elias said. "We had one of our organizers visit a woman at a nursing home where she lives. And she told us that her signature was indeed different than the one on file with the county and that was because she had suffered a stroke . . . Her ballot didn't get counted—yet," he said, for effect, leaving open for assumption that he would make sure that it would be counted soon. He then dropped the recount's first bombshell. The Franken campaign was about to file a Minnesota Government Data Practices Act (a state version of the federal Freedom of Information Act) lawsuit in Ramsey County because its chief election official and the county attorney refused to turn over the names of absentee voters in the county in which St. Paul resides. He said that the Franken campaign had been making these Data Practices Act requests to other counties over the past two days. Some, such as Beltrami County in northwest Minnesota, had complied. Others, such as Ramsey County, had not. The hope was that if Franken won in his St. Paul effort, other counties would fall in line.

He went on to call the woman in the nursing home "an eighty-four-year-old stroke victim" from Beltrami County. The goal of the legal action was obvious: if Franken's campaign had the names of all absentee voters and not just a few little old ladies, then it could begin the absentee-ballot chase that Reese had recommended days before.

"This is not a lawsuit about putting ballots in the count for nothing," Elias said. "This is about giving us access to the data that will allow us to determine whether or not there are lawful ballots." You could almost see his adrenaline beginning to pump. Elias's volume increased. His words came faster. Perhaps to make it seem as if he were a Minnesotan, he began dropping the *g* at the end of words.

"Honest, hard workin' men and women, who did everythin' right, they played by the rules, they went to the secretary of state's Web site, they read how to submit an absentee ballot, and yet their ballots weren't counted," he said, his voice moving from a 6 to a 10 on the volume scale, as he asserted that Coleman was trying to stop the count while Franken wanted "every legally cast ballot to count."

After a while, Elias took questions from the reporters. Minnesota nice wasn't in the room that day. What about Ritchie saying absentee ballots weren't a part of this phase? Do you intend to contest this election in court? Will you take this to the U.S. Supreme Court? The questions rained down.

"Right now, we are preparing for a recount," Elias said, attempting to calm the journalists.

The *Star Tribune*'s chief political correspondent, Patricia Lopez, was aggressive. "Could you answer this question please?" Lopez asked. "Is there a mechanism for counting those absentee ballots short of going to court?"

"Yes," Elias replied.

"What would that be?" Lopez asked impatiently.

"We believe that if they are brought to the attention of the Canvassing Board they can be counted," he said.

But Ritchie said that's not so, she volleyed back. "So what do you know that he doesn't know?" The room turned frosty.

"Why," Lopez asked a minute later, "is it so difficult to say that legal action may be an option?" She was baiting him. Elias had heard from the Franken communications team that this press corps was timid. This was timid?

"Look, before we jump four steps down the road as to what might happen, what might be necessary, let's start with first principles . . . This eighty-four-year-old woman had a Constitutional right to vote. Let's start with that . . . A state may not devise an election regime where a woman, because she had a stroke, no longer gets the right to vote."

OK, you get these lists, so you're going to contact voters, the reporters surmised. "Might that be seen as some level of intimidation?" Lopez thrust. "Uh, no," Elias parried. "Just asking," she said. "And I'm just answering," he replied with a chuckle that belied his own impatience.

By the end of the day, it got worse for Elias, who had been victimized by very bad information from the Franken field staff about the alleged elderly voter. Lopez's skepticism was warranted. She proceeded to do her job well and found out from the Beltrami County auditor, Kay Mack, that, as Lopez wrote, "her office hadn't rejected any ballots because of mismatched signatures. Mack said there was one instance of an eighty-seven-year-old woman in an assisted living center whose ballot was rejected because it bore no signature or mark. The law, Mack said, is 'very clear' about not accepting such ballots."

Oops. Credibility was considered the key to the Franken recount effort and here, in his first media encounter in the Land of 10,000 Lakes, Elias's credibility was under water. Despite the nonexistence of the eighty-four-year-old stroke victim and the campaign's embarrassment, the mainstream news organizations soon did what mainstream news organizations do, even in the face of cutbacks and layoffs. In the days that followed Elias's news conference, reporters from the *Star Tribune* and the *Pioneer Press*, using some of the same data that the Franken campaign received voluntarily from some counties, found real people whose real votes were in real doubt. As the journalists performed their watchdog role, triggered by mistrust of Elias, they created an odd, backdoor bit of progress for Elias too.

A hard lesson was learned. In the wake of the embarrassment, the Franken team tightened fact-checking around the veracity of voters whose ballots had been rejected. The distance the Franken force went to ensure accuracy revealed its boundless resources. Hamilton brought in a Perkins Coie partner from Seattle, a former Department of Justice attorney and former vice president for internal investigations at Fannie Mae named Fred Rivera. Rivera, aided by campaign volunteers, investigated and documented the facts of each potential voter–plaintiff whose ballot was rejected. This was not for media consumption. This was to generate affidavits so these voters could, at some point, have their ballots counted. This was evidence development. When Rivera had to return to Seattle, the Franken team employed a succession of other Perkins Coie partners, all of them, male or female, nicknamed "new Fred" or "new, new Fred" — a code name for whoever was currently serving as the elite vetting czar who would allow no more fictional nursing home residents.

Really, there was no need for fictional voters because there were hundreds, maybe thousands, of real votes that had been wrongly rejected for reasons other than the four statutory ones: improper name and address on the application and ballot envelope; signature doesn't match with the ballot's application; is not a registered voter; and voted in person on Election Day. As reporters kept finding wrongly rejected voters, as lawyers chased for affidavits, as election officials statewide began to wonder themselves about turned-down ballots, a public relations buzz grew that could trigger a political climate that might force a legal solution. Elias and friends wanted that conversation to travel from average citizens to talk show hosts to blogs to the state Canvassing Board. At the same time, Coleman's team worked hard to swat away all the discussion of the absentee envelopes.

"The Franken campaign is shamelessly trying to strong-arm local officials into counting invalid ballots in order to influence the outcome of the recount," Coleman's campaign manager, Cullen Sheehan, said. "This is a new low. This tactic is simply designed to shove more rejected ballots into the ballot box before the recount takes place . . ."

The recount tug-of-war was soon to be waged on 106 fronts, that is, recount locations. The recount of ballots counted on Election Night was set to begin with Franken still behind. There was a slight risk in seeking to rejuvenate rejected absentee ballots. If the absentees statewide leaned in the Republican direction, it could come back to bite Elias and Franken. They could be opening votes for Coleman. But if Franken's lawyers could win their Data Practices Act lawsuit, then they could begin to examine the names and locations of all the rejected voters. The DFL had far better voter identification data than the GOP. How much better was unclear. The Franken lawyers assumed that, if and when absentee voter lists became available, Coleman would engage in his own absentee-ballot chase, gathering his own additional votes. "There's a train a-comin'," Hamilton told Franken staffers in their headquarters, readying for Coleman's absentee-ballot offensive. But Coleman's absentee-ballot train never left the station. The Coleman side was confident they wouldn't need more votes — overly confident, as it turned out. They didn't know the DFL's data-gathering machine was only beginning to rev up, and not just for those absentees, but for the recount of all 2.9 million ballots cast on Election Night. Another pearl of wisdom from Democratic recount expert Sautter, written in 1994, was spot-on in November of 2008: "If the election is too close to tell who is ahead, opt for a broad recount on the assumption that the opposing side will not be as well organized as you are."

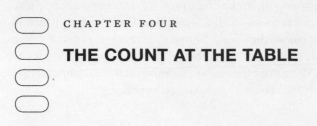

CHAPTER FOUR

THE COUNT AT THE TABLE

"Why would you ever want less information?"

Al Franken's list of contributors was pretty cool. Hundreds of pages in the Federal Election Commission's files detailed nearly fourteen thousand names and about twenty million dollars to back the rookie candidate. A browse through the list revealed donors such as musician Don Henley of the Eagles rock band, TV journalist Jane Pauley, financier George Soros, movie mogul David Geffen, husband-and-wife actors Ted Danson and Mary Steenburgen, and film star Michael Douglas, to name a few. As the recount effort got underway, with Franken needing volunteers and staff at 106 different locations statewide to monitor the hand counting of nearly three million ballots, spectacle and buzz were to be expected. Even more money was needed.

On Saturday, November 15, eleven days after Election Day and four days before the Great Minnesota Recount was set to begin, more than one thousand volunteers descended on Macalester College's Campus Center in St. Paul to receive training on how to monitor elections officials' actions, how to collect critical data, and how to challenge ballots. Elements of Paul Wellstone's legacy were present. Jeff Blodgett, Wellstone's former campaign manager, was Barack Obama's Minnesota campaign manager. He helped with training. Dan Cramer, a skilled trainer and organizer, Franken's field operations consultant, and the political director of Wellstone's maiden 1990 Senate campaign, led many of the sessions, along with Sautter.

The gaggle of energetic volunteers received handouts with information about their tasks. They prepared for breakout groups and mock recount sessions so they could then fan out to recount locations days later. Before the important work began, they were greeted by Franken himself, along with two of his close pals. One was former Clinton administration political aide and CNN talking head Paul Begala. The other was Bradley Whitford, the dashing actor who played deputy chief of staff Josh Lyman on the *West Wing*. The show-biz buzz was in the house. The three pumped up the crowd with an instructional chant, led by the candidate himself.

"What do we want?" Franken shouted to the supporters in the auditorium.

"Patience!" the troops responded.

"When do we want it?" the underdog trailing by 215 votes asked again.

"Now!" they replied.

"Patience now." That was a purposely oxymoronic notion, but it was an appropriate call-and-response for all that was in store over the next seven weeks of the recount, let alone the next seven days. Over the course of the next week, a blizzard of legal documents would whip around the state Canvassing Board as the Franken team pushed the absentee-ballot chase to the next level. A hurricane of activity kept both campaigns moving as if it were the preelection final-days rush, and not an unprecedented postelection frenzy.

Between this busy Saturday and Tuesday, November 18, Sautter, Cramer, and others trained more than two thousand volunteers in St. Paul, Minneapolis, Duluth, Grand Rapids, Little Falls, Rochester, Moorhead, and Worthington. Add another four hundred volunteer lawyers from inside Minnesota and beyond. Among the skills taught were how to challenge ballots that appeared to have fuzzy voter intent—at least those that were Coleman votes—and how to mark down as accurately as possible what election judges decided when confronted with challenged ballots.

On the Coleman side, similar, but less extensive, training was underway. According to legal team members, recount captains were trained for the various sites; then, when these leaders arrived at recount locations, they trained others that day. Coleman lawyers Matt Haapoja and Tony Trimble conducted training sessions for "hundreds of volunteers" at Coleman's St. Paul campaign headquarters and the GOP's Fifth Congressional District offices in Minneapolis.

What might an odd ballot look like and what might be one worthy of a challenge? The oval next to the other guy's name wasn't fully filled in. The oval was filled in, but an X was written across it and the oppos-ing candidate's oval was completed, suggesting a change-of-mind in the voting booth. Errant marks were on the ballot, such as an "OK" next to a name. Oddball names—from football stars to cartoon super heroes—were written in as candidates, even if Franken's or Coleman's oval was also filled. Half an oval was completed. A candidate's name was circled rather than his assigned oval filled. Scrawl covered an oval, as if colored by an angry two-year-old.

For Franken, Sautter was the expert and master trainer. Using tem-plates from *The Recount Primer,* the recount bible he coauthored in 1994, Sautter distributed forms for volunteers to use and complete when they arrived at their recount sites. The forms aimed to detail the number of precincts counted at a recount table, the total numbers of votes, the total numbers of votes for each candidate, and the specifics of challenged bal-lots. At Macalester, the Franken volunteers, often directed and led by labor union officials or political activists who had received more exten-sive training the night before, broke up into twenty-five-person groups and simulated what was to occur at recount tables from Minneapolis to Moorhead beginning in a few days.

Challenging questionable ballots was one thing—and zealots from both sides would go on to challenge too many ballots frivolously, ballots that were clearly marked for one man or another and absolutely reflected a voter's intent—but Sautter's major issue was this: keep impeccable track of what the election judges ruled at the recount tables.

Here's what it will look like, the volunteers were told. Ballots from individual precincts will be removed from large envelopes. There will be one or two election judges on duty. A Franken representative, but more likely two, will also be at the table, along with Coleman observers. Most ballots will be easy to determine. An oval to the left of the candidate's name will be completely filled in. The voter's intent is certain. When the election official declares, "Franken," mark it down for Franken. When the official declares, "Coleman," record it for Coleman.

When a voter's intent is unclear, be alert. If it's hard to decipher—and seemingly leaning toward Coleman—challenge it. Assume the Cole-man campaign will act similarly with votes that seem to be intended for Franken, challenging an imperfectly filled-out ballot because it wants to eliminate a potential Franken vote. No matter which side challenges, the election judge will make a determination right there at the table as to which candidate, in the judge's opinion, was the intended vote-getter.

The local, nonpartisan, civic-minded election judge will make his or her own "call at the table" of the voter's intent, giving the vote to Coleman, Franken, or other, in most cases, Dean Barkley. Those challenged ballots will then be set aside until mid-December for the members of the state Canvassing Board to make final decisions on challenged ballots and on which candidate received the most votes. Before this recount was completed, 6,689 Election Day ballots were, at some point along the way, challenged, a number that would, thankfully, be reduced before landing on the desks of the Canvassing Board members.

(By the way, that 6,689 figure was a pittance compared to the feisty 1962 gubernatorial recount in Minnesota. With only 1.3 million voters, more than one hundred thousand votes were challenged during that recount.)[1]

On all challenged ballots, the Franken volunteers were told, be obsessive and compulsive about recording the nonpartisan judge's decision at the table. The mantra was: "Keep track of the call at the table." Observe everything, preserve all documentation. Why? Sautter's experience taught him that what a local judge decides during the hand recount is almost always what the more centralized Canvassing Board decides once the process moves to the next level and the votes are formally and finally counted. As Elias, the New York Giants fan, explained, a challenged ballot is not unlike a video challenge by a head coach in pro football. In an NFL game, the ruling on the field stands unless there is indisputable evidence on video that the play should be overturned. Most times, the ruling on the field holds up.

"We all know that sometimes instant replay overturns it," Elias said of questionable calls by a referee. "But, as a baseline, the NFL could say we'll assume every call on the field is correct or every call is incorrect. It's more sensible to start with the proposition that they're probably correct in the first instance." The Franken team embraced the NFL assumption that the judges' rulings at tables from Roseau to Albert Lea would be ultimately accepted by the state Canvassing Board. On this meticulous exercise, the Coleman team fumbled the ball. According to Coleman staffers and lawyers who were interviewed, his campaign was not diligent in tracking every day exactly how the recount went at all 106 recount sites.

Dan Cramer, who helped organize the field troops for the Franken recount, explained the thinking on requiring as much information as possible as quickly as possible. "Why would you ever want less information? You don't have to act on information, but if you have it, you can act on it. You can inform your press strategy. You can inform your fundraising. You can inform the deployment of your resources. You can inform what you're doing with absentee ballots. You don't have to do anything with it, but information gives you options."

As both campaigns organized for the November 19 recount kickoff, the number was set. After all the county and local election officials gathered all their ballots, after the canvassing of election machine tapes, Coleman held an official 215-vote lead. Franken needed at least that many votes to overtake the incumbent. Patience now would be a recount virtue for the candidates, their volunteers, elections judges, and Ritchie's office. But this was no waiting game. Coleman–Franken 2.0 was underway, and the pace was dizzying.

Elias had legal experience at a handful of recounts, but he had never been a foot soldier training observers and analyzing challenged ballots. He had always been counsel to campaigns. Hamilton tried the Washington State gubernatorial election contest and won, but he wasn't a precinct-to-precinct recount infantryman. Schriock worried about a recount in her 2006 U.S. Senate race in Montana, and that's why she was so eager to be prepared this time, but she had never managed one of these things before. Lillehaug, for all of his work in the past as a debate coach and lawyer to Paul Wellstone, Amy Klobuchar, and Franken, had not found himself in the throes of a recount. The state of Minnesota, through all of its elections, hadn't faced a statewide, general election recount since that 1962 row between Elmer Andersen and Karl Rolvaag.

That left Sautter, fifty-nine years old, as the go-to guy on the Franken legal team. Unlike Elias, Hamilton, and Lillehaug, he was not a partner in a gigantic law firm with fancy offices. He was a sole practitioner, a law school instructor, and one-time campaign manager and media consultant. Besides Sautter's regular recount gigs dating back to 1984, he had produced political commercials and award-winning film documentaries. He was the creator of the first radio commercials in 2000 for an unknown Illinois state senator named Barack Obama who ran for U.S. Congress, and lost; years earlier, Sautter worked with David Axelrod, who would go on to become Obama's top political adviser. Sometimes, to hear the other Franken lawyers speak, Sautter's contributions were deemed a bit pedestrian. It was as if they were generals dressed in their pressed uniforms in the safety of headquarters and he was the smudged Marine, kicking down the door, telling the others on the commando unit it's safe to move in. A Franken staffer, who wasn't quite sure of Sautter's role, asked him, "What do you do here?" Sautter replied, "I'm the security blanket."

Growing up in Illinois and Indiana, Sautter emerged from an unusual ancestry for the Franken legal team: his parents were Republicans. By the time he got to high school, he was improbably preparing for this *Saturday Night Live*-linked recount. One of his neighbors, football teammates, and pals was John Belushi, the wacky comedian who went on to work with Franken on the NBC television show. Another neighbor was a less-funny fellow named Bob Woodward, he of the fabled Watergate journalism team of Woodward and Bernstein.

By 1968, eighteen years old and an Indiana University student, Sautter was a Democrat working on Robert F. Kennedy's presidential primary campaign. Since working on his first recount, that super-close congressional race in Indiana's Eighth District, he has been called in by the Democrats on virtually every nail-biter since. In 1989, he helped Douglas Wilder win a recount in Virginia and become the first African-American governor of that state. He worked on the 1994 congressional recount for Connecticut's Sam Gejdenson, who won by four votes. He met Elias for the first time when helping Harry Reid win his Senate seat in Nevada in 1998. Election Night 2000, Sautter watched returns of the George Bush–Al Gore battle at the Democratic National Committee headquarters in Washington with Elias's mentor, Bob Bauer. As the night wore on, most of the calls started coming from Florida. The next day, Sautter flew to Florida to help oversee the likely recount. At strategy sessions in Tallahassee attended by top Gore aides—such as Warren Christopher and William Daley—Sautter urged them to seek a statewide hand count of all six million votes cast. The Gore strategy team rejected Sautter's advice, deciding instead to seek hand counts in only four counties. You know the rest.

There were no limits in Minnesota in 2008. This project required enormous resources, and Schriock made sure they had them. Because of the politics of the race, its national importance, the watchful eye of Democrats in Washington, and Schriock's and Franken's ability to raise large sums of money, this recount was fully funded. The lawyers would tell Schriock, "I think we need it." She would ask, "Why?" They would say because real-time information is critical, and she would say, "Approved." When it was over, the Franken team had raised about eleven million dollars after the election to cover the costs of the recount, including the fees for all the lawyers. (Coleman's side raised more in the range of eight million dollars.) Sautter was paid $225,000 for his work, and his advice to the campaign to track the calls at the tables made it all worth it. He worked closely with Franken's recount field director, Alana Petersen, who, of all the Minnesota-based members of Franken's team, was the only one with recount experience. She led the recount for Congressman David Minge when he lost to Mark Kennedy in 2000; Coleman lawyer Trimble was Kennedy's attorney.

Because information informs quick reaction tactics and even long-term litigation strategy, Sautter had a notion that all the data compiled daily at each recount site needed to be transmitted instantly to Franken's St. Paul headquarters. At first, he suggested to Petersen that the campaign acquire scanners at every recount location and electronically deliver each challenged ballot. Petersen, who lived in rural Minnesota and was a member of Congressman James Oberstar's staff, scoffed at that. Broadband capabilities were less than adequate in various parts of Greater Minnesota, she told him. "I'll get them to you fast. It might be the middle of the night, but you'll have them." To fulfill that promise, Petersen, Schriock, and others devised what they called "the Pony Express." Petersen delegated to a campaign operative named Dusty Trice the major task of gathering, purchasing, and organizing supplies for volunteers and then developing a network of drivers to bring data back to headquarters for an around-the-clock ballot analysis operation.

"Alana was marching through the offices like a general on the eve of battle," said lawyer Kevin Hamilton. "Jesus, get out of her way."

Trice was the Pony Express guru, a shaved-headed North Dakotan who during the two-year-long campaign was Al and Franni Franken's trusted driver. Trice, a twenty-eight-year-old one-time Young Republican, was the third person hired by Franken after early campaign managers Andy Barr and David Benson. Throughout the campaign, Trice, driving the Franken's black Chevy Tahoe hybrid, survived fog, endless chicken dinners, and wee-hours treks to get the candidate and his spouse to their appointed rounds. Once, in a late-night drive through parts of desolate western Minnesota, with Al snoring in the back seat, Franni Franken kept Trice awake at the wheel by reading aloud juicy news from trashy tabloids about Britney Spears, Ryan Seacrest, and Alex Rodriguez. Trice was Franken's trusted "git-er-done" miracle worker during the campaign, and perfect for this recount role.

As the volunteers fanned out, they needed supplies to document this recount. Trice assembled 106 self-contained mini-offices in large white cardboard bankers' boxes that recount volunteer drivers delivered to their counting sites. Each set of boxes included a rented laptop, a cell modem, two cell phones, dozens of pens, two staplers, and five clipboards, the latter with the template work sheets that Sautter devised so that the volunteers could record every move or event at their respective recount sites. Some of the supplies were hanging around from the just-completed campaign. Some were acquired from friendly organizations. For other stuff, Trice said, "We went to like fifteen Office Maxes. We bought every single clipboard in the Twin Cities. It was nuts."

All told, Trice's team assembled and stacked more than 300 boxes, each weighing about 20 pounds. They filled three twelve-by-twelve-foot offices in Franken's campaign headquarters and rose six feet high. They then were placed in trucks, which Trice rented, and distributed like clockwork to volunteers or recount sites across Minnesota. Sautter had seen dozens of recounts. None was better organized, he told Franken, who crowed about his recount operation at just about every gathering he spoke to during this period.

As Operation Recount Storm was about to invade the hills and dales of Minnesota, the Franken team kept pounding away on the other front, wrongly rejected absentee ballots. Hamilton, who was leading the litigation effort, believed in swarming and surrounding his legal opponents. The absentee-ballot hunt was about to operate on two tracks. In the days after the Franken lawyers became aware of the growing number of inexplicably rejected absentee ballots, Lillehaug began to pepper county and local election officials with Minnesota Government Data Practices Act requests. These requests sought the names and addresses of absentee voters whose ballots had been rejected by local election judges and the reasons for the rejections. When a ballot was not accepted, and so not counted, the local election official — or, in some cases, a local absentee-ballot board — was required to mark on the outside envelope of the absentee ballot why it had not fulfilled the statutory guidelines.

Some counties and municipalities gladly replied and supplied the voter information Lillehaug and Hamilton sought. Others, citing privacy concerns, did not, including Ramsey County, where St. Paul is located, and where Joe Mansky, the dean of the state's voting experts, was the elections manager. The Franken theory was that if Mansky were forced to turn over the data, other reluctant elections officials would follow. After Knaak and Trimble's Saturday Sneak Attack a week earlier, it was the Franken legal squad's turn six days later to run into Ramsey County District Court for relief.[2] The Data Practices Act requests were fundamental to Franken's strategy to expand the playing field. If successful in shaking all that information loose from the counties, Franken's campaign would be aided by the Democrats' significantly more exacting voter information lists. If the Franken campaign knew who voted via absentee ballots, it could begin to seek out the voters. There were votes in them thar rejected envelopes. Perhaps even more than 215.

The Canvassing Board met for the first time on November 18, 2008. The members staked out the seats they would fill at their meetings for the next seven weeks. In room 10 of the State Office Building, a venue usually reserved for legislative hearings, Judge Kathleen Gearin sat to the far left of the audience made up of journalists, lawyers, campaign staffers, and a revolving group of recount junkies. Chief Justice Eric Magnuson sat to Gearin's left and the audience's right, and then Secretary of State Mark Ritchie, Justice G. Barry Anderson, and, finally, Judge Edward Cleary. This first meeting started routinely enough with State Elections Director Gary Poser sitting twenty feet in front of the board members at a witness table. Poser was the fellow who walked into Ritchie's office sometime in August 2008, and told his boss, "We should prepare for a recount," and Ritchie's office did, beginning with the training of election officials across the state. Now, three months later, Poser droned off the results of other elections, a report on the general accuracy of voting machines statewide, and the details of the recount plan that was to take shape the next day.

From these opening minutes of the board's first session, it was impossible to know that this was going to be the place and these were to be the judges whose decisions and actions would determine the outcome of this election. A trial would ensue. The Minnesota Supreme Court would weigh in at a handful of key moments. There would be all sorts of noise about how the U.S. Senate was to intervene. But this battle for potential control of the U.S. Senate was in the hands of the Minnesota State Canvassing Board, and its five members sculpted a record that laid the foundation for all that came after. Technically speaking, this body was ministerial, that is, not a court, not a finder of facts, but a mere approver of ballots. Before long, this Canvassing Board stepped out of its lane, pushed the absentee ballot envelopes the way that Franken wanted, evaluated challenged ballots with scrupulous fairness, and opened the door for Franken to gain more votes than Elias, Hamilton, Lillehaug, Sautter, and Schriock ever dreamed of. This election was won at this board. The persuasion began at this first meeting.

David Lillehaug was center stage. He preferred it that way. Lillehaug was the local face of the Franken campaign, but after Election Night, he was pushed aside when Elias arrived. The two men denied it, but others saw tension between them. Lillehaug was initially threatened by Elias's presence, reputation, and big personality. Franni Franken, Al's wife, quickly nicknamed Elias "Mr. Larger Than Life." In a room with Schriock, Hamilton, and Elias, Lillehaug often found himself as the fourth-biggest personality. He wasn't used to that. Seeing Elias meet the local media, chat on the phone with the bloggers at the *Washington Post* and *Politico*, and make the final decisions took some getting used to.

The two were opposites. Elias was a pacing, f-bombing New Yorker whose shirt tail was often hanging out of his pants and whose emotions were just as apparent. Lillehaug was the son of the municipal band director of Sioux Falls, South Dakota. He went to Augustana College in his hometown and then off to Harvard Law School. His note taking was exacting. His speechifying was deliberate and delivered in full sentences. Knaak said that he thought Lillehaug was always in a "slow burn." A Franken colleague described Lillehaug as always "zipped up," but this recount and election meant a lot to him. Lillehaug loved Paul Wellstone, had been his debate coach during his campaigns, and was elevated to U.S. attorney because of Wellstone's recommendation. Lillehaug may have been cool as a cucumber, but he was fighting from his heart for Franken.

All the judges on this Canvassing Board knew Lillehaug as one of the state's most respected and liberal lawyers and as the Clinton administration's U.S. attorney in Minnesota from 1994 to 1998. Representing Franken before this board at this introductory stage was a good role for him, and a chance to prove himself to Elias and Hamilton, who underestimated him and wondered just how aggressive a South Dakotan could get. He was a moderating force, believing that Minnesota was under a microscope and that he, particularly in such a volatile political environment, needed to be the low-key, local counsel, avoiding theatrics while putting a Minnesota face on this Minnesota case. Unlike everyone else on Franken's legal team, Lillehaug was no stranger to Minnesota's powers-that-be.

After the Canvassing Board completed its housekeeping measures, Ritchie asked if representatives of the campaigns cared to comment on any matters. Lillehaug left his seat in the audience, approached the chair where Poser had sat, and, in the straightforward fashion he felt was necessary, reading from a tightly prepared script, presented the Franken side's first oral argument in a legal forum that wrongly rejected absentee ballots must be included in the recount. Franni Franken labeled Lillehaug "The White Knight." His brilliant white hair was never out of place. He was squeaky clean. He was pleasant, but formal. "It is an honor to appear before you on such an historic occasion," Lillehaug began, and he meant it.

Lillehaug took his place in front of the two Supreme Court justices and two county judges knowing he had a legal mountain to climb. A day earlier, the office of Minnesota Attorney General Lori Swanson, a Democrat, had provided an advisory opinion to the Canvassing Board that greatly concerned the Franken team. That three-page document, written by Assistant Attorney General Kenneth E. Raschke Jr., was surprisingly shallow in its legal analysis; months later, members of the Canvassing Board expressed dismay at how insubstantial a piece of work the Raschke memo was, and how it adversely affected them. "I was not impressed," said Gearin. "It was not as good a work product as I expect with the stakes this high," said Cleary. The Raschke memo was so lacking in deep analysis that it seemed to militate against his credibility and, instead, tilted Gearin and Cleary toward a sympathetic ear to Lillehaug, even before he opened his mouth.

In his memo, Raschke argued that "Only the ballots cast in the election and the summary statements certified by the election judges may be considered in the recount process," leaving unsaid whether wrongly rejected absentee ballots were "cast" or not. Raschke quoted from Ritchie's "Recount Guide," a document developed in anticipation of this eventuality, which stated that an administrative recount is "*not* to determine who was eligible to vote. It is *not* to determine if campaign laws are violated. It is *not* to determine if absentee ballots were properly accepted. It is *not*—except for recounting the ballots—to determine if judges did

things right. It is simply to physically recount the ballots *for this race!*"
[Emphasis was in Ritchie's original guide.] "Further," Raschke wrote
to Ritchie, "your office has not advised us of any previous recount in
Minnesota that has included reconsideration of rejected absentee ballot
return envelopes."

Raschke's conclusion: the only forum for Franken to raise the absentee-
ballot issue was at a subsequent election contest, or trial; and the only
way for an aggrieved voter to seek a remedy for his wrongly rejected
ballot was also to start an election contest. This Canvassing Board was
not the right place for the rejected absentee ballot issue, Raschke wrote.
The message: if the vote wasn't already counted, it surely couldn't be
recounted.

In his gentle, exacting approach, Lillehaug laid out the Franken position that would endure for months to come and that would live on the
public relations level every time the more animated Elias opened his
mouth at a news briefing. "We submit that every valid vote cast in this
election should be counted in the canvass," Lillehaug told the Board,
adding that those who voted and followed the law "have a right to have
their votes counted, not later, but now." He asked the Canvassing Board
members to "correct administrative errors."

He noted that in 1962, in the last major statewide recount, ten counties reexamined absentee ballots because of suspected errors by election
judges. Specifically, Lillehaug pointed to four affidavits that the Franken
campaign had offered to the board just that morning, statements from
people in places like Willmar and Thief River Falls, stating that they had
followed all the absentee ballot voting rules, but that their votes had been
rejected. "These people are real people," Lillehaug said, getting a bit
feistier than he wanted, adding, "You have the power to get to the truth,"
gesturing his right hand toward the panel, putting them on the spot.

For the first time in the recount, Lillehaug raised the eight-hundred-
pound gorilla in the room, the 2000 presidential recount case of *Bush v.
Gore*. He quoted from the United States Supreme Court's majority opinion in that matter, the opinion that allowed George W. Bush to become
president. Lillehaug said that the nation's high court opined in 2000 that
there must be "equal weight accorded to each vote and . . . equal dignity
owed to each voter" and that a state "may not . . . value one person's vote
over that of another."

In ten clear minutes of persuasion, Lillehaug performed his duty. He
didn't overtly blast the attorney general's office in the process, but just

as the Franken campaign sent a warning shot over Ritchie's head a week earlier about the makeup of the Canvassing Board, this presentation was a salvo at Swanson's office. Franken's legal team muttered about a Democratic attorney general stinging them with a memo like Raschke's. They were going to fight it. Justice Anderson asked if Lillehaug would object to the panel spending some time thinking about it, and, of course, Lillehaug did not.

Knaak was next. He went out of his way to praise the DFL attorney general's office for its "simple, elegant opinion," not knowing that at least two of the judges he faced thought it was a subpar piece of work. Knaak then hammered home the Coleman position on rejected absentee ballots. Only ballots "actually cast at the election" should be counted, he said. If they were not counted in the original local tally and the later county canvass, then their inclusion was the stuff of an election contest trial down the road, not for this state Canvassing Board to consider. "There is no precedent—let me emphasize that—there is no precedent for what's being requested of this body by the Franken campaign," Knaak said. There may not have been a precedent, but there was a consistent public relations and legal breeze picking up. Elias started it, albeit poorly, with the alleged eighty-four-year-old stroke victim from Beltrami County. Now, Lillehaug put the same issue on the Canvassing Board's plate.

Sautter, the recount expert, worried about opening the absentee-ballot door. He knew from experience that seeking an opening for your side can provide opportunities for the other side, but Sautter understood the power of the politics of seeking votes, not blocking votes.

"We wanted to count votes and that's what the public wants," Sautter said. "In the end, no matter what the law was, these are judges. They knew the public would want anything that's a legitimate ballot counted . . . It's an old adage: 'I'd rather have a good set of facts on my side than the law.'"

After a series of meetings and conference calls between both campaigns and Ritchie's office, sixteen ground rules were established for the recount. These set up standards for the process, which complemented established laws about the guidelines for absentee ballot acceptance. The recount rules were all quickly approved by the Canvassing Board, including the one known as Rule Nine. It dealt with how so-called duplicate ballots would be handled during the recount.

From time to time at polling places, local election judges created duplicates of original absentee ballots. Remember, these were ballots that had been folded and mailed in. The most common scenario was that a ballot was too torn or wrinkled to navigate its way into the feed chute of the voting machine. When that occurred, poll workers grabbed a blank ballot and filled it in just as the voter did. The duplicate was marked and sent through the machine. The original was set aside and placed in an envelope with other slightly damaged or ripped ballots. When best practices are followed, the duplicate is the only ballot counted and reported on Election Night.[3]

Occasionally, poll workers "clean up" damaged absentee ballots that can't go through a voting machine. With such a tattered ballot, it might be difficult to decipher a voter's intent. The election official fills out a duplicate, but independently determines the intent of the voter in filling out the duplicate. It has been known to happen.

Shortly after Election Day, Franken's lawyers heard of an unusually large number of duplicate ballots in Wright County, just west of Minneapolis. If that was the case, any cleaning up of those ballots would likely go for Coleman; Franken received about 29 percent of the vote in Wright County, barely nudging out Barkley, with Coleman garnering more than 50 percent of the vote. Similarly, the Coleman lawyers believed there was hanky-panky among election judges in Minneapolis, where Franken dominated.

As the rules for the recount were developed, the Franken side wanted originals to be counted in the recount, not the duplicates that were counted on Election Night. Originals reveal more closely the actual intent of voters. At the same time, they might not be as clearly marked as a duplicate and, so, could be more easily challenged. Another thing: Coleman had the lead after Election Night when duplicates — not originals — were counted. It was in Franken's interest to alter the method of counting in the recount. Franken's lawyers expected Coleman's lawyers to take the opposite position. From Coleman's perspective, why not replicate the way votes were counted on Election Night? Strategically, Coleman's lawyers should have worked hard to ensure that the recount rules mirrored Election Night counting methods.

But when the negotiations over Rule Nine came up during a conference call, it was Coleman lawyer Trimble who was adamant that originals be counted in the recount, and that any ballots marked "duplicate" be set aside. He agreed that voter intent could be better discerned with originals. Gary Poser, from the secretary of state's office, opposed that idea, asserting that the duplicates would be clearer to evaluate in a recount. Poser wanted a recount free of controversy. No, Trimble said, originals should be counted. Fine with us, said Lillehaug, as the other Franken lawyers listening in giggled amongst themselves.

What developed was this: "As the Table Official sorts the ballots, he or she shall remove all ballots that are marked as duplicate ballots and place those duplicate ballots in a . . . pile. At the conclusion of the sorting process, the Table Official shall open the envelope of original ballots for which duplicates were made for that precinct and sort the original ballots in the same manner as they sorted all other ballots. The Table Official shall disregard this step if there is not an envelope of original ballots, in which case the duplicate ballots will be sorted."

Trimble's preference, though well-meaning, would turn sour for Coleman. The recounting of ballots was about to begin with the universe slightly changed by the wording of Rule Nine. That shift to counting the original absentee ballots could only be good for Franken. Eventually, it was the Coleman lawyers who felt their candidate lost out on this, and that there was double counting in big-city precincts where election officials didn't properly mark and separate originals and duplicates.

One rule that Franken's side wanted, especially Sautter, wasn't adopted by Ritchie's office. Sautter wanted the secretary of state to keep track of the calls at the tables and report those results to the public and the media. Sautter was told that would be too difficult. Instead, when the recount began, Ritchie's office posted votes for Coleman, votes for Franken, and challenged votes by both camps. This way of keeping score made the scoreboard unreliable.

On November 19, the recount began in about 50 locations across the state, and, with it, challenges by both sides. By the secretary of state's count, Coleman representatives challenged 146 votes that local election judges called for Franken, and Franken observers called into question 123 Coleman-bound votes. The game of tit-for-tat began slowly, but it would build to such absurd proportions that keeping track of who was picking up votes was nearly impossible with all the challenges. But Elias, Sautter, Lillehaug, Hamilton, and Schriock knew the count as the Pony Express kicked into service and, with it, Franken's data operation.

At each site, any vote that was challenged was photocopied by election officials and handed over to the on-site representatives of both campaigns. Sautter and Elias wanted to know as quickly as possible how those challenges were being determined by local election judges. Franken operatives Petersen and Trice, via relays of rented and borrowed cars, zoomed the challenges back to Franken headquarters in St. Paul.

Trice divided the state into regions. Some hauls, say, from Thief River Falls and over to Detroit Lakes and down to St. Paul, were seven-hour trips. Feeder routes were established, moving challenged ballots from smaller villages to a hub, such as Thief River Falls, population 8,377. When the ballots got to St. Paul, in the darkness of night, staff members scanned the ballots, created PDFs, moved them onto a Linux server, neatly set aside the originals, made paper copies, and began to categorize each challenged ballot and digitally tag it for location, reason for the challenge, and identifying marks, such as a folded corner, a coffee stain, an errant pen mark, an *X* through two boxes, or whatever.

Meanwhile, volunteer lawyers were brought in to also analyze and tag the ballots by category, but, mostly, to grade the credibility of each challenge. Elias's Washington, D.C., associate Ezra Reese oversaw that exercise. Reese was told by the volunteer lawyers that the Franken (and Coleman) operatives in the field were too often making overly aggressive and silly challenges. Franken tech and data staffer J. D. Schlough and Andy Bechhoefer, a Washington, D.C.–based voter information expert, led the effort to categorize what would become a total of nearly 6,700 challenged ballots, which, during the recount phase, were about evenly divided between the two candidates. Spreadsheets blossomed.

On the Coleman side, there was not as much of a rush to get the ballots to campaign headquarters, about a mile to the east of Franken's. The challenged ballots were scanned and PDFed. Groups of Coleman attorneys examined the challenges closely, but not with the digital detail used by Franken's side. A month later, when the board began counting, the uploaded algorithms of Franken's data team scored points.

On the very day the recount began, Franken won his first major ruling in Minnesota's courts. Ramsey County District Judge Dale Lindman ordered that the names of citizens who cast their votes via absentee ballots were subject to the state's Data Practices Act and should be made public.

"The harm that [Franken's campaign] would suffer absent a temporary restraining order and temporary injunction far outweighs any harm to [Ramsey County]," Lindman wrote. "With each passing hour, the Franken campaign is irreparably harmed in its efforts to ensure that each valid vote is properly counted and to prepare for the procedures that will decide this election." For Franken, this was a huge victory. The names of voters who submitted absentee ballots, the envelopes of absentee ballots that had not been opened, the data compiled by election officials about the number of absentee votes and voters, and the existing written information that explained why a ballot was rejected were to be handed over to Franken.

Knaak seemed unaffected. He tartly accused the Franken campaign of planning to "pound on people's doors and ask, 'How did you vote?'" No, he said, even if Coleman's campaign received the same lists of voters, it wouldn't do that. As time wore on, the question became, Why not? Why not explore all their avenues for more votes? Elias, enjoying a chance to poke Knaak, countered: "I promise you I will not knock on Mr. Knaak's door in order to avoid frightening him."

Knaak should have been frightened. The Franken camp now began to gradually receive data from all the counties. Bechhoefer and others began to match up names with extensive Democratic Party voter lists, lists that showed voters' preferences. No Canvassing Board or court had yet determined that these rejected votes would be included in the recount tally. Raschke's opinion remained an obstacle, but Franken's lawyers had an inkling that what was inside many of these envelopes would be good news. Young, first-time, Obama-supporting voters were likely to be the sorts of voters who didn't exactly color within the lines. If a court wouldn't let Franken include these votes in the count, perhaps, as Raschke suggested, each voter should contest the election. As they gathered more affidavits and learned firsthand of more Franken voters who felt their votes had been blocked, an idea to bring a citizen-generated lawsuit gestated in Franken headquarters. Why not have aggrieved voters themselves ask the courts to count their wrongly rejected ballots?

Another reason Knaak pooh-poohed the door pounding was that Coleman's campaign didn't have that depth of data and the hunting-and-gathering DNA in its organizational blood. During the 2008 campaign—unlike 2000 and 2004—the national and statewide Republican Party failed miserably in developing these detailed lists of their potential voters. John McCain's presidential campaign didn't promote a write-in effort like Obama's.

The landscape of the postelection battle was quickly beginning to take shape, and the recount was but one full day old. Except for the Raschke opinion, Franken seemed to own a bit of momentum. The numbers were sure to change over the next few weeks, but one immutable fact couldn't be denied, one piece of data couldn't be spun, one question still could not be answered. In a blue state, with a charismatic progressive presidential candidate at the top of the ticket, against a flip-floppy Bush supporter who had been accused of being linked to corruption, Al Franken, with a twenty-million-dollar treasury, garnered about 42 percent of the vote. Why couldn't he knock off an incumbent as vulnerable as Coleman? Why had it all come to this?

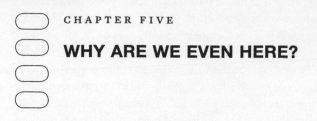

CHAPTER FIVE

WHY ARE WE EVEN HERE?

"Really, Minnesota deserves better than this."

What I do is jujitsu. [Republicans] say something ridiculous and
I subject them to scorn and ridicule.
—Al Franken, interview with *Star Tribune,* October 19, 2008

The origins of this recount can be traced, oddly enough, to Valentine's
Day 2007, when Franken announced his run for the Minnesota U.S. Senate seat held by Coleman. With an eight-minute video on his Web site,
Franken outlined his political philosophy and displayed his passion
for issues, such as the stability of the middle class, health care reform,
affordable college tuition, and the growth of the green economy. Toward
the end of the monologue, Franken declared, "My political hero is Paul
Wellstone."

For an opening argument, it came off as sincere and vulnerable. He
might have smiled a bit too hard and spoken, literally, too much out of the
side of his mouth, but he appeared relaxed and personable, not the angry,
biting, foul-mouthed, satirist, talk-radio host, and liberal flag bearer of
the previous thirty years. Franken acknowledged he wasn't a politician,
presumably a good thing. With bookshelves visible in the background and
looking directly into the camera, he showed that he was something more
than a comedian. For years he had campaigned for Democrats, including
Wellstone, and in 2006 he traveled statewide, preparing to run, listening
to voters. He heard they wanted a change in Washington. He didn't mention Coleman in the video, but of course he would be Franken's opponent come November 2008. This assumed Franken could outdo a list of
challengers, including high-powered and right-of-Franken Twin Cities

lawyer Michael Ciresi and left-of-Franken University of St. Thomas Professor Jack Nelson-Pallmeyer, to gain the official endorsement of the Minnesota DFL delegates at their convention in June 2008. After living for three decades in New York, Franken had moved back to Minnesota in 2005 with the Senate seat in mind and Coleman in his sights. From the moment he stared into that camera on Valentine's Day and said he was running, Franken ignited a fundamentally personal, scandal-peppered, forty-million-dollar campaign that was destined to be too close to call.

Four years before that introductory video was released, and not nearly as politely, Franken's ideological, and sometimes name-calling, campaign against Coleman began. It reared its head first in a sarcastic Op-Ed piece in the Minneapolis *Star Tribune* that reacted to a pointed comment Coleman made to *Roll Call,* the Capitol Hill publication. Just three months after formally assuming Wellstone's seat, in a story noting Coleman's rapid rise to prominence among Republicans, the new senator told *Roll Call,* "To be very blunt and God watch over Paul's soul, I am a 99 percent improvement over Paul Wellstone. Just about on every issue."[1]

Such puffery—from a man who jumped parties to aid his ambition, who lost in 1998 to former wrestler Jesse Ventura in a gubernatorial election, and who was an accidental senator because of Wellstone's untimely death—rankled liberals. It flabbergasted Franken, who grew up as a middle-class Jewish kid in the Minneapolis suburb of St. Louis Park in the 1950s and '60s and who had come to adore Wellstone. It got the creative writer in Franken to fantasize aloud in his Op-Ed piece about a phone conversation he said he had shared with Coleman.[2] In it, Coleman called Franken to chat, somewhat apologetically, about the "99 percent" comment and to explain the remaining 1 percent in which Wellstone bettered him. As the imagined conversation unfolds, Coleman acknowledges, with little debate, many attributes at which Wellstone bettered him, from passion to authenticity to integrity to humility to independence. The 99 percent keeps melting away until Franken has, pretty much, gotten Coleman to admit that Wellstone was head-and-shoulders better than Coleman in, well, just about every possible category.

"I'm going with 68," Coleman tells Franken in this faux phone call. "I'm a 68 percent improvement over Wellstone. That's still a big improvement."

"Yes. Yes, it is. Norm, can I ask you a question?" Franken asks.

"Sure, Al."

"Besides lack of independence and ability not to be offended, can you tell me another area where you're an improvement over Paul Wellstone?"

"Oh, that's easy," Coleman said. "I'm very smart."

Later that fall, Franken's book *Lies and the Lying Liars Who Tell Them*—part satire, part diatribe, part truth-squading—was released to much critical acclaim. In the book's angriest, but most touching, chapter, Franken reported on the Republican misinformation virus that spread in the days after a memorial event for Wellstone. The senator died, along with his wife, daughter, three aides, and two pilots on October 25, eleven days before the 2002 election. Four days later, a jam-packed memorial event was staged at the University of Minnesota's Williams Arena, usually the basketball home of the Golden Gophers. Franken, as a private citizen and friend of Wellstone, attended the service–rally–community hug along with his brother and an estimated twenty thousand others who filled the arena and an adjacent smaller sports hall. Thousands stood outside just to be close to the spirit of it all.

In the *Lies* chapter titled "'This Was *Not* a Memorial to Paul Wellstone': A Case Study in Right-Wing Lies," Franken engaged in some solid journalism in tracking how a smattering of boos directed toward Republican Senator Trent Lott somehow morphed into an orchestrated crowd of twenty thousand booing the senator, the latter inaccuracy according to conservative radio talk shows, TV pundits, and newspaper columnists. Franken also analyzed the speech by Wellstone's best friend, Rick Kahn, that raised all sorts of hackles because it took a turn from distraught, heartfelt eulogy to passionate partisanship. Franken writes that it "ended with a political call to arms that went over the top...Yeah, it had some inappropriate moments. But I assumed that people would understand, and cut the man a little slack." Instead, Republican opinion makers, on local television and in local newspapers, saw an opportunity to blast the Democrats for using the Wellstone memorial as a partisan stage and to turn that somber event to Coleman's advantage in the closing days of the 2002 campaign.

Franken's sense of outrage about the entire turn of events jumped off the pages of *Lies*. There was barely a joke in the twenty-eight-page chapter. One paragraph, on page 187, stands out. Franken wrote:

The last time I saw Paul was in the late summer of 2002, about six weeks before he died ... It was an evening event in the Twin Cities. Paul was in the middle of an intense, dead-even Senate race. He'd been targeted as vulnerable by the national Republican Party and money was flowing in from around the country for his opponent, a suit named Norm Coleman.

Franken went on to write about how the Republicans, in his view, capitalized on Wellstone's death, with Coleman "taking every possible opportunity to show voters that he was not exploiting Wellstone's death for political gain," all the while appearing on national TV news shows exploiting Wellstone's death. Disdain dripped from Franken's words. He zeroed in on Coleman while making himself an even bigger target for right-wing commentators.

About the time *Lies* topped the New York Times best-sellers list in the fall of 2003, Franken visited Minneapolis to attend a release party for a book of photos honoring Wellstone and his wife, Sheila. Franken spoke emotionally at the jam-packed gathering on the University of Minnesota campus, and, for the first time, someone mentioned that he should consider running for office. A year later, he told the *Star Tribune* he was pondering a run, which triggered this response from Minnesota Republican Party chairman Ron Eibensteiner: "After a failed movie career and a failed radio career, maybe Al Franken wants to top things off with a failed political career."[3] In retrospect, the 2008 campaign had begun.

In his 2005 book, *The Truth (with jokes),* Franken wrote about Coleman's chairmanship of the Senate Subcommittee on Permanent Investigations, a panel charged with looking into, among other things, corruption in defense and security contracts in Iraq. Asserting that Coleman had failed to hold "a single hearing on postwar corruption," Franken called Coleman "one of the administration's leading butt boys," and wondered if Coleman's ambition was "to become vice president in the third Bush administration."

Thus the emotional and personal groundwork was laid for a brutal campaign years before Franken announced his own ambitions. Franken–Coleman 2008 was not Wellstone–Coleman 2.0, but the pugnacious spirit of Paul Wellstone hovered above Franken and his campaign, a spirit that must have seemed more like a ghost to Coleman. The fundamentals were different from 2002. Coleman was now the incumbent. Handpicked by Vice President Dick Cheney six years earlier, such a connection at the hip was ball-and-chain. In his early years as a senator, he voted more than 90 percent of the time with Bush. He backed the Iraq war. He cozied up to conservative special business interests. Franken's background and previous writings became targets for his lack of decorum, his tendency to polarize, and, so the argument went, the lack of readiness and temperament to be a U.S. senator. Franken had no experience. Coleman said he knew how to "get things done" if everyone "worked together."

Franken was opposed to the Iraq War and opposed to Bush's tax cuts for the wealthy, which Coleman backed. Franken stood for universal health care, Coleman did not. These themes prevailed for the entire campaign, but issues became muddled amid a volley of wicked television commercials that dumbed down the debate and turned it all personal. Franken may have switched careers, but not his political compass. Coleman was a career politician who had often changed positions.

The energetic remnants of the Wellstone coalition rallied around Franken as the far-right news and information machine vigorously attacked him for his leftist politics and trail of obscenity-laced, sex-act-peppered writings and television work. Before too long, Franken's narrative about Coleman's affection for Bush was drowned out by the fruits of Coleman's opposition research. In the early months of the campaign, Franken, the challenger, was on the defensive. That wasn't the way it was supposed to be. A series of rumbles and mini-scandals — some new, some rehashed — ensued. An incumbent who couldn't be trusted faced off against an inexperienced candidate who couldn't be liked. They competed for who had the lower negative ratings, a recipe for an ugly, sometimes stomach-turning, campaign and for a razor-thin result as many voters came to prefer "None of the above."

Much like a recount effort, a campaign needs to make strategic decisions on day one that come home to roost in the closing "final argument" days and, ultimately, on Election Day. A U.S. Senate campaign requires experience and a sense of how the candidate's takeoff connects every step of the way with his landing in the days leading up to the voting. Franken was new to the game, and so were his campaign co-managers, Andy Barr and David Benson. Barr had been his student, researcher, and protégé, but had never run a political campaign. Benson had worked on a few campaigns in South Dakota. Both men were in their twenties and worked for Franken after he formed (in 2005) his Midwest Values Political Action Committee, which soon raised more than one million dollars for progressive candidates nationwide.

With his New York and Hollywood pals, his great sense of humor, his chutzpah and celebrity, raising funds was Franken's strength. Sculpting a major-league campaign that could lift the Democrats to a filibuster-proof majority was not. From the start, experts in Washington, D.C., and the Minnesota DFL community, such as longtime Wellstone campaign manager Jeff Blodgett, urged Franken to hire a pro to run his operation. Franken resisted, not wanting to fiddle with his close-knit team of loyal youthful aides, but the hits started coming and kept building toward a need to dramatically adjust.

In June 2007, Franken was punched by a story in the *Star Tribune* about his drug use during his time on *Saturday Night Live*. The article that appeared on June 28, 2007, was triggered by a five-paragraph item a day earlier on a *Star Tribune* political gossip blog called "The Big Question." The blog item reported that a former college pal of Coleman's at New York's Hofstra University posted an open letter on a pro-marijuana Web site detailing Coleman's pot smoking while in college in the 1960s. The letter writer, a marijuana rights activist, challenged Coleman's twenty-first-century position as a senator opposed to legalizing marijuana. The whole thing was five paragraphs and, seemingly, barely significant. Coleman's hippie past as a rock music roadie had been chronicled, and a joint here or there didn't prevent him from running for other public offices or working for the Minnesota attorney general's office for fifteen years.

The next day, that *Star Tribune* blog post developed into a full-blown story in the newspaper bearing the headline, "Candidates' Past Use of Illegal Substances Surfaces." It devoted more words to Franken's admitted drug use during his *Saturday Night Live* years than to Coleman's inhaling. How did that happen?

Ninety minutes after the "Big Question" item by *Star Tribune* Washington bureau intern Jake Sherman was posted, a fellow named Michael Brodkorb added a reader comment. Brodkorb was then Minnesota's most active right-wing blogger, and the purveyor of all things negative at Minnesota Democrats Exposed, his Web site. In his day job, he worked as a researcher for the Minnesota GOP. Brodkorb rehashed information to which Franken had years ago admitted, including cocaine and LSD use.

Star Tribune editors gulped, felt pressured to react to Brodkorb, and decided to re-craft Sherman's Web post into a "balanced" fifteen-paragraph story for the newspaper that incorporated Brodkorb's historical information about Franken, with bows to Coleman's smoking past and Ciresi's pot dabbling. Barr, who handled the follow-up phone calls from Sherman, was ticked off that the news outlet would use an open letter about Coleman's pot smoking to dig up old Franken news. No mention was made that since his *SNL* days, where drug use was rampant among cast and crew, Franken had written two movies about addiction and its horrors.[4] His wife, Franni, had struggled with alcoholism. Drugs were no longer a laughing matter to Franken.

When the full newspaper story was published, it was buried on Page 5B of the newspaper, but it devoted six of the fifteen paragraphs to Franken's drug-linked past and only four to Coleman's, including a mea culpa statement from a Coleman spokesman. *Star Tribune* staffers viewed Barr as "an amateur," but Barr thought the newspaper, which was swerving from its traditional liberal bent under some more conservative-minded editors and owners, was out to get Franken. And Franken, for all of his ability to dish out harsh criticism of others, is not known to possess the thickest skin on the planet. It got so tense that, days later, Franken campaign leaders met with *Star Tribune* editors in Minneapolis to complain about the drugs story, small as it was, and to attempt to make peace. It was a telltale early event that soured the relationship between the Franken campaign and the state's largest news organization, a relationship that was never repaired, and that frayed even more during a recount that no one could have seen coming in June 2007. The episode also served as an early indication of how effective Coleman supporters could be in attacking Franken.

By the summer of 2007, Franken, with a grassroots campaign, had been gathering support for the DFL's 2008 state endorsement convention. More-traditional Democrats feared his candidacy and his reputation for lashing out at opponents, believing this baggage could harm him in a contest with Coleman and, à la Jesse Ventura, demean the political process by elevating celebrity over substance.

By the fall of 2007, it was clear to Barr, Benson, and others who had joined the campaign, such as press secretary Jess McIntosh, that they alone couldn't handle the rigors of running a full-blown U.S. Senate campaign. Perhaps they could carry Franken through the 2008 DFL endorsement convention, but they would need a real pro to carry him across any finish line. Barr began making phone calls within the professional campaign community in search of help. No correct fit could be found. At the Democratic Senatorial Campaign Committee (DSCC), Chairman Charles Schumer and others were concerned. Coleman was vulnerable, his Bush-linked record a liability in blue Minnesota. The promised land of sixty Democratic senators was imaginable. There was a presumption that the Democrats' presidential campaign scrum between Barack Obama and Hillary Clinton would reach a conclusion in early 2008, and that professional talent from the losing campaign would be available to work on Franken's campaign. Unfortunately, the Obama–Clinton battle wore on, as did Franken's public relations woes.

In January 2008, Franken received a mention in the *Star Tribune*'s "C.J." gossip column, a space usually reserved for minor-league local celebrities and late-night sightings. This time, however, C.J. scored a high-profile scoop. While campaigning for a DFL state legislative candidate on the Carleton College campus in Northfield, Minnesota, Franken had a snarky run-in with a student who was identified as a Republican, C.J. wrote. According to the report, Franken made fun of the conservative student and refused to shake the kid's hand. As just about everything would in the campaign, this incident rolled around the Internet, fanning the flames of Franken's reputation as a difficult jerk.

That was sophomoric compared to what was to come: Franken's miscues on tax payments. The revelations were broken — again — by blogger Brodkorb, whose entire reason for being seemed to be tarnishing Democrats, and he was quite good at it. Unlike the drug story, in which he recycled very old news, this time Brodkorb was the first to expose Franken and set the agenda for the mainstream media via his Minnesota Democrats Exposed Web site.

"Franken Faces Penalties for Lack of Workers' Insurance," screamed a *Star Tribune* headline on March 5, a day after Brodkorb's exposé. According to the Brodkorb reporting, which was confirmed by other news outlets, Franken owed a twenty-five thousand dollar penalty to the New York State Workers' Compensation Board for failing to carry workers' compensation insurance for employees of his corporation from 2002 to 2005. Barr was quoted as saying Al and Franni Franken didn't know anything about it and it was a "misunderstanding."

News reports said the Workers' Compensation Board began sending notices to Franken as early as April 2005 after discovering that the insurance hadn't been paid for nearly three years. Penalty notices went unanswered and unpaid. The candidate for the working man wasn't paying his workers' comp insurance, the bloggers screeched. This man wants to be a senator?

When Coleman officially launched his reelection campaign a few weeks after the taxes stories hit, campaign manager Cullen Sheehan was already regularly referring to Franken as "Angry Al"—an instant Coleman campaign theme—and Coleman, distancing himself from his consistent Bush support, claimed to be "a voice of optimism in cynical times." "This race is about tomorrow," Coleman told reporters when he announced the kick off of his campaign. "Al's running against yesterday." The battle was on.

In April, Franken himself released more tax data showing he had overpaid personal income taxes in some states and underpaid in others. He blamed his accountant. In this go-round, Franken finally got ahead of Brodkorb, but an experienced candidate would have addressed these matters months, if not years, earlier. Cumulatively, headlines about drugs, run-ins with students, and unpaid taxes defined Franken in the media, rather than Coleman's allegiance to an unpopular George W. Bush. Not surprisingly, at the DSCC in Washington, conversations about drafting a seasoned campaign manager for Franken heated up. There were also discussions about seeking a replacement for Franken. Franken visited Washington and met with DSCC leaders, who were troubled about the wide gap in poll results between him and Coleman. He was told to get his act together. No other winnable DFL candidate emerged. Mike Ciresi, Franken's toughest Democratic rival, never won the blessings of the DSCC in Washington. Ciresi dropped out of the DFL endorsement race in March. Nelson-Pallmeyer, the University of St. Thomas justice and peace studies professor, who pitched himself as a sincere, pure, Wellstone-like maverick college professor, gathered grassroots support too, a reaction to Franken's ornery personality and Hollywood glitz. But Nelson-Pallmeyer's statewide name recognition and fundraising capabilities were limited. If Franken was going to be the Democrats' guy in Minnesota, he needed help.

It was at this point that DSCC lawyer Marc Elias, close to DSCC chairman and New York Senator Charles Schumer, contacted Stephanie Schriock, the chief of staff to Montana Senator Jon Tester. He asked about her availability. Born in Mankato, Minnesota, and a graduate of Minnesota State University, Mankato, Schriock was the mastermind behind Howard Dean's revolutionary Internet fundraising efforts during the 2004 presidential campaign. She then managed Tester's upset victory over incumbent Conrad Burns in 2006. Franken had surrounded himself with a first-class stable of Washington and Minnesota political consultants, many with Wellstone pasts, such as pollsters Diane Feldman and Roy Temple, Mandy Grunwald and Saul Schorr on media, and Dan Cramer and Andy Bechhoefer for targeting potential voters. It was like Noah's Ark as Franken had two of each, but, as Blodgett noted, no one was "saying hard things" to Franken; no one was managing the candidate.

As April stumbled along, J. B. Poersch, the DSCC's executive director who worked directly with Elias and Schumer, urged Schriock to join the Franken campaign. Barr called too. Schriock was reluctant. Tester was still settling into his life as a senator. Schriock was recovering from the recent death of her mother. "If this is going to happen," Schriock told Poersch, "then someone needs to talk to Senator Tester, and it ain't gonna be me." Poersch selected the most powerful messenger he could to break the news to Tester. Schumer himself "asked" Tester to lend Schriock to the Franken campaign, a difficult request to refuse for the organic farmer turned freshman Montana senator. Democratic leaders wanted Franken's campaign to stabilize, and they saw Schriock as the captain to right the complicated and listing ship. (Months later, coincidentally or not, Tester was appointed to the influential Senate Appropriations Committee.)

In early May, after the second wave of tax stories hit, Schriock and Franken met to discuss her possible involvement. They knew each other. With her Internet fundraising expertise, Franken had asked her to run his Midwest Values PAC in 2005, but she declined. Their urgent 2008 meeting occurred at, of all places, a McDonald's restaurant in New York City. Franken was in New York to raise money for his campaign. Schriock arrived from Washington late, so they wandered to the fast food outlet for her coffee and his Diet Coke. They discussed what she could add, how he could win, why he wanted to be a U.S. senator, and if he was ready for all that was to come. "I'm not sure if I really need you right now," he said, but Schriock and her D.C. backers convinced him. On May 15, it was announced that Schriock would manage the campaign — and Franken. At that time, Coleman was ahead in a *Star Tribune* poll by seven points. Schriock walked into a rugged situation that wasn't going to get better anytime soon.

Schriock's political career began when she was in high school. In a tactic that previewed her adult savvy and persistence, Schriock targeted voters in her campaign to become student body president of her Butte,

Montana, high school. She had lost contests for freshman and sopho-more class president. The freshmen, sophomores, and juniors voted for student body president. Schriock focused on the freshmen and sopho-mores and let her three opponents battle for popularity among their own junior class. Her instincts were good: go after new voters and expand the voter pool. On her third try, she won.

Her family had moved from Mankato to Butte when she was an infant so her father, Jim, could get a job as a medical technician in the highly unionized town. But for college, Schriock, a top high school swimmer, decided to return to Mankato and compete for the Mavericks' swim team. She dived into politics too. Her opposition to the first Gulf War led her to become active with the Mankato campus Democrats. She volunteered for political campaigns back home in Montana. Before long, at the age of twenty-three, she became the finance director for the 1996 campaign of DFL First Congressional District candidate Mary Rieder. Rieder lost, but Schriock's experience in raising money for candidates and her addic-tion to the election cycle meant she was about to become a political vagabond.

Next stop was as the finance director for the South Carolina Demo-cratic Party. Then, back to Minnesota to run the campaign of Bill Luther in the Sixth Congressional District. By 1999, she had become the South-ern region finance director for the Democratic Senatorial Campaign Com-mittee. In that role, she crossed paths for the first time with the DSCC's young lawyer, Marc Elias. He was 30. She was 26.

By 2004, Elias was John Kerry's general counsel for his presidential run. Schriock was the finance director for Dean's insurgent effort. She was a trailblazer in using the Internet to raise funds, overseeing a tech squad of more than thirty people while raising fifty-two million dollars for the Vermont governor, forty million more than Dean expected. Her reputation was staked and then enhanced with Tester's victory, which was close enough that she prepared for a statewide Senate race recount in 2006. Her recount legal consultant was Elias.

From all of her campaigns, Schriock learned one basic lesson. "They are all about narratives." As soon as she moved back to Minnesota in late May to help Franken, she walked into a narrative controlled by the Cole-man forces and a blast of unseasonably cold air. Weeks before the DFL endorsing convention, which was supposed to be Franken's finest hour, the Minnesota GOP dug up and circulated an eight-year-old *Playboy* magazine story Franken wrote.[5] Titled "Porn-O-Rama," it envisioned a futuristic virtual sex lab at MIT, or the "Minnesota Institute of Titology," in which Franken "sat back and enjoyed the amazingly realistic cyber job. It was every bit as good as the last real blow job I had gotten 23 years earlier—if not better—because when I shot my wad, the virtual mouth swallowed."

Far from senatorial, the article triggered attacks from the Republicans and scorn from key Democrats, including U.S. Representative Betty McCollum, the Democrat from St. Paul, who questioned Franken's ability to be a strong candidate and said, "This isn't satire. It's a serious political problem."

With Nelson-Pallmeyer his only opponent when the state convention opened, Franken dodged the intraparty skirmish. He won the DFL endorsement by acclamation on the first ballot after Nelson-Pallmeyer withdrew, seeing he couldn't garner enough votes to push a second convention ballot. Nelson-Pallmeyer also had fundraising issues, having raised about one million dollars in the year leading up to the convention, almost all from Minnesotans, compared with Franken, a virtual political ATM who would go on to raise twenty million dollars to take on Coleman, with most of his contributors from out of state.

The convention's controversies brought to a head Franken's weakness among women voters. As he won the DFL nomination, he told the delegates, "It kills me that things I said and wrote sent a message . . . that they can't count on me to be a champion for women, for all Minnesotans. I'm sorry for that. Because that's not who I am . . . I wrote a lot of jokes. Some of them weren't funny. Some of them weren't appropriate. Some of them were downright offensive. I understand that."

McCollum was right. As the real head-to-head battle with Coleman was set to begin, all of Franken's previous writings, satirical, hysterical, whimsical or not, were now political problems that especially turned off women voters.[6]

With the nomination in hand, Schriock needed help in crafting the Franken narrative and assembling a Franken rapid response communications team. Schriock hired Eric Schultz, a twenty-eight-year-old bomb-thrower extraordinaire. His first experience in the political media realm came as a tracker helping in Hillary Clinton's 2000 senate campaign in New York against Republican Rick Lazio. Trackers are "spies" with video cameras who operate in plain view. Still a student at Washington University in St. Louis, Schultz, video cam in hand, attended Lazio campaign events for Clinton, just in case Lazio said or did something stupid. If he does, when he does, you jump on it. Clinton's communications strategist was Washington big hitter Howard Wolfson. When explaining the task of a communications department, Wolfson held up a baseball bat and told the troops, "We're going to take this to Rick Lazio every day." Schultz inhaled that mentality. Trackers, he knew, created important intelligence and content for a campaign.

By 2008, Schultz, the son of a Democratic judge in Syracuse, New York, had a lengthy résumé despite his age. He was a Kerry spokesman in 2004 in New Hampshire, worked in Schumer's Senate office in communications, and then joined the 2008 John Edwards presidential campaign. Recently arrived in Minnesota, Schultz viewed the local media corps as timid and the Franken media relations team as quaint. In Minnesota, for instance, photo opportunities and news conferences are generally expected to be events, with chanting supporters waving signs; a candidate can't simply step out of his SUV, stand in front of a Perkins restaurant in Fergus Falls, and jabber to the two cameras and one local reporter. Schultz didn't get why the media team would plan these rah-rah events: this is a war, not a bake sale. Before Elias arrived, Schultz was the king of impatience. Among his first moves was to plant a George W. Bush look-alike at Coleman campaign events as a reminder of the incumbent's ties to the White House. As if it were sport, Schultz kept standings of wins and losses for each news cycle, and that included national mentions of Franken. Schultz was a solid source for key political bloggers at the *Washington Post, Politico,* and Huffington Post. As bold as Franken was in his own writings, as stinging as his books were, even Schultz topped him in his disdain for Republicans. "Al always wanted to do what was right," Schultz said. "I wanted to win."

The summer heated up with Schultz's arrival, as did scrutiny of Coleman's connections and his ties to generic "special interests." The first blast came days before Schultz's arrival when the *National Journal,* hardly a left-wing rag, detailed Coleman's arrangement with a shadowy Republican telemarketer named Jeff Larson, who was Minnesota based but had close ties to the Bush White House and the president's political mastermind, Karl Rove. As the *Journal* quoted Coleman on Larson, "He's the most connected person in D.C. that nobody in Minnesota knows," but Coleman knew him well.

Coleman intermittently, and sometimes belatedly, paid rent to Larson to live in a basement bedroom of a Washington townhouse Larson owned, the *Journal* reported. By Washington standards, the six hundred dollars per month rent was at best odd, and some watchdog groups said below market value, for a nearly one-million-dollar home. Larson's wife also worked for Coleman, the publication said. Coleman was instrumental in bringing the Republican National Convention to St. Paul for September 2008, and Larson was named CEO of the convention's host committee. Coleman's Northstar Leadership Political Action Committee and his campaigns had paid about $1.6 million to FLS Connect, Larson's fundraising firm, between 2001 and 2008. Larson was the fellow who eventually was reported to have paid for thousands of dollars of clothing for vice presidential candidate Sarah Palin during the St. Paul GOP convention.

By some estimates, before it was over, more than ten thousand television commercials aired in Minnesota from the candidates and their surrogates. The attacks were relentless. Coleman was responsible for the deaths of American service people for his support of the Iraq war. Franken was an angry, out-of-control personality, an extremist. Coleman didn't investigate waste in Iraq even though he chaired a committee that should have. Franken attacked Coleman's wife unfairly. True, false, outrageous, or squishy, the effects were obvious. A May 2008 *Star Tribune* poll of registered voters showed Coleman ahead of Franken with 51 percent approval versus Franken's 44 percent. Not surprisingly, a mid-September poll showed Coleman ahead with a 41 percent approval rating over Franken's 37 percent. The margin had narrowed, but more significant, Independence Party candidate Dean Barkley had cut support for both major-party candidates. Much of that had to be attributed to a two-week period in September when Coleman and the National Republican Senatorial Committee (NRSC) went over the top in smearing Franken, and Franken and his allies responded in kind.

It was all so poisonous, beginning on September 12 with a commercial called "Angry Al," which began with Norm Coleman stating, "I'm Norm Coleman and I approved this message because I thought it was important for you to see it."

The words *Does Al Franken Have the Temperament to Be U.S. Senator?* then flashed on the TV screen. What followed were quick audio excerpts from confrontations or interviews or his book in which an agitated, argumentative, profane Franken is exposed. At the end of the thirty-second spot, the words *Al Franken. Reckless. Ridiculous. Wrong.* are displayed.

Five days later, Franken's campaign punched back with a calm, senatorial Franken responding. "Look, I'm not a politician and I guess I get outraged, and sometimes I've gone too far," he said, adding that with gas, grocery, and health care costs soaring and "special interests" succeeding, "My question is . . . [w]hy isn't Norm Coleman outraged?"

Two days later, Coleman jabbed back, sitting in his dining room, a cup of coffee in front of him, dreamy piano music playing under his words, "Al Franken talks about outrage, but there's a difference between outrage and being out of control . . . People out of control can't get things done . . . If we keep working together, we can lower gas prices, crack down on corporate greed, and fix the health care mess . . . Outrage isn't leadership. It's what you do that makes the difference."

Three days after that, the NRSC released a gauzy, horror movie–like spot asking, "Is Al Franken fit for office?" He wrote pornography, he speaks profanity, he is subject to violent outbursts, he didn't pay his taxes, the ad said. "Al Franken, degrading to women, to us all," the voiceover stated, as the words *Rape Jokes. Physical Assault.* flashed on the screen. "Al Franken, Frankly . . . Unfit For Office," it ended, with a photo of Franken behind bars, as if a prisoner. This was a low point, but not the end point.

Five days later, the Franken campaign released a new ad that featured women legislators and a union leader defending Franken and a narrator noting that independent media labeled the "Unfit" ad as misleading. Franken's ad asked, "Is there anything Norm Coleman and his allies won't say to get reelected? . . . Norm Coleman should be ashamed and it would be a shame for Minnesota to send Norm Coleman back to the U.S. Senate."

Only the crash of the New York Stock Exchange in the closing days of September and early October could shut down the gunk flying through Minnesota's airwaves. Electorally speaking, the tumbling of the economy was very good for Franken. As the electorate's concerns switched from the war and national security to the economy, Coleman's support eroded. As the toxicity of the campaign degraded both men, Coleman's association with Bush couldn't be denied. Bush promoted a bailout of banks and Wall Street financial firms. Coleman supported the $700 billion package. Franken opposed it. In the next weeks, the polls soared in his favor, with one *Star Tribune* poll showing a thirteen-point surge from mid-September to early October. It felt like a game changer in Franken's favor.

As economic issues began to favor Franken, there was also time to revisit his temperament. One day after Coleman voted to bail out Wall Street, Franni Franken got into the political commercial act in a dramatic way. It was October 2, which happened to be the couple's thirty-third wedding anniversary. She was alone on the screen, looking to her left as if speaking to an interviewer off camera, as she delivered a heartfelt testimonial to her spouse. It was about as un-pornographic, as un-outrageous, as a commercial could get. She spoke of her alcoholism and her husband's support during her period of struggling with the disease.

"How could a mother of two fabulous, healthy children be an alcoholic?" Franni Franken asked, as snapshots of their son, Joe, and daughter, Thomasin, flashed on the screen. "When I was struggling with my recovery, Al stood right by my side . . . The Al Franken I know stood by me through thick and thin, so I know he'll always come through for Minnesotans." It was a home run of a commercial that could only help Franken with his lagging women's support.

Four days later, the Franken campaign got another shot in the arm. *Harper's* Ken Silverstein dropped a mini bombshell.[7] "Senator Norm Coleman Gets by with a Little Help From His Friends," the headline read, and in the story, Silverstein reported that sources told him that Coleman friend and contributor Nasser Kazeminy purchased expensive suits for the senator at the upscale Neiman-Marcus department store, gifts that could be in violation of Senate ethics rules. "Having a private businessman pay for your clothing is never a good idea if you're a public official," wrote Silverstein, a respected and veteran investigative newspaper reporter.

This was the very same Iran-born, UK-educated, Minnesota entrepreneur Kazeminy who had provided Coleman and his family with expensive private jet trips to the Bahamas and Paris in years past, gifts that also raised ethical eyebrows, but no violations.

Silverstein went on to further report that Laurie Coleman, Coleman's wife, was employed by Minneapolis-based Hays Companies, a risk management, commercial insurance, and employee benefits firm, from which Coleman received $20,700 in campaign contributions between 2002 and 2006. Mrs. Coleman, an actress, was not a risk management expert, he pointed out.

The tidbit about the suits would not have been so dramatic had the Coleman campaign's response been more mellow and transparent. But

Silverstein was stonewalled when he asked about it before he published his story. He simply asked a Coleman spokesman, "Has Nasser Kazeminy paid for clothing for Senator Coleman and/or his wife at Neiman-Marcus?" A Coleman PR flak e-mailed back, "As required, any gift Norm Coleman has received from his friends has been fully reported."

When it came to fashion, the incumbent wasn't talking, and it put the Coleman campaign on the defensive with the election in sight. At a State Capitol news conference that Coleman campaign manager Cullen Sheehan conducted two days later, he refused to answer specific questions about the Neiman-Marcus mystery. Peppered repeatedly by Capitol reporters, Sheehan said twelve times to variously worded questions, "The senator has reported every gift he has ever received." He also added a few times, "We are not going to respond to unnamed sources on a blog," even though *Harper's* is a respected outlet and Silverstein a former investigative reporter for the *Los Angeles Times*. The tailored response raised more questions than it answered and laid the groundwork for more Coleman ethics woes in the weeks to come.

While Sheehan dealt with that kerfuffle, Schriock, on the very next day, advised lawyers Marc Elias in Washington and David Lillehaug in Minneapolis that she had designated Alpha Lillstrom, on Franken's staff, as the lead on election law issues. That same day, October 9, Lillstrom and Lillehaug began planning how to relate to canvassing boards—those bodies that examine ballots and certify election results—and for a possible recount.

On the Coleman side, there were some preparations for election protection, to make sure votes were secure on Election Night and that there was no hanky-panky by any local election officials in Franken-dominated precincts. That prep began about two weeks before Election Day. As for recount prep, it was minimal. Internal polling showed the incumbent eking out a victory as did most public polls. But another Coleman insider said that as Election Day approached, "We anticipated a recount, but we didn't prepare for it."

On October 10, in a grandstanding move that people close to him insist was his sincere recognition that the voters were "fed up" with the mudslinging, Coleman announced an end to negative ads from his campaign. In what the *Star Tribune* called a "somber" news conference at his headquarters, Coleman said that after observing the Jewish high holiday of Yom Kippur, a "time of fasting, soul-searching, and refocusing on your life," he had chosen to reset the tone of the campaign.[8] "We're in a place that I don't think any of us of this generation, this time, have ever seen before," Coleman said of the economic downturn. "At times like this, politics should not add to the negativity. It should lift people up with hope and a confident vision for the future."

Reporter Patricia Lopez noted in her story that Coleman was slipping in the polls and that his negative ads were creating more of a backlash against him than against Franken. "While 42 percent of respondents [to a *Star Tribune* poll] said ads critical of Coleman were 'unfair personal attacks,' 56 percent said that about ads aimed at Franken," Lopez wrote.

The Franken team, with notable fervor, blasted Coleman with one of the better lines of the entire two-year-long saga for "a stunt . . . [that] rings as a cynical ploy designed to change the subject and avoid scrutiny of his own record. It's like an arsonist burning down every house in the village and then asking to be named fire chief." Like the *Star Tribune* poll, a Minnesota Public Radio–Humphrey Institute poll in the closing days of the campaign showed that negative ads had hurt Coleman far more than Franken: "Coleman loses twice as much support as Franken because of his negative television advertisements," the pollsters found.[9]

Franken's communications SWAT team began feeding information to the news media to show that Coleman's call for the end to negativity was phony. Communications leader Eric Schultz launched the "Wink Watch," so named because the Franken side claimed Coleman winked while his allies continued to thrash Franken. According to that tracking, groups such as the NRSC, U.S. Chamber of Commerce, and National Federation of Independent Business spent more than five million dollars in TV, radio, Internet, and direct mail advertising attacking Franken in the three weeks after Coleman said he wanted to end such attacks. Coleman wanted voters to think he would eschew negativity, but in this bumpy roller coaster ride of a political battle, that would be impossible to the very end.

An unlikely element contributed to the closeness of the Coleman–Franken contest. The national Obama organization wanted nothing to do with Franken.

As Barack Obama's momentum picked up, his Chicago-based political organization didn't seek to help Franken. Obama was a candidate who reached people who didn't usually connect with politics. Franken's standoff with Coleman was the worst, really, of modern politics, nasty and devoid of hope. Blodgett, the former Wellstone campaign manager who advised Franken, was Obama's state campaign manager. He repeatedly asked Obama's headquarters in Chicago to send the presidential candidate to Minnesota to boost enthusiasm in the state that has voted for a Republican presidential candidate only once since 1960 (Richard Nixon in 1972), and to help Franken. It was not going to happen. They were on a fifty-state-strategy mission, believed Minnesota was secure for them, and didn't feel a need to visit the state. When Michelle Obama, the candidate's wife, campaigned at St. Paul's Macalester College in September, Franken attended, but wasn't on the stage with her.

Even the door hangers distributed to homes for all the Democratic candidates highlighted Obama while minimizing others on the ballot. In the final days, Blodgett, who was frustrated by the Obama campaign's lack of support for Franken, went rogue, or as rogue as he could. He redesigned the Minnesota door hangers to make Franken's photo as big as Obama's, almost as if they were running mates. No one in Chicago noticed.

In the final, out-of-control six days, it was as if the campaign were in a cup and the candidates were two dice shaken and tossed every which way. Franken's lead in the polls, propped up by the bailout fallout, slid away. Competing polls had differing numbers, but an average of the scientific polls compiled by the Web site Real Clear Politics showed Coleman ahead by about 3 percentage points. Internal polls in both campaigns jumped up and down, a point here, a point there. Endorsements by major newspapers statewide went heavily to Coleman, with only the likes of the *Winona Daily News;* weekly *Tower Timberjay;* and ethnic *American Jewish World, La Prensa,* African-American *Insight News,* and Somali *Wardheer News* providing editorial page victories for Franken.

The once-liberal *Star Tribune* enthusiastically endorsed Coleman, even going so far as to call him "the Minnesota maverick" and quickly dismissing Franken in two paragraphs with, "He's an effective critic. It isn't as easy to envision him as a constructive force for bipartisan legislation." That editorial two Sundays before Election Day further chilled relations between that news organization and the candidate. Three days later, all hell broke loose with the state's largest newspaper smack-dab in the middle of it.

Why Are We Even Here?

The theater unfolded in St. Cloud, where the *Star Tribune*'s investigative reporters Paul McEnroe and Tony Kennedy were in pursuit of Coleman. In their hands they held a copy of a lawsuit filed in Texas days earlier. In the complex case, a Texas businessman alleged that Nasser Kazeminy, Coleman's benefactor, used a Houston company to funnel seventy-five thousand dollars to Coleman via a Minneapolis insurance company where Laurie Coleman worked. In the matter, Kazeminy's lawyer was Robert Weinstine, a close Coleman friend and former legal associate. The lawsuit, based on a sworn statement, alleged that funds intended for Coleman were sent in three installments of twenty-five thousand dollars in 2007 to the insurance broker that employed Mrs. Coleman.

For two days the intrepid reporters attempted to get a comment from the senator, but, for some reason, no one returned their phone calls; thus, the need to chase him down. A video of the attempt by McEnroe and Kennedy to confront Coleman about the charges was taken by a tracker for the Franken campaign. It is for moments like these that trackers exist, earning their measly pay and producing great fodder for their candidate. It was moments like this that Franken media soldier Eric Schultz lived for. This video was particularly chilling, even Hollywood movie–like. It was cinema verité, and almost made it seem as if Coleman were on a perp walk. Coleman, surrounded by security and media relations aides, was whisked out of a St. Cloud restaurant after a campaign appearance. McEnroe, a well-known, dogged *Star Tribune* muckraker, yelled out to him from a few yards away, "Senator, I'd like to ask you questions about a lawsuit...What are the allegations about your wife receiving seventy-five thousand dollars, Senator..." Coleman and his entourage kept moving.

The shaky but clear video chased Coleman to his black SUV, where a back passenger door was opened and Coleman hopped into the vehicle, with McEnroe and Kennedy in pursuit, still asking their questions. "Why won't the Senator answer the questions?" McEnroe asked, and then, talking through the window to Coleman demanded, "Can you roll down the window?...Can you answer the questions in the lawsuit? Why won't you answer the questions?"

The car's motor started, the car moved, "Please answer the questions, Senator!" McEnroe hollered as the SUV moved out of the picture and the reporter, shoulders hunched, stomped off.

Instantly, the video hit YouTube, thanks to the Minnesota DFL. Quickly, a story about the failed confrontation appeared in the St. Paul *Pioneer*

Press, the *Star Tribune*'s competition. McEnroe and Kennedy didn't get their story into the newspaper until two days later. Soon, the entire scandal was the buzz of the Internet and a collection of local blogs.

The Coleman campaign blamed the newspaper. The Coleman campaign called the allegations in the lawsuit "baseless and false." But Coleman then took the next step, claiming Franken was behind it all. "If my opponents have any shred of decency left in this campaign—stop attacking my family," he said in a statement.

Quicker than a New York minute, the DSCC in Washington put together a television ad with excerpts from the McEnroe–Kennedy ambush, asking, *Why Is Norm Coleman Running From Reporters?* The thirty-second spot reviewed the Texas lawsuit, the alleged free clothing, and the vacations, all with Kazeminy links. It ended with that excerpt of the tracker's video of McEnroe's pleading, "Please answer the question, Senator!" Throughout the early part of the fall, the Franken communications team had thought the Minnesota media soft-pedaled any Kazeminy stories and didn't dive into Coleman's connections. Not any more.

Saturday, three days before voters would go to the polls, Coleman turned in an extraordinary performance for his campaign's final TV ad, doing pity quite well. With Laurie sitting beside him on a sofa in their home, a sober and hurt Coleman called the recent events "Al Franken's eleventh-hour attack . . . [a] vicious personal attack on my wife. This time Al Franken has crossed the line."

As he said those words, he turned to his right to gaze into his wife's eyes and she into his. "My name's on the ballot. I'm fair game to his ugly smears, my wife and family are not. In Minnesota this is as dirty as it gets," Coleman said.

It stunned even the aggressive Franken campaign that Coleman played the spouse card. It caught them off guard because they actually had nothing to do with the Texas lawsuit or the allegations. This wasn't their idea, although they were thrilled that Kazeminy's name had reemerged. Earlier in the week, in another commercial, Franken's campaign called Coleman "the fourth most corrupt" U.S. senator. Coleman's questionable connections were a Franken campaign theme. But for Coleman to assert that Franken was behind this most recent Kazeminy turbulence was too much for Franken. Minutes after Coleman's commercial first appeared, Franken raced to DFL headquarters in St. Paul, Franni at his side, his seething obvious. This was like the denouement to a very bad B movie on Fox. In an election cycle filled with joy because of Obama's freshness, the Franken–Coleman war was markedly joyless and so unbecoming to Minnesotan's sensibilities that, it seemed, only Barkley benefited from the flying mud and last-hours mayhem. The third party candidate stood for "A pox on both your houses." By this point in the campaign, that was a popular point of view.

Of Coleman's TV ad trashing him, Franken told reporters, "In this ad, Senator Coleman looks the people of Minnesota in the eye and lies by blaming me for something that I had absolutely nothing to do with... This isn't about me. This is about money... This is about a lawsuit filed against Nasser Kazeminy by the Republican CEO of a company in Texas that I have never heard of... For Norm Coleman to try to deflect attention from this incredibly serious matter by attacking me with false claims is simply insulting to voters who have a right to know the facts before the election... I am not a politician and thought I had seen everything there was to see in this race, but, really, Minnesota deserves better than this." Soon, at Schriock's urging, Franken produced his own commercial, reiterating in thirty seconds what he said at the news conference, kicking off the spot with this: "There is no other way to put it. Norm Coleman is looking you in the eye and lying."

The next morning, the *Star Tribune*'s headline read, "Coleman Calls on Foes to 'Stop Attacking My Family.'" The Franken campaign workers were incredulous about that message and Coleman's ability to spin the controversy sympathetically to him. The explosiveness of the final days knocked aside Franken's "closing argument" supporting the middle class and small businesses and alleviating college tuition worries, an argument that he thought was gaining traction. He never believed this was what an election campaign was going to feel like.

Al Franken's journey to his first Election Day had begun with the death of Paul Wellstone and with his outrage at the way Wellstone's memory was treated by Republicans, especially by Coleman. For Franken, lies, and the lying liars who tell them, had come full circle.

After a final tense debate on Sunday night, both men went on marathon statewide campaign tours to try to close their deals. How the final week shook out, no one was sure. Internal Franken polls had his support waning in the final hours. Schriock and the experts at the DSCC were in the dark; it was the only U.S. Senate race that the DSCC numbers wonks couldn't call. Coleman staffers believed their man was going to eke it out. The voters had whiplash.

This race was close because it became a painful, personalized mess; however, the Iron Range, a traditional DFL stronghold in northeastern Minnesota—ethnic, populist, union-heavy—played a role too. By the time Election Day ended, Minnesota voter turnout reached nearly 78 percent. It was the highest turnout in the nation, but 2 percentage points lower than Obama state campaign manager Jeff Blodgett hoped for—and some of that turnout shortfall was on the Range. Those additional voters could have put Franken over the top. There was a certain New York–celebrity aura to Franken that Rangers didn't tolerate well, even though Franken worked the region hard for two years. Perhaps his strong environmental stance troubled the many hunters and anglers there.

Obama didn't supply the substantial coattails that many presidential candidates have, but enthusiasm for him could only have helped Franken, who was seen very negatively by voters. If Obama underperformed in key DFL strongholds, Franken was punished more by that same DFL base. A Minnesota Public Radio–Humphrey Institute poll showed that, as Election Day approached, an astonishing 25 percent of voters identified as Democrats said they didn't plan to vote for Franken. Statewide, Obama took Minnesota with 54 percent of the vote and dominated in key areas. Franken managed just shy of 42 percent, or almost 361,000 fewer votes than Obama. Obama scored 66 percent in strongly Democratic Ramsey County, home to the city of St. Paul, and Franken got just 52 percent; in Hennepin County, home to Minneapolis, Obama received 64 percent of the vote, Franken just 50 percent; in St. Louis County, home to Duluth, Obama outpolled Franken 65 to 55 percent.

In the critical Eighth Congressional District, the historic DFL hotbed that includes the Iron Range and is home to Democratic Congressman Jim Oberstar, who was winning his eighteenth term that night, Obama received 34,000 more votes than Franken did. In the closing days of the campaign, Republican vice presidential candidate Sarah Palin's snowmobiling husband, Todd, made a visit to northern Minnesota, connecting with voters, but Obama never made a visit to the important Eighth, whose voters wanted to see him, to feel wanted by him. They got also-ran Hillary Clinton as a surrogate on the Monday before Election Day. Franken needed Obama on the ground to help with his closing argument, there in the Eighth and in the Twin Cities.

Why Are We Even Here?

On Election Night, as the returns streamed in from the state's 4,130 precincts, 58 percent of Minnesotans voted against Coleman and against Franken. Neither could generate 42 percent of the vote, with Barkley gathering a remarkable 15 percent. Because they were so divided and so dissatisfied, Minnesota's voters did something they really didn't want to do. They extended the brutal campaign. They placed the election into the hands of judges and lawyers.

CHAPTER SIX

NO RUBBER STAMP

"It would be unjust and disrespectful to those voters to not count those votes."

Two weeks after Franken explained in the wee hours of Election Night that a hand recount was required by state law, and after Coleman said he would step back if he were behind, the recount was underway. It felt like two years. It was November 19, and thousands of partisan volunteers and hundreds of fair-minded election judges began to examine millions of ballots, with every move witnessed by media members and most of the action televised and streamed online for the entire world to see.

In Minneapolis and St. Paul, Fritz Knaak and Marc Elias engaged in dueling news briefings most days. For the ten or so local journalists who covered every nook and cranny of the recount, the days leading up to Thanksgiving owned a rhythm. Each morning, e-mails from one campaign arrived in reporters' in-boxes announcing, in boldface capital letters, "AN UPDATE" conference call or in-person news conference. Minutes later, the other campaign responded with notice of its own briefing, set for about an hour after the rival's so there could be a response.

Most times cheerful, sometimes stern, Coleman's Knaak placed both of his hands on the lectern and methodically read from sharply worded statements, often poking Elias for his ties to "East Coast" Democrats and his "strategy to ignore the will of the Minnesota voters." As for Elias, passion and arm movements always accompanied his focused words, as if he were conducting the Saint Paul Chamber Orchestra rather than a recount legal team. He projected a purposeful politeness as he complimented the state's election officials, expressed confidence that Minnesota's system would work, and constantly jabbed at the Coleman team's reluctance to count every lawful vote.

To a citizenry that was turning its attention to a nose-diving economy, the celebrity of its first African-American president, and the inconsistent Minnesota Vikings, it felt as if the process was dragging, but that was okay because the Minnesota public was now just one of the audiences for the campaigns, and not necessarily the most important. There were other demographic slices to reach, such as election officials from the state's eighty-seven counties working tirelessly to get the recount right while responding to waves of Data Practices Act requests. There were the donors, locally and across the nation, who had already contributed during the election cycle, and who needed to be goosed to reopen their checkbooks to back their favorite runner in this electoral ultramarathon in Flyover Land.

As November moved toward December, the most highly targeted niche was the five-person state Canvassing Board, which included four experienced judges and Secretary of State Ritchie. For the Franken side, Chief Justice Eric Magnuson was the looming question mark. A former law partner of Governor Tim Pawlenty, Magnuson was appointed by Republican Pawlenty to chair the state's Commission on Judicial Selection, and then in June 2008 to be chief justice. Even before being named to the Court, he was an appeals court expert and one of those calm leaders who waits to speak. When push came to shove, if the board needed to make a close call, Elias and others in the Franken camp expected Magnuson to side with Coleman and assumed that the Coleman side was relying on Magnuson to lean its way. G. Barry Anderson, the associate Supreme Court justice, was the only member of the Canvassing Board with election law experience, and that was as counsel to the Republican Party of Minnesota. He first served on the Minnesota Court of Appeals, to which he was appointed by former Republican governor Arne Carlson, and then was elevated to the state's high court by Pawlenty.

Neither Ramsey County Judge Kathleen Gearin nor Ramsey County Judge Ed Cleary was appointed by a Democrat, but both were good, old-fashioned St. Paul Irish Catholic DFLers. Gearin was kicked out of a class at the all-female College of St. Catherine in the 1970s because she disagreed with a conservative professor over the Vietnam War. Gearin went on to become a social studies teacher who once was threatened by a high school kid pointing a derringer at her. "I looked at him, my knees were shaking," Gearin said, "and I told him, 'If you're going to carry a gun like a man, treat it like a man and not like a baby. Now, put it away!'" He did. Soon after, she entered law school, became a prosecutor under a Republican county attorney, and then ran for an open seat on the Ramsey County bench in 1987.

Cleary was a former Ramsey County public defender and for five years had been the director of the state's Office of Lawyers Professional Responsibility, an agency of the state Supreme Court, which oversees the conduct of lawyers. He was also the author of a highly-regarded book, *Beyond the Burning Cross,* about his defense of a white teenager in St. Paul who burned a cross on the lawn of an African-American family. Cleary fearlessly challenged the city's ordinance prohibiting such a hateful act as violating the First Amendment of the U.S. Constitution. In a landmark case, *R.A.V. v. St. Paul,* Cleary successfully argued before the U.S. Supreme Court that the ordinance should be struck down, and it was by a unanimous vote of the nation's highest court. He was appointed to the bench by Independence Party Governor Jesse Ventura.

And then there was Mark Ritchie, arguably the most politically progressive elected official in Minnesota. A farm policy expert, for eighteen years Ritchie was the executive director of a Minneapolis-based global nonprofit called the Institute for Agriculture and Trade Policy, which, by its own description, "works locally and globally at the intersection of policy and practice to ensure fair and sustainable food, farm and trade systems." Ritchie had been a Franken supporter and appeared at Franken campaign events. For the Coleman forces, Ritchie was a natural enemy. When he ran in 2006 against Republican Secretary of State Mary Kiffmeyer, Ritchie wrote of what motivated him to aspire to the state's top elections job:

> In the early 1980s, I became active in a movement to save family farms and rural communities. The challenges facing Greater Minnesota had quickly ballooned into an economic disaster...During this important—yet challenging—time I had the opportunity to work closely with a political science professor from Carleton College named Paul Wellstone...a strong believer in the need for voter registration and "Get Out the Vote" drives. He taught me that every voice—and vote—mattered and that everyone should be included in the political process...Paul's death was a true turning point in my life.

It pushed Ritchie to leave the farm policy think tank and lead a voter registration campaign in 2004, and then run for office on the DFL ticket. His victory elevated him to chairman of the state Canvassing Board, whose job was to certify the winner of the 2008 senate race between a Wellstone rival and a Wellstone ally. Hate mail directed at Ritchie was common, and included the "Pissing on Obama" drawing he received by fax. In the cartoon, a gallows labeled "Marxist Ritchie" was depicted in a woodsy scene, as if the site of a lynching. The caption read "Death to All Marxists." It arrived at 3:43 p.m. on November 19, the first day ballots began being counted and challenged around the great state of Minnesota.

On November 26, the state Canvassing Board met to tackle the issue of the improperly rejected absentee ballots that it had set aside eight days earlier at its initial organizational meeting. Since then, the advisory letter from Assistant Attorney General Kenneth Raschke stating that rejected absentee ballots were not part of the Canvassing Board's jurisdiction had been getting trashed in Democratic legal circles. DFL Attorney General Lori Swanson was receiving pointed phone calls from influential members of her party asking, How could the AG's office allow such an opinion to be written? How could a Democrat turn her back on voters?

While Swanson was feeling the political heat, Team Franken was compiling affidavits from voters who said their votes had been rejected for unclear reasons. A comprehensive, three-page affidavit from a DFL operative named Will Howell, who was helping with the investigation of rejected ballots, outlined eighteen different categories of inexplicable rejections from Hennepin to Itasca counties, mostly because of simple clerical errors by harried election judges examining more absentee ballots than ever before. Judges looked up a voter's name on the precinct roster, couldn't find it and rejected the ballot, but later realized the voter's name was listed there. County officials sent envelopes of absentee ballots to the wrong precinct, so the votes weren't counted. Howell wrote that voter registration cards were inside the secrecy envelopes with the ballots, and the votes were wrongly rejected. The most blunt reason for a ballot rejection that Howell wrote of was, "The Itasca County list states that Jonas A's ballot was rejected because: 'We messed up and somebody put [it] in the reject pile.'" "We messed up" was, of course, not one of the four statutory reasons to reject a citizen's vote.

As Franken's lawyers scoured those gems from counties responding to Data Practices Act requests, some counties on their own began to review and sort their piles of rejected absentee ballots. Hennepin County Attorney Mike Freeman, a DFL partisan, sent a letter to the Canvassing Board proposing a uniform statewide solution to the problem. In a plan developed with other county attorneys, Freeman suggested that election officials in all eighty-seven counties statewide reexamine rejected absentee ballots and place them in five piles, not just the four that aligned with the legal reasons for rejection. Those four reasons to discard a ballot were: the voter's name and address on the outside return envelope were not the same as on the ballot application; the voter's signature on the return envelope did not match the application signature; the voter wasn't registered; the voter also voted in person. Freeman's additional pile would include ballots for which "the election judge cannot determine any basis for rejecting the absentee ballot"; that is, the "we messed up" pile. In a sense, this new pile was filled with uncounted ballots, rather than rejected ballots, because they had been tossed aside without any statutory basis.

Under the Freeman proposal, the rejected ballots would not be opened, but would be "securely retained in their separate piles" until "an agency, judge, board or other with authority" determined they should be opened and counted. That letter from the son of the late Governor Orville Freeman, one of the founders of Minnesota's DFL Party, grabbed the attention of board members Cleary and Gearin as they digested it before their November 26 meeting. "I read it and thought, 'You know, he's got a good point,'" Gearin said months later.

Cleary carried the ball for the notion that the absentee ballots, if wrongly turned down by election officials in the precincts, should get a second look. In pushing for that, he ran up against Justice G. Barry Anderson, the former GOP attorney, in a fast-paced meeting that revealed the smarts and biases of the panel members and in which Ritchie, the alleged leftist of the group, served as the consensus builder.

The Canvassing Board session began with Anderson offering a motion to reject the Franken side's request of November 18 that some wrongly rejected absentee ballots be included in the recount. Magnuson quickly seconded the motion, and Anderson went on to explain that his opposition was "purely procedural," and that any "irregularities" should be addressed in what was sure to be a subsequent election contest trial. "The statute does not directly grant authority for this body to accept and include rejected absentee ballots," Anderson said. "The relief that is requested of this board [by Franken] is extraordinary... The jurisdiction and authority of this board is limited." This was the Coleman position.

Because of Minnesota's open meeting law, the five board members were not allowed to gather privately to debate the issues, and Ritchie, Gearin, and Cleary said after the case concluded that board members vigilantly followed the law. Any debate executed in public was extemporaneous and raw, but these Canvassing Board disputes were conducted by four judges, who, in their day jobs, made their livings in constant give-and-take with lawyers and other judges. The thrusts and parries were impressively articulate and painfully polite, but Cleary was the most dogged.

Cleary instantly challenged the associate justice's motion to block all of the absentee ballots from consideration. Cleary agreed with Anderson that the board had no authority to make "findings of fact and conclusions of law" on which absentee ballots should be included in the recount. But Cleary, raising the index finger of his right hand for emphasis, said that all of the rejected ballots should be reviewed for the four statutory reasons, plus, "It appears there is a fifth pile," and he meant those ballots rejected for no legal reasons.

With that, Cleary conceived a new Minnesota election law concept and coined a new phrase, the "fifth pile." No one knew then that its inclusion in the recount would open a floodgate of votes, a flurry of litigation, and a new term in the recount lexicon. Soon, Gearin joined Cleary's position. "We do not have the authority to review rejected absentee ballots [and] I'm not particularly happy about that," she said, but Cleary's "fifth pile" should be sorted, she said. Gearin's comments seemed to sway Anderson, who allowed that "there's no problem in sorting," but his concern focused on actually opening and then counting the ballots that had been previously rejected. He wasn't ready to go that far.

Magnuson, listening carefully throughout, sat motionless between Gearin and Ritchie, looking at photocopies of Minnesota Supreme Court cases from 1858 and 1865 that he had discovered. Nearly thirty-six minutes into the discussion, the state's highest-ranking judge finally spoke. "I don't hear anyone on the Canvassing Board quarrelling with the notion that the right of every citizen to have their ballot counted is a vital and important right," he said, sounding a bit like Marc Elias. Magnuson then embraced the position proffered in the Raschke opinion, that "the Canvassing Board only counts cast ballots. Rejected ballots are not cast ballots, and we act in a ministerial capacity and not an adjudicative function." This was an administrative process, he was saying, not a full-blown court taking evidence and hearing sworn testimony. As for the absentee ballots, "the right body can look at them at the right time," he said, but for now, Anderson's motion should be approved, and the rejected absentees barred from the recount.

"I just want to respond briefly," said Cleary, not backing down to Supreme Court justices used to getting their way. "I do believe that the ministerial capacity the chief justice is referring to has been expanded by statute since those cases of 150 years ago." Times change, Cleary implied, but, apparently, not enough. Ritchie, taking a cue from Magnuson, recrafted the Anderson motion with something more succinct: "The state Canvassing Board will reject the request to include rejected absentee ballots in the recount," Ritchie said.

Cleary protested. He would be willing to agree with that resolution, but only if ballots in that fifth pile were considered "uncounted" and not "rejected." "By voting for this I am not agreeing that the fifth group is out of our purview," Cleary insisted.

"I agree with you," Ritchie said, finally staking out a position.

"I agree," Magnuson said.

"I agree," Gearin said.

"Fine," Anderson surrendered.

In this quick hour, the formal vote by the board did bar rejected ballots from the recount, but the issue had migrated toward Franken's legal position. The board had agreed that a fifth pile—that is, a set of wrongly rejected ballots—existed; Knaak even told journalists after the vote that he agreed that such a category existed, but with only a handful of votes, not the "five hundred to a thousand" ballots that Ritchie estimated. The distinction, articulated best by Cleary, was that there was a difference between a ballot rejected for one or more of the four statutory reasons and an uncounted ballot, which was turned down for no apparent reason. The question now was whether the board could force, or even request, that local election officials sort their rejected ballots and create local fifth piles so everyone could get a feel for how many uncounted absentee ballots were out there. Furthermore, if and when a fifth pile of wrongly rejected ballots was formed, could those votes be counted and included in the recount that the Canvassing Board was bound to certify? Republican Supreme Court Justice G. Barry Anderson sought additional guidance from DFL Attorney General Swanson's office. It wouldn't come for a while, but when it did, the fifth pile would gain a life of its own.

The decision by the Canvassing Board not to include rejected absentee ballots in the recount was reported in the media as a defeat for the Franken forces. "Franken Loses Bid to Add Ballots," said the *Star Tribune*. "Franken Loses a Round over Absentee Votes, Canvassing Board Won't Add Rejected Ballots to Recount," screamed the *Pioneer Press* headline.

Elias didn't see it that way. If a legal ballot had been wrongly rejected, then, as Cleary noted, it was simply uncounted. If it was uncounted then, under Minnesota case law, there was time to get it counted and included in the tally. That's where, it seemed, Cleary and Gearin stood. Anderson and Magnuson weren't prepared to take that position, not yet. Ritchie, playing facilitator and chairman, didn't tip his hand.

Back at Franken's headquarters in Minneapolis, Lillehaug and Hamilton were among those who urged Elias to appeal the board's decision to the state Supreme Court. They couldn't risk losing the absentee-ballot fight, the other lawyers argued. Typically impatient Elias opted to play it cool. The board members had not shut down the path to counting wrongly rejected absentee ballots. With the birth of the fifth pile, they gave life to some of the rejected ballots while punting the matter down the road for another meeting and another opinion from the attorney general. The political scientist in Elias trumped the lawyer in him on this day. His instincts drove him to reduce the legal temperature on the Canvassing Board, but turn up the media and public relations pressure.

"Look, this is an elected judiciary," Elias said at a meeting of key Franken leadership soon after the Canvassing Board session. "This secretary of state runs for office too. You get enough people on TV saying, 'My vote was not counted for no reason,' and it will affect them. The more we can show them there were real voters disenfranchised, the less likely it is that this issue will go away." This was no time for "legal mumbo jumbo," Elias said, but rather, an opportunity for a full-court PR press on the decision makers in this recount.

First, he went out to his daily news briefing and instantly generated some news. He knew that in six days a runoff election was set for the open Georgia U.S. Senate seat. That state went to a second election, not a recount. If Democratic challenger Jim Martin could somehow unseat incumbent Republican Senator Saxby Chambliss, then Franken would represent the Democrats' hopes for their coveted sixtieth Senate spot. Speaking to reporters after the Canvassing Board meeting, Elias began his briefing with this provocative statement:

> By the end of this process, Minnesotans' votes will be counted and today makes me more confident than ever of that. There are a number of ways this can happen, whether it is at the county level, before the state Canvassing Board, before the courts of Minnesota, or before the United States Senate, we do not know . . . The [Canvassing] Board's consensus that there is a problem and that all of the votes have not been counted only bolsters our resolve to pursue this matter further.

His first hint that he might take the Franken case to the U.S. Senate floor was a real eyebrow raiser and was soon echoed by Democratic Majority Leader Harry Reid, who issued an orchestrated statement in Washington backing his friend Elias. "Today's decision by the Minnesota Canvassing Board not to count certain absentee ballots is cause for great concern," Reid said, adding, "As the process moves forward, Minnesota authorities must ensure that no voter is disenfranchised."

Coleman's campaign manager Cullen Sheehan yelled back, "This is a stunning admission by the Franken campaign that they are willing to take this process away from Minnesotans if they fail to win the recount. It is even more stunning that the Democratic Senate leader would inject himself into the Minnesota election process."

Elias's words stirred the pot, but he wasn't about to leapfrog into a Senate battle with the Republicans — not yet, anyway. Instead, he was merely cranking up the significance of this Minnesota fight as Martin campaigned against Chambliss in Georgia and as donors everywhere kept receiving phone calls from Franken fundraisers. He also assigned the campaign's new-media consultant and tech whiz J. D. Schlough to begin production of a video of voters whose ballots were rejected. Schlough was to make one-dimensional affidavits about rejected ballots come to life. The idea was to produce a minidocumentary and to post it at Franken's campaign Web site and YouTube, the video-sharing site, before the next Canvassing Board meeting on December 12. It would show real people whose votes hadn't been counted and challenge the sitting Senator Coleman to oppose the inclusion of valid votes. Elias, the New York Giants fan, was spreading out his offense.

At a gathering of some staffers in Franken's campaign office war room, Elias got overly dramatic as he marshaled the troops for the days to come. "We're here to fight for the enfranchisement of voters," he told staffers. "We're here to make sure that voters who did everything right, and through no fault of their own haven't had their ballots counted, will have their voices heard." As he spoke, he bowed his head, his chin resting on his chest, and, like a righteous demonstrator from the 1960s and '70s, Elias raised his right fist in a symbol of defiance. It was a fun, theatrical moment on a day that marked his best legal non-decision of the recount. There was no reason to run into court willy-nilly, no sense in looking overly litigious. There was no payback in ticking off the Canvassing Board, not now, not when it felt as if things were moving in his direction.

A few days later, to get a jumpstart on the fifth-pile possibility, Ritchie's office asked county and city election officials to begin sorting each of their jurisdiction's rejected absentee ballots into five distinct piles. It was an action that caused Coleman's lawyers to angrily assert, as Knaak did in a letter, "No evidence exists that any, much less 'many' absentee ballot envelopes were improperly rejected by any local election officials." But Ritchie's office knew — and the Franken campaign's hunt revealed — there was growing evidence that more than 10 percent of the 11,000 or so rejected absentee ballots, or more than 1,100 votes, might have been wrongly rejected by local officials. Elias did not need the courts to tell the Canvassing Board what to do. The numbers were beginning to speak for themselves.

Thanksgiving meant a break in the recount and, everyone hoped, a peaceful weekend. The calendar was turning to December, a month for both campaigns to convince the public that victory was at hand and to lay the groundwork for litigation, just in case this all wound up in court. December was about perception molding reality, particularly as the December 5 deadline approached for all counties to have their hand recounts completed.

Franken was on the telephone from his downtown Minneapolis townhouse up to six hours a day seeking financial help from supporters. He was back and forth to Washington to fund raise and kiss the rings of Charles Schumer, Harry Reid, and others. Coleman, still the sitting senator, worked his money-raising magic too. By the time this case ended,

Franken raised about $11.3 million to pay for post–Election Day expenses. Coleman, with fewer telemarketing costs, whipped up about $8.7 million. Before it was over, the election campaigns and the recount would cost Franken and Coleman a combined $61.8 million.

The changing of the calendar did not reduce the Franken campaign's general animus toward the *Star Tribune,* with its Sunday circulation of 500,000 newspapers statewide, and its Web site, StarTribune.com. The enthusiastic endorsement of Coleman and dismissive attitude toward Franken was one thing, but a story that ran in the November 30 newspaper shoved the campaign into a tizzy. Stripped across the top of the local news section on that Sunday was a story written by reporters Pat Doyle and Glenn Howatt stating that Franken wasn't winning the recount, and, what's more, it was unlikely that he could recover to win. A fancy, but complicated, chart accompanied the article, which revolved around the challenges by both camps and the presumption that all challenges were created equal, which they weren't. Franken was actually winning more challenges at the recount tables statewide than was Coleman. Franken's people knew it.

In addition, during the meticulous hand recount Franken was picking up new votes that weren't being challenged. One factor was the voting machine used in some St. Louis County precincts, the so-called Eagle machine: the Optech Eagle III-P tabulator. Ballots used with the Eagle required voters to complete a tiny image of an arrow, with the arrowhead pointing to the left. Between the arrowhead and the back end of the arrow was a half-inch gap. The voter filled in that gap to record his vote. Those machines were known to be less accurate in their optical scanning than the more widely used M100 and Accu-Vote machines, whose ballots required filling in an oval. Of the thirty-three precincts statewide using the Eagle machines, thirty-one were located in DFL-leaning St. Louis County.

From the start of the recount on November 19, Franken data gurus Schlough and Andy Bechhoefer had developed a computer model to project how the recount might unfold. Acquiring nearly real-time data allowed that model to be formulated quickly, and to evolve. Using numbers from the recount's first days, they began to notice a "pace of pickup" for Franken; that is, he gained a vote here or there over and above what the initial election returns showed. When you're behind 215 votes, and there are more than four thousand precincts and nearly three million votes, it doesn't take much to begin chipping away at the deficit if you pick up, for example, one vote in every ten precincts. The Franken team grew increasingly optimistic the election could swing to their guy. It was invaluable knowledge to possess, but Elias and others didn't want to share their projections, not yet anyway.

As they felt they were gaining on Coleman, the Franken side was totally frustrated by the recount reporting method of the secretary of state's office, and the local media that regurgitated it. Under Ritchie's tabulation system, when the recount began on November 19, "the score was zero–zero," Ritchie said. The official tally was as if no original counting had ever been done. Every night at 8 p.m., Ritchie's office posted where things stood in the recount after that particular day. Sometimes the precincts were in parts of the state that favored Coleman on Election Night. Sometimes they were from Franken precincts. But in reporting the tally, the secretary of state's office stripped out the challenges of both sides. By the Thanksgiving break in the statewide recount, with about 85 percent of the chore completed, the campaigns, in a tit-for-tat dance, had challenged a total of more than 6,600 ballots. By not factoring in how election judges were ruling on challenges, however, Ritchie's office created an inaccurate scoreboard.

If one candidate challenged more ballots, frivolously or not, that wasn't reflected in the recount tally. Much to Team Franken's dismay, challenges were set aside and not included in Ritchie's calculus. When recount rules were established in early November, Sautter told Ritchie's people that the call at the table should be used for a public tally; he lost that argument. Challenges mounted, even as Ritchie and his aides kept complaining to the campaigns about them.

"What is driving the challenge strategy is the way you are reporting it!" Franken lawyer Kevin Hamilton told Ritchie deputy Jim Gelbmann one day. "Look, if you want to win the day's recount totals, all you've got to do is challenge the other guy. Like, duh! Hello?"

Both legal teams acknowledged that their volunteers on the ground got feistier than they hoped. For his part, Ritchie blamed both campaigns for gaming the system, and local election officials got fed up with all the challenges. Some temporarily suspended recounts in their county buildings and city halls until volunteers learned how to behave.

In Elias's view—and this would be borne out—Franken's challenges were better; that is, according to the election judges at tables across the state, more of the Coleman-leaning ballots that Franken's volunteers challenged presented legitimate questions about a voter's intent. The perception problem was this: the more Coleman's side challenged Franken ballots, the more they removed likely Franken votes from the secretary of state's nightly scoreboard. Anyone looking at the "official" running results on Ritchie's Web site would think that Coleman continued to lead, and would likely win.

The *Star Tribune*'s method was a bit different from Ritchie's. Rather than report the recount as an entirely new calculation with a zero–zero tie on the first day, the newspaper compared the recounted results in each precinct with the original results from Election Night, did the math, and reported that new margin as the daily recount score. If Coleman won a precinct in St. Cloud by ten votes on November 4, but only by nine when Stearns County conducted its recount, the *Star Tribune* subtracted a vote from Coleman's tally. That at least took Team Franken's "pace of pickup" into consideration, but still did not take into account the real effects of the challenges on the tally.

This calculation confusion came to a head because of the November 30 *Star Tribune* story, which pushed Elias to come clean with his internal numbers. Headlined "For Franken, a Math Problem," with the subheadline, "Challenged ballots may offer the Senate challenger a path to overtaking Coleman, but numbers indicate it would be a tough route," the story read:

> While a tiny margin separates the candidates in the Minnesota U.S. Senate race, it is wide enough that Democrat Al Franken faces a daunting task in challenging votes to erase Sen. Norm Coleman's lead . . . To win his case before the state Canvassing Board, Franken must prevail on more than 6 percent of his challenges of Coleman votes even if Coleman fails to succeed on any of his challenges, a *Star Tribune* analysis shows . . . If the outcome of past election disputes provides a clue, Franken will have a hard time reversing enough votes to win, said one veteran elections official who has been involved in the Senate recount.

The article was accompanied by a chart with eleven columns and eleven rows that needed a 150–word explanation of what it meant. It looked like one of those mileage charts on a road map, telling travelers the distances between Omaha and Des Moines, or Omaha and Minneapolis, or Omaha and Dallas. The chart supposedly projected Franken's chances of winning the recount if a sliding index of percentages of his challenges prevailed. The entire package of story and chart made very little sense, but in a campaign, election, and recount battle flamed by the Internet, the *Star Tribune* story stating that the odds against Franken's climb were "daunting" instantly circulated nationally. The Franken side went bonkers.

"A nightmare," campaign manager Schriock said later. "Everyone was doubting us." Calls came in from DSCC leaders, including Senator Charles Schumer, the man who had urged her to take the Franken campaign manager job six months earlier.

"Are you sure?" they asked Schriock and Elias, as in, "Are you sure you can win this thing, and is it worth it for us to keep raising money?"

"I swear we are right on the numbers," Schriock pleaded, numbers she had been sharing with key Washington Democrats since Schlough and Bechhoefer began noting the pick up of votes.

"Then you have to change the press," she was told by at least one DSCC leader, who said the message had to change, and now.

"There's nothing I can do to fix this press," she replied. "You have to keep the caucus behind us."

Franken was "going insane," one staffer said. He was conducting his continual fundraising, calling his core donor constituents in places like New York and California. In the days after the Doyle and Howatt story, Franken was told more than once, "But the Minneapolis *Star Tribune* says you can't win."

While he was pulling out whatever hair he had left, Elias knew it was time to disclose what the campaign already knew. In that November 30 story, he told the *Star Tribune* that, using internal data, he believed Franken was behind by 73 votes, not the 282 that the newspaper reported. That was the first time he revealed the campaign's recount tally. To help Schriock and Franken in their high-pressure race to raise money and keep their important Washington support, Elias thought back to a tactic that Barack Obama's campaign used as his nomination effort built. Primary after primary, caucus after caucus, Obama regularly announced how many Democratic Party delegates he had corralled. It built momentum and credibility. It gave real information for voters and the media to get their heads around.

The Tuesday after the *Star Tribune* story appeared, Elias told reporters in a briefing that the Franken team believed it was down by fifty votes. By Friday, December 5, when the recount was over—or, rather, was supposed to be over—the secretary of state's office said Coleman was ahead by 192 votes. Elias, using the campaign's method, claimed

Franken led by four. Neither of those "final" numbers meant a darn thing because of what occurred on that Thursday, December 4, hours before the completion of the hand recount. In Minneapolis, the largest electoral jurisdiction in the state, 132 ballots went missing. An envelope with eighty votes for Franken, thirty-four for Coleman, and eighteen for others had, apparently, disappeared. Poof, gone. A search was underway at the church where the votes were cast and at the Minneapolis ballot warehouse. Never a dull moment.

First, there was the birth of the fifth pile. Now, recount lore was set to embrace the mystery of the fifth envelope, a missing Tyvek envelope that couldn't be found in time for the December 5 hand recount deadline. The disappearance occurred in Minneapolis's Ward Three, Precinct One, near the University of Minnesota campus, and, so, a bundle of Franken votes was at stake.

It all began on December 3 as Minneapolis elections officials were set to complete their hand recount. As many times as counters calculated and recalculated, Minneapolis Elections Director Cindy Reichert said, nothing seemed to add up. The hand-signed rosters of voters who were checked in at Minneapolis W-3 P-1 on Election Day added up to 2,028 votes. When officials went to recount the results of the precinct, only 1,896 votes could be found, a shortfall of 132 ballots. Calls were made to the election judges at the polling place, the University Lutheran Church of Hope, to its pastor and building custodian, and to the person who drove the ballots to the Minneapolis election warehouse. The ballots were mysteriously missing.

They had been packaged in five Tyvek envelopes, those white, shiny, slippery, waterproof envelopes often used by overnight mail services. Four of the envelopes could be found, and they were labeled "2 of 5," "3 of 5," "4 of 5," and "5 of 5." Logically, Reichert and others believed, and one of the election judges confirmed, on Election Night there was a fifth envelope and it was marked "1 of 5." But it was gone, not in a trunk of a car, not on a floor in the church, not behind a filing cabinet in an office somewhere. What's a democracy to do when ballots disappear? That was the next dilemma of this recount that seemed to have no boundaries for complexities, frayed nerves, and over-the-top accusations. Even as Reichert, Gelbmann, and others scoured the Minneapolis elections warehouse, looking behind every pallet, under every stack,

Elias lashed out, saying, "These ballots must be found. The outcome of this election is at stake . . . The integrity of this election is also at stake, as is the integrity of Minnesota's electoral process. We won't stand for the disenfranchisement of 132 Minnesota voters, and neither will the people of this state. Find the ballots."

Elias then proposed a series of marginally Draconian steps to find the ballots, such as interviewing every person who worked at the precinct on Election Day, every person who had a role in setting up or cleaning up at the church, and every person who touched or transported the ballots either on Election Day or at any point afterward. He called for a "systematic forensic search" of the church, and of any vehicle used to transport ballots or other elections materials. He sought the release of the names, addresses, and phone numbers for everyone who worked at the precinct on Election Day and every county employee who might have touched the ballot envelopes. Elias wanted those votes badly, and demanded that officials "move heaven and earth" to find the ballots.

Perhaps it was the mention of heaven, but Minnesota Republican Party Chairman Ron Carey came out swinging against Elias. "Demanding that the government invade a place of worship — and require taxpayers to foot the bill for that invasion — is bizarre and repulsive," Carey said. "In addition to a loud slap in the face of local election officials, the Franken campaign's demand for information on the administrator of the church is simply tantamount to government-sponsored persecution." The headline that the state GOP placed on top of Carey's written statement read, "Franken Campaign Calls For Government Invasion Of A Church!"

Despite all the verbiage, a profound problem was at hand. Elias knew from his campaign's internal count that the statewide margin was narrowing. The forty-six-vote net gain for Franken in Minneapolis W-3 P-1 could be the difference in the entire election. How should the state Canvassing Board react to receiving official results that had no tangible ballots backing them up? Knaak argued in a letter to Reichert and the Canvassing Board that "the only legally recognizable number to be submitted is the recounted number and *not* the election night total." With the 132 ballots missing, their voters' intent unknown, and citing an earlier Minnesota case, Knaak added, "probability is not enough to ascribe these votes to one candidate or the other."

On the other hand, there was Minnesota case law that seemed to favor the Franken position. If the ballots were missing, a previous case said, "the next best evidence" was the totals provided by officials on Election

Day. An Illinois case, which Lillehaug cited in his memo to the Canvassing Board, was more on point, saying, "While the ballots are original evidence, the official results are *prima facie* evidence of the votes cast. Where the original ballots cannot be deemed trustworthy, or . . . are missing, the official results are the best evidence." The burden, the Franken team was saying, was on Knaak and his Coleman comrades to prove that the official results were wrong. The ballots were never found. The Minneapolis 132 became a dangling detail. It was a mystery to be solved at a later date, and another legal hill for Coleman's lawyers to climb.

Even a studious and rabid follower of the recount needed a GPS system to keep track of all the pathways the Great Minnesota Recount was now traversing. Four piles were becoming five, lost envelopes with more than a hundred votes were being hunted on hands-and-knees as if colored eggs on Easter Sunday, thousands of challenged ballots were being returned from the hinterlands for central examination, and the state Canvassing Board—once a twenty-minute commitment with cookies for busy judges—was about to meet again to make a fundamental ruling on the fate of absentee ballots that Franken wanted and Coleman didn't. Elias, Schlough, and others in Franken's communications shop kept their eyes on the prize: continue to push the Canvassing Board toward including the legal votes in those envelopes in that fifth pile.

That push came in the form of a six-minute-long video piece called "My Vote," which put emotional meat on the bones of their argument that real votes of real people were being denied. Getting out of campaign mode was a tough adjustment for staffers in both camps, but the Franken crew came the closest to a political ad with its Web-posted video. It began with a black screen and white typeface, the words silently fading in and out. No voices, no music.

"In the closest Senate race in Minnesota history, every vote should be counted fairly," the first screen said. "But there are Minnesotans who had their votes thrown out, even though they did nothing wrong . . . They voted absentee, but their ballots were improperly rejected because of someone else's mistake . . . And in the closest Senate race in Minnesota history, their votes remain uncounted."

Cut to sixty-nine-year-old Jane Bolter of Minnetonka, who voted absentee because her husband was scheduled to have open-heart surgery. Their votes were rejected because it seemed as if they weren't registered, but they were. Cut to Erick Garcia Luna, thirty-one, with a noticeable Latino accent, who became a U.S. citizen in 2008. His vote was rejected too, he explains, because of a registration error. Cut to forty-six-year-old quadriplegic Mike Brickley, lying on a couch with a Minnesota Vikings–logoed pillow under his head. His was rejected for a signature mismatch; he signed the absentee ballot application with his mouth.

Extreme? You betcha. Effective? The video presentation, first posted on YouTube, received a link in the story about it in the *Star Tribune*. Minnesota Public Radio posted the video on its highly read, up-to-the-minute News Cut blog. MSNBC, the national Web site and cable channel, posted the video. In the first day, "My Vote" received about fifteen thousand hits on YouTube. Elias and company sent DVD copies to the Canvassing Board members along with a written brief about why improperly rejected absentee ballots should be counted.

Months later, Canvassing Board members Cleary, Gearin, and Ritchie, in separate interviews, said they never looked at the Franken DVD and couldn't even remember receiving one. Gearin acknowledged hearing about it and seeing an excerpt on the television news. "I didn't like that," she said. "It seemed to be an emotional play, and I don't like emotional plays." It might not have helped, but the buzz it created among Franken boosters sure didn't hurt. Recounts, Elias understood, were not won by legal mumbo-jumbo alone.

At the Canvassing Board, the missing Minneapolis ballots were addressed and, following precedent in previous cases, the 132 votes were included in the board's recount tally. Reichert testified before the panel, provided her troubling but believable story, and there was, surprisingly, limited debate. There went a key issue for Coleman, and a huge chunk of votes. In those 132, Franken held a forty-six-vote advantage. Coleman lawyer Tony Trimble sat a few rows directly behind Reichert in the hearing room as she faced the board. He looked disbelieving as she spoke and as the board, especially Chief Justice Magnuson, decided that Reichert's explanation and presented data were "prima facie evidence" that, in fact, those 132 ballots, now in election heaven, did once exist.

The matter of the fifth pile was raised again with some compelling news from Deputy Secretary of State Jim Gelbmann. This matter of wrongly rejected absentee ballots was not just a few here and a few there, Gelbmann implied. He told of the case of Duluth, in which 127 ballots were rejected by local officials because of a lack of a date on ballots; witnesses and voters are not required to date the envelope. So, roughly forty percent of the absentee ballots in Duluth were improperly rejected, Gelbmann told the board. "I could see the faces of the members of the Canvassing Board," Gelbmann remembered. "I knew from their faces they weren't just going to say, 'Let's forget about it.'"

Add to Gelbmann's news a completely new spin from Attorney General Lori Swanson's office, which unveiled a second advisory opinion. This time, Swanson appeared at the Canvassing Board to support it. The attorney general's office had changed its mind, and dramatically. The Raschke view — that wrongly rejected absentee ballots should be considered at an election contest and not at this Canvassing Board forum — was, essentially, refuted. A month earlier, Raschke wrote, "Only the ballots cast in the election and the summary statements certified by the election judges may be considered in the recount process," and he added a sentence from the secretary of state's *2008 Recount Guide* that the recount "is *not* to determine if absentee ballots were properly accepted."

Now, there was a 180-degree reversal, written by Swanson's top deputy, Solicitor General Alan I. Gilbert. Gilbert wrote to the board, "There is no doubt that voters who have complied with all legal requirements, but whose ballots were improperly rejected, should have their votes counted. Minnesota courts have long expressed the importance of the right of the citizen to vote and to have his or her vote counted."

Coleman's side was convinced that powerful Democrats had gotten Swanson's ear. "Political pressures reached their zenith," Trimble said later, "and they weren't just Minnesota pressures," but in this slice of the recount, the Minnesota Republicans were disappointed even more by Magnuson, whom they saw as one of their own. Knaak, Trimble, and others, including Elias, presumed Magnuson would err in Coleman's favor. Any illusion that that would occur ended on December 12 at the board's meeting, this time in a new hearing room in the basement of the State Capitol, down a flight of steps from Swanson's corner office.

After Swanson outlined Gilbert's revised opinion, a discussion ensued about just how far the board could take it. Could this "ministerial" body order county election officials to actually open and count rejected ballots? A Minnesota Supreme Court decision during the 1962 gubernatorial recount allowed for the correction of errors, and this sure seemed to be a similar case now. Why not allow local officials to sort and open the fifth pile, amend their recount tallies, and send them off to the state Canvassing Board?

The four sitting judges on the board began to weigh in. They were used to ordering people and corporations and local governments to do all kinds of things. But as Canvassing Board members, they weren't judges, and this board had no authority to order anybody to do anything, but it could request or recommend. Cleary was once more the most forceful advocate for including the wrongly rejected ballots. He reiterated his stance from the November 26 meeting.

"I don't believe those to be rejected ballots," he said of the now-familiar fifth pile. "I believe them to be uncounted ballots . . . There is absolutely no reason why that fifth pile should not be submitted to this board . . . The fifth pile — those that have been identified by election officials, not by either candidate . . . as having been put improperly into the rejected pile and are uncounted votes, in my opinion, should come to us, they should be opened and should be counted . . . The bottom line: I think we're disenfranchising voters who followed the command of the law, who submitted the absentee ballots according to law, and it would be unjust and disrespectful to those voters to not count those votes."

Magnuson indicated to Ritchie that he wanted to speak. "Please," Ritchie said, extending his hand to offer the floor to the chief justice of the State of Minnesota. Magnuson had something important to say. "Mister Secretary and other members of the Canvassing Board, I agree wholeheartedly with Judge Cleary," he said "The idea here is to count ballots that were properly cast. I believe that the election officials are making a good faith effort to go back, figure out where they may have missed the boat, and fix it, and I would be very surprised if they refused to submit to us amended returns."

When she heard Magnuson agree with Cleary, Gearin leaned back in her chair, digesting the moment. Cleary said later he was surprised at Magnuson's agreement with him. Because of the state's open meeting law, the panelists hadn't discussed Gilbert's new advisory letter in private. These decisions and pronouncements were occurring in real time. "Eric and I butted heads in the first couple of meetings," Clearly remembered later, "I'm not thrilled about butting heads with the chief justice. But it felt to me that Eric was making a concerted effort to walk a line, and when I saw that I began deferring to him . . . If he had shown strong partisan tendency, this could have been a mess."

Ritchie was the chairman of the panel, but, as time wore on, it became clear that the others looked to Magnuson for signals. His wholehearted agreement with Cleary would ring long in the ears of Republicans statewide. Not only was the Pawlenty-appointed Supreme Court justice aligning himself with the Democratic Irish Catholic judges from St. Paul on this critical absentee ballot issue, but he would soon be operating on the same wavelength on other matters too. A majority coalition was forming on the Canvassing Board, and it wasn't to Coleman's advantage. Magnuson had only been a judge for six months, but Gearin, who had been on the bench for twenty-one years, knew what happened to lawyers who became jurists in Minnesota. "You really become apolitical the longer you're a judge," Gearin said. "Sometimes, it happens really quickly."

Four days later, the board began its glacial examination of the already recounted but challenged ballots from 106 locations statewide. More than 6,600 challenged ballots still remained in the system. If the board were to spend even one minute on each challenged ballot, that could amount to a week's worth of fourteen-hour days. Ritchie had set aside four days. The challenges had to be reduced.

For weeks, Knaak had been telling the news media that he thought both sides should trade challenges. That was a method used in 1962 during the Elmer Andersen–Karl Rolvaag gubernatorial recount when more than one hundred thousand ballots were challenged. Wide categories were reduced by one side or another via electoral horse trading. Elias kept saying he was open to some negotiations, but he resisted Knaak's overtures because of the way Knaak delivered them. Knaak's suggestions came via letters that were simultaneously released to the news media. That really pressed Elias's buttons. He found such public offers annoying, so he refused to respond to them.

When the hand recount ended on December 5, and there were still more than 6,600 challenges in play, Deputy Secretary of State Jim Gelbmann telephoned both sides and implored them to reduce the numbers by throwing out their respective frivolous challenges, such as tiny marks on ballots. Elias finally broke down and called Knaak to figure out a way to respond to Gelbmann's demand.

On Thursday night, December 11, Gelbmann received a call from Elias and Trimble. The conversation had to remain "top secret," Gelbmann was told. The opposing sides had agreed to meet and negotiate the reduction in challenges, but neither side trusted the others' copies of the ballots. What if Franken doctored a ballot, then Coleman withdrew it and later learned that could have been a Coleman vote? Or vice versa? Trimble and Elias asked Gelbmann if he could do them a favor and produce two sets of copies for each campaign of the 6,689 challenges, or about 27,000 pages.

"As much as I'd like to help, that's going to be very expensive," Gelbmann said, and, what with state procurement rules, he would have to send the job out to printers for bidding. Gelbmann offered a solution: he could simply deliver to them computer disks with PDFs of the ballots, and the two sides could take care of the printing costs on their own. No taxpayer dollars, no prolonged open bidding. Swell, the lawyers said.

A meeting was set for 10 a.m. the next day at the Crowne Plaza hotel in St. Paul, a location on which Elias insisted because it was a union hotel and he wanted to tweak Republican Knaak. Gelbmann delivered the disks to the printer for the lawyers, picked up the copies for them, and dropped off six boxes of ballots at the hotel. "They were so suspicious of each other," he said. As he departed from the Crowne Plaza's conference room about 10 a.m., Gelbmann remembers saying, "Good luck!" He returned to his office, and assumed he would hear from the campaigns after a weekend of wheeling and dealing.

Elias delegated Chris Sautter to oversee the challenge dismissals. Bill McGinley of the Washington law firm of Patton Boggs was in the conference room for Coleman. Kevin Hamilton was scurrying to the hotel to aid Sautter. As he left the keys of his rental car with the parking ramp valet, the man asked, "How long you gonna be here?"

"All day," Hamilton replied, and paid for the full parking rate. But when Hamilton entered the conference room, he was confronted by McGinley. There was a noisy disagreement as to what it was they were to discuss. Coleman's side believed Elias had previously agreed to reduce sweeping ballot categories; for example, any Coleman challenges of Franken votes for identifying marks would go away if Franken challenges of Coleman votes without filled ovals were accepted. But the Franken side believed each ballot needed to be examined individually, not in groups. The categories themselves couldn't be agreed to, and some ballots were challenged for more than one reason. Besides, the Canvassing Board had said it was going to examine individual ballots, and that's the way other challenge-dismissal sessions had gone in Sautter's long recount career. (This was the first signal that Coleman's lawyers were thinking about groups and categories of ballots, not individual ballots, a theme they would reprise when the matter went to court a month later.)

Even if there was an honest misunderstanding between the two parties about dismissing categories or individual ballots, Franken's side also believed that Knaak and Trimble had previously agreed to reduce all the so-called process challenges, such as the issue of those lost Minneapolis ballots and the allegations of double counting of votes. The latter was a particularly important issue to the Coleman side, especially to Trimble. He firmly believed that ballots had been double counted in Franken-friendly precincts when election judges occasionally made mistakes.

"No way," said McGinley, Coleman wasn't going to drop those double counting challenges.

"Yes way," said Hamilton, in a fifth-grade-like exchange that triggered a frantic phone call to Elias, who, on the speaker phone of Hamilton's Blackberry, accused the Coleman team of reneging on its deal to drop the process charges. He also declared the exercise over. Everybody up and left. Elias called Gelbmann by 11:00 a.m., and said the two sides couldn't strike a deal. Could Gelbmann retrieve the ballots?

As for Hamilton, he barely had his overcoat off, but he was already headed out of the hotel and back to his car. "That valet guy was surprised to see me so soon," he said.

"Kumbaya" was not a song on this recount's playlist. With compromise impossible, each side began unilaterally withdrawing challenges to satisfy the desire of Ritchie's office and the Canvassing Board. On December 16, finally, the board began reviewing challenged ballots, with Coleman still prepared to challenge about 1,100 Franken votes, and Franken challenging about 400 Coleman votes. The numbers were ever changing. J. D. Schlough was ready with the database of electronically tagged ballots that he and Bechhoefer developed with the help of volunteer attorneys. Also, on the night before the board met, Schlough, Sautter, and Perkins Coie lawyer Ezra Reese performed a mock Canvassing Board, further reviewing ballots. The Franken side was set. A team of Coleman lawyers had also analyzed challenged ballots, but not with the digital compulsiveness of Schlough et al. The Coleman lawyers, particularly Trimble, remained concerned about alleged double counting of votes. Minutes before the Canvassing Board began ruling on voter intent on all the ballots, Trimble told that panel that he believed there were "137 instances" in which original absentee votes and their duplicates made by election judges on Election Day were both counted. Whether that alleged double counting all benefited Franken was unclear, but the possibility that votes were counted twice continued to be one of Trimble's pet issues throughout the process. Even one Franken lawyer acknowledged privately that there might have been double counting, but, as time wore on, the Coleman side was never able to prove it.

In theory, if the board took three minutes on each ballot, that would have added up to about seventy-five hours of wondering about voter intent, "until Christmas," said Canvassing Board member G. Barry Anderson, *next* Christmas." Thankfully, almost half of the ballots were withdrawn during the four days of counting, and the five members picked up a rhythm of mowing down their evaluations. Still, it was a dreary exercise. State Elections Director Gary Poser or Jim Gelbmann read out the city, precinct, and assigned number of the challenged ballot. The ballot was then projected onto large screens in a hearing room. The same proceedings and ballots were streamed onto the Minnesota House of Representatives' and Senate's Web sites, which hosted the state's Web cast. Other outlets, such as the UpTake, the left-leaning news and video Web site, streamed the proceedings live too. Minnesota's ballot review was free and open to the planet's public.

Board members also received paper copies of the ballot in question. The Canvassing Board assumed that most challenges would, in fact, be rejected, just as Elias had believed in constructing Franken's tracking of the recount vote tally at the tables statewide. With that baseline, Secretary of State Ritchie, the board chairman, went into a monotonous default mode before every ballot was reviewed. "Lino Lakes 5, Challenge 2," he said, declaring the label on the ballot. "I want to move to reject the challenge and assign this vote to Senator Coleman." (This ballot was clearly marked for Coleman, but the voter wrote in Ronald Reagan for some lesser offices.) "Is there any discussion to my motion? . . . Hearing none, all in favor of my motion to reject the challenge, and to assign this vote to Senator Coleman, signify by saying, 'Aye.'"

There were four "Ayes" and Ritchie did not vote.

"Opposed, same sign," he said. There was silence. "We're moving to Glenwood . . ."

On some occasions, board members requested to examine the original ballots, and not the photocopied version. Judge Gearin said it was sometimes necessary to touch and feel the erasure on a ballot to better determine the voter's intent.

And the process continued. And continued.

In nearly 96 percent of the challenges over the next four days, the board members would unanimously say "Aye," thereby rejecting most of the challenges that were made by volunteers in November and continued to be pursued by the legal teams into mid-December. Patterns developed, and that's why Schlough's database was so important. Chief Justice Magnuson was developing his own informal crib sheet, trying to keep the board as consistent as possible on similarly marked ballots. He developed a document filled with what he called hieroglyphics to track ballot oddities.

On the first day of the board's review of challenges, some bloggers believed they saw patterns emerging, with Cleary, Gearin, and Ritchie forming a sort of leftish, pro-Franken wing of the board. That didn't prove to be true. For his part, Ritchie said later that because he was sitting to Anderson's right, whatever the Associate Justice ruled, he generally went along with, the liberal secretary of state and conservative Supreme Court justice in harmony.

It was Magnuson who set the tone early on the first day of evaluating challenges. On one ballot that seemed to have been cast clearly for Coleman, there were initials, *TD,* near the presidential section of the ballot. The Franken side challenged the ballot. Such initials fell into the category of an "identifying mark," a major no-no under Minnesota Statute § 204C.22, subdivision 13. That entire law lists fifteen different ways that elections officials and Canvassing Board members can determine a voter's intent. The identifying mark has long been scrutinized on ballots; in some cities, a voter who initialed his ballot or otherwise marked it distinctively, did it so that corrupt party bosses could know that a friendly vote had been delivered. A payoff followed.

In this particular case, Elias told the board that *TD* was an obvious identifying mark. Trimble opposed that idea, saying it was just a voter emphasizing his choice for Coleman. Magnuson countered: "It's difficult to take someone's vote away because they did something extra. On the other hand, I can't for the life of me figure out what those initials are there for other than to identify them as the voter." In the end, Coleman did not get the vote, and Franken won the challenge.

On a decision like that, Schlough made note and then, with his database of tagged ballots, he advised Elias when similar ballots popped up throughout the review process. "Should I say something, should I challenge their ruling?" Elias asked Schlough on close calls. Schlough then called up previous rulings on look-alike ballots to advise Elias.

Various local news organizations got into the act of asking Web site visitors to weigh in on how, if they were Canvassing Board members, they might rule on ballots, a sort of recount Fantasy League. While most challenges from both sides were picky, determining voter intent on some ballots was not an easy task. Some voters marked their choice for Senator with an *X* rather than filling in the oval. (Such an *X* marking was anticipated by lawmakers years ago in state statute and is considered a clear sign of a voter's intent.) Some voters marked *No* next to a candidate, even though they filled in the oval next to his name. Some had dots in one oval, suggesting the beginning of a vote, but then another oval on the ballot was fully completed, more firmly showing voter intent. Some made mistakes and wrote notes to explain what they really meant by their markings. The board had to address all of these oddities, and do it live under the watchful lenses of video cameras. Members felt the palpable public scrutiny.

On day one, widely read Twin Cities blogger David Brauer of Minn-Post.com, watching the board on his computer screen, described G. Barry Anderson as "sour-seeming." Anderson read that, turned to Cleary, and said defiantly, "I'll show him sour!"

"Some of the ballots were really close," Gearin said later. "The tension grew for all of us. We're all used to tension, but you begin to look at a ballot and you're thinking, 'Could this be the one that could determine who the Senator will be?'"

By day two, the Canvassing Board's ballot-review-and-voter-intent show contained these sorts of pressures for the judges, but also all of the spectator excitement of watching people watching paint dry. The board continued on its slogging mission of evaluating ballots as real courtroom drama was set to begin one block away in increasingly chilly St. Paul.

Minnesota Supreme Court Justice Paul Anderson knew election law. In 1990, in one of the most sordid episodes in Minnesota political history, conservative Republican gubernatorial nominee Jon Grunseth dropped out of the race nine days before Election Day because of damning allegations, including one that he had been swimming naked with teenage girls who were friends of his daughter. The man who finished second in the Republican primary that year, moderate Arne Carlson, fought to be placed on the ballot. Two hearings before the Minnesota Supreme Court were needed. Among the lawyers who aided Carlson then was Paul Anderson (no relation G. Barry Anderson), a South St. Paul real estate and construction lawyer. Carlson eventually named Anderson to be the chief judge of the Court of Appeals, and then in 1994 elevated Anderson to the state's Supreme Court.

On December 17, 2008, Anderson was looking forward to hearing Roger Magnuson argue Norm Coleman's case seeking a temporary restraining order to bar any local canvassing boards from opening and then counting any of the rejected absentee ballots in the fifth pile. It was Magnuson's position, as it was Knaak's before the Canvassing Board, that if a vote wasn't counted on Election Night, it couldn't be "recounted" now. Only in an election contest—a full-blown trial—could this group of rejected absentee ballots be considered and counted, Coleman's lawyers believed.

Out of court, Anderson and Magnuson were cordial acquaintances. They were both active in promoting goodwill visits to the Twin Cities by lawyers from developing nations and then hosting and mentoring the guests. Everyone on the Supreme Court knew of Roger Magnuson's reputation as a confident and witty courtroom advocate, without using written notes. Minutes before he entered courtroom 300, Anderson made himself a promise. "I like to ask questions. I don't like to get in the way of the attorneys," he explained later. "I said to myself, 'Paul, you're not going to ask any questions to the attorneys for the first five minutes. Don't do something right out of the box.'" Sometimes, even Supreme Court justices don't keep their promises.

"May it please the Court," Roger Magnuson (no relation to Eric) began, as the five Supreme Court justices readied for the first argument before them in this historic recount. (Because the Supreme Court was to evaluate Canvassing Board actions, justices Eric Magnuson and G. Barry Anderson voluntarily removed themselves from these hearings.)

"On December twelfth, the state Canvassing Board, with the best of intentions, accepted an invitation, we believe, to go to Florida," Magnuson said. "And as tempting as that invitation is, given the weather outside the courtroom today..."

Anderson couldn't help himself. He smashed his five-minute rule. His first reaction to Magnuson came exactly twenty-seven seconds after the lawyer uttered those first provocative words suggesting that Minnesota's Canvassing Board was leading the state toward a "legal thicket" in this election recount just as Florida's 2000 recount raised Constitutional issues during the presidential election. Anderson, with Minnesota ancestral roots dating back to the 1855, took offense, and had no patience for being mentioned in the same breath with the botched Bush–Gore recount.

"Counsel . . . I know you've been to Florida," Anderson said. "This is not Florida, and I'm just not terribly receptive to you telling us that we're going to Florida and we're comparing to that. This is Minnesota, we've got a case in Minnesota, argue the case in Minnesota."

Roger Magnuson, who was used to being the smartest guy in the room, was surprised by Anderson's dramatic push back. He recovered, "I appreciate that admonition," he said respectfully to Anderson, and then went on to field a slew of question from the justices in the next twenty-five minutes, answering consistently that those ballots in the fifth pile just weren't the stuff of a recount.

Justice Lorie Gildea focused on the *Andersen v. Rolvaag* 1962 recount decision, in which the Supreme Court allowed the fixing of "obvious errors" in that election. Was that still good law? Magnuson questioned what an "obvious" error was.

Paul Anderson wondered about some definitions, such as "validly cast." Magnuson took the hard line that "a ballot that . . . has never been counted on November 4 has not been cast . . . A recount is to count again." Besides, the Canvassing Board is administrative, not evaluative. It's not the board's job to make determinations about the validity of rejected ballots.

Justice Alan Page turned the tables a bit on Magnuson. The Coleman side had been arguing that the fifth pile matter was for a court to tackle, not the board. Well, Page wondered, if the rejected ballots are allowed into the recount now, wouldn't Coleman have the right to challenge that at trial?

Justice Christopher Dietzen, addressing equal protection concerns, wondered if the Supreme Court had the authority to order all counties and municipalities to review rejected absentee ballots. That is, if the Canvassing Board couldn't order the review of these rejected ballots, what about this high court? Sure, Magnuson said, but there would have to be clear applications of any order so that there wouldn't be eighty-seven different processes in the state's eighty-seven counties, differences that could trigger claims of equal protection and due process violations.

Paul Anderson shot back. Why should the Supreme Court get involved in this thicket right now anyway, he wondered. Minnesota election law gave great authority to the county canvassing boards and local election officials. "What you're asking us to do is a little bold and brassy, beyond what courts should do in a situation like this," Anderson said. As Magnuson's twenty-five minutes were expiring, there was no doubt that the Supreme Court justices were fully engaged.

William Pentelovitch, a Minneapolis attorney, was brought in to argue Franken's position that the Canvassing Board was on the right track in requesting that election officials statewide begin to sort and count the fifth pile. To Pentelovitch, the group of uncounted ballots was a set of obvious errors that needed to be included in the recount.

Soon, Justice Helen Meyer, who had been appointed by Independence Party Governor Jesse Ventura six years earlier, weighed in. Meyer seemed to be seeking some sort of settlement to the matter. She offered a moderating suggestion. In a sense, she wondered if the two sides couldn't get along. One statute allowed the correction of so-called obvious errors if the two candidates agreed that such errors existed. Was that worth looking at? "There may be some we can agree on," Pentelovitch replied, referring to previously rejected ballots.

Page raised another issue: what's the difference if either side wins now before the Canvassing Board, or later in a trial? What's the big deal here and the urgency? Pentelovitch was blunt. If the Canvassing Board certified a victor, that person immediately gained a major leg up. As the U.S. Supreme Court said in *Bush v. Gore*, "The certified winner would enjoy presumptive validity, making a contest proceeding by the losing candidate an uphill battle." That's why Elias wanted these fifth pile votes. That's why neither side wanted the board to get to a final number, not yet. The winner before the Canvassing Board was also sure to be the victor in the public's eyes, unless the loser could somehow undo that reality and perception in court. If you win before the board, chances are you win among donors, you win among editorialists, and your battle at any trial is less daunting. Pentelovitch's time was up. He wasn't nearly as articulate as Magnuson, but he had held his ground. He was on the side of counting all legal votes, a more appealing side than Magnuson's.

Magnuson was now back at the lectern, staring at the five justices about fifteen feet in front of him. Anderson, picking up on Meyer's thread, wanted to know if Magnuson agreed that there were, in fact, wrongfully rejected ballots that were obvious errors out there in the state's electoral universe. Magnuson wouldn't give in. "All I can say on that, Justice Anderson, is that when people are making decisions there are likely to be some that everybody would agree on."

Here came Meyer again, looking for the two campaigns to find common ground. She wondered if both sides agreed that if there were "five hundred votes . . . that should have been counted because they contained obvious errors, is there still no mechanism at this point to amend the local canvassing board returns to reflect the agreement of the candidates?"

"I think that's an interesting question, as to whether or not there could be an agreement," Magnuson said, tap dancing. He went on to say that the Minnesota "statutory scheme" for evaluating ballots wasn't obvious and, so, obvious errors couldn't be assumed. Magnuson had his story, and he was going to stick to it.

The hour-long hearing revealed that Magnuson acknowledged, but grudgingly so, that some fifth-pile ballots were likely valid. Meyer was in search of a middle ground. Anderson was eager to count votes of citizens who had followed the absentee ballot rules. Gildea seemed troubled by the details of the law and how it seemed to direct the Court to halt the Canvassing Board's potential activism. When she noted those details, Pentelovitch suggested she was being "hypertechnical." Gildea took offense at that. Page was baffled by Magnuson's immovable stance on obvious errors, including the most obvious: a voter is duly registered, the local election official's voter roster says the voter is not registered, the secretary of state's master list says the voter is. Isn't that an obvious error? No, Magnuson told Page, which didn't score any points with the former NFL star, or, for that matter, with any of the justices. One of Minnesota's most prominent lawyers had managed to annoy five Supreme Court judges in one performance.

"Counsel, your time has expired," Page pronounced curtly. "The decision will be forthcoming."

When the oral arguments ended, the justices retreated to their conference room in the secure area of the Judicial Center, a short walk down the hallway from the courtroom. The dynamics of a five-person decision-making conversation were unfamiliar to the group accustomed to seven personalities. This was their first conference without Chief Justice Magnuson and Associate Justice G. Barry Anderson, the Canvassing Board members who removed themselves from any Supreme Court actions related to the recount. In recusing themselves, Magnuson and Anderson left it open for their Supreme Court colleagues to evaluate their Canvassing Board work, an odd position and a tricky job for the remaining five, who now had to figure out how to play nice under such a microscope.

Then, there was the politics. Minnesota's judicial system has an enviable record for fairness, for judges putting aside their partisan pasts once they don their robes. In this case, backgrounds mattered. In the years before they were named to the bench, associate justices Christopher Dietzen and Lorie Gildea contributed to previous Norm Coleman campaigns for other offices. Justice Helen Meyer contributed to Paul Wellstone's 2002 U.S. Senate campaign, which Coleman won after Wellstone's death. Page had considered running for the Senate in 2002 in the wake of Wellstone's death. Justice Paul Anderson was once a close adviser to former Minnesota Governor Arne Carlson, a moderate Republican.

The time pressures on this odd Gang of Five were severe. The Canvassing Board and the secretary of state's office signaled that they wanted the recount completed by the U.S. Senate's swearing-in date on January 6. If there were no election contest trial — if neither Coleman nor Franken challenged the board's conclusion as to which of them had garnered the most votes — the winner could represent Minnesota on time, and the state would not go without full representation. That was all wishful thinking. This Court, like most Supreme Courts, often took six or eight months to read briefs and related case law, hear oral arguments, confer, exchange drafts of opinions, and issue orders. The Christmas and New Year's holidays approached. County election officials, who had been working tirelessly on the recount for a month, waited for guidance. This newly configured five-member Minnesota Supreme Court had to make a decision instantly on a matter that could determine the outcome of the Senate race.

Coleman filed his petition for an emergency temporary restraining order of the Canvassing Board's decision on the fifth pile late in the day on December 15. The Supreme Court ordered oral arguments for two days later, and, soon after, the justices scurried to issue an order about the unknown number of wrongly rejected absentee ballots in play. Scurry they did. Scuffle, too. Generally, the justices' post-argument conferences are remarkably formal. As if around a legal campfire, justices speak in order of seniority—from most senior to least—offering their positions on the issues in a case. The chief justice always speaks last. It is in the privacy of their conference room that disagreements are expressed, coalitions form, and writers of opinions are assigned. Justices claim that little lobbying occurs outside the conference room. There are no secret gatherings in restrooms, parking ramps, or dark coffee shops. Perhaps before oral argument, as they each prepare, casual conversations take place among a couple of them in their offices about the complexities of a new case, but the persuasion ensues when the club meets behind closed doors, and again as the prevailing opinion is reduced to a document.

In most cases, that initial opinion is circulated among the justices and can become a ping-pong ball with footnotes. Handwritten notations, corrections, and dissents on the margins are added by colleagues as the process unfolds and opinions or orders are honed and clarified. Disciplined and strategic, some justices are known as coalition builders, such as Associate Justice Paul Anderson, the guy who barked at Roger Magnuson when he attempted to link Minnesota's recount with the Bush–Gore Florida recount. With all the time they spend together, they are familiar with each other's tendencies. An edit here, a footnote there, can bring a colleague to forge a majority or, better yet, a unanimous opinion. Historically, the Minnesota Supreme Court works diligently to achieve unanimous agreement. In 2008, for instance, out of 102 full opinions issued, only 18 included dissents.

Much like the voters, who were sharply divided on Election Day, the slimmed-down Supreme Court was horribly splintered on this absentee-ballot issue and Coleman's attempt to shut down the counting of them. How would a new coalition be formed? With Eric Magnuson's recusal, it was Alan Page who became the acting chief justice, his sixteen years on the bench making him the most senior. As chief justice, Page got the last word in the conference room. It must have been a doozy.

Things were gettin' weird. Over at the State Office Building, the tired Canvassing Board was continuing to review the intent of voters who just couldn't get it right. Filling an oval seemed to be an intellectual challenge for some. Thousands of people from across the globe tuned in to watch this daily democracy reality show on various Internet feeds, from the upstart UpTake to the mainstream *Star Tribune*. Minnesota's transparency standard meant that every minute of the process was streamed live on the state legislature's Internet TV system. A social network of recount addicts developed at various Web sites, including the tongue-in-cheek Washington, D.C., blog Wonkette.com. For political junkies, one commenter wrote, watching the tedious evaluation of ballots was "kinda like a Chiefs–Bengals [NFL football] game. We hate both teams but we're watching . . . because it's the only game on." Every once in a while, entertainment happened.

"Bemidji, Ward Two, Ballot One," Deputy Secretary of State Jim Gelbmann pronounced, sounding like an old-fashioned train conductor alerting passengers to the next station. This was the next ballot on this wild ride called the Review of Challenged Ballots. Already, Jesus, Mickey Mouse, Satan, and some of Hitler's henchmen had gotten a few votes.

Around 9:30 a.m. on December 18, as most recount insiders anxiously awaited the Supreme Court's ruling on the absentee ballots, that challenged ballot, Bemidji, Ward Two, Ballot One, moved to center stage. There, for all to see, was the oval to the left of Franken's name, filled, but not very exactly. A faint *X* leaked out from the top and bottom of the scribbled-in oval. Plus, on the write-in line beneath the U.S. Senate candidates' names, the words *Lizard People* were casually hand printed. This voter also wrote in Lizard People for president, U.S. representative, mayor of Bemidji, two Soil and Water Conservation supervisor posts, and Bemidji School Board. But Franken was the only candidate's oval that the voter also filled. For others, Lizard People was the only vote cast. The ballot had been challenged by a Coleman observer way back in November because "voter intent was not clear," according to a note by an election judge at the bottom left side of the ballot.

"Well, let's have a discussion," Ritchie said with a chuckle, as the ballot was posted on the large monitors overhead.

"I guess," said Gearin, not eager.

"It's a Jim Morrison reference," Cleary softly said, meaning the former lead singer of The Doors, a sign that the judge had a rock 'n' roll past.

"The motion would be to reject the challenge, and to allocate this vote to Franken," Ritchie said.

Elias rose in the half-empty hearing room, the boredom of thousands of challenged votes being reviewed having kicked in. Elias wanted this vote to count because even though the voter's intent might be in doubt, "My argument would be that Lizard People is not a genuine write-in, in other words, it's not a person," he said.

Cleary: "Do we know that for sure?"

Chief Justice Magnuson jumped in: "If it said, 'Moon Unit Zappa,' would you say there is no such person?" (History might record that no other American Chief Justice ever uttered the words, "Moon Unit" in public.) Others laughed, but Elias, still standing, trying not to smile, always lawyering, said, "Actually, I think that would be permissive."

Magnuson, baiting Elias: "But you don't know that there's someone named Lizard People . . . You don't, you and I don't."

Elias: "I wouldn't disagree with your honor."

Gearin: "Can we take another second to look at it? . . . It's the weirdest thing."

Magnuson: "No, it's not the weirdest."

Gearin, exasperated: "If somebody's going to vote and they want to make some kind of statement . . ."

Magnuson: "They may not get their vote counted."

And the vote for Lizard People wasn't counted.

Minutes later, Gelbmann declared: "Sauk Rapids, Precinct 3, Ballot 1. Here someone voted for the Flying Spaghetti Monster."

Gearin: "Flying Spaghetti Monster? Geez . . ."

Cleary: "Middle name, Spaghetti."

By December 18, the Canvassing Board was almost finished with its work. A certain esprit de corps had developed. The board members shared pizza and sandwiches with each other in Ritchie's office in the State Office Building. They all expressed concern for Justice G. Barry Anderson, who was running a high fever throughout the proceedings. This collegiality was reflected in the final tally of the board itself: despite all the mind-numbing details, despite looking at about 1,500 challenged ballots, the board split to a 3–2 vote only fourteen times, and on only forty-five occasions was there a single dissenter and four ayes. By the way, of those fourteen 3–2 votes, Secretary of State Ritchie voted with the "left-leaning" Gearin and Cleary seven times and with the "right-leaning" Magnuson and Anderson seven times, straight down the middle. Overall, when determining the status of ballots, the five Canvassing Board members agreed about 96 percent of the time. Not so the Supreme Court, which was a house divided.

The written order in the matter of *Norm Coleman, et al., Petitioners, vs. Mark Ritchie, Minnesota Secretary of State, the Minnesota State Canvassing Board, Isanti County Canvassing Board, et al., Respondents, Al Franken for Senate and Al Franken, Intervenor-Respondents* was issued the very next day, December 18, barely twenty-eight hours after the oral argument. For the Supreme Court, it was warp speed. Their head-scratching 3–2 decision straddled a confusing line.

On the one hand, the majority of Dietzen, Gildea, and Meyer agreed with Coleman's side that opening and counting the wrongly rejected absentee ballots was the stuff of an election contest and shouldn't be the purview of the Canvassing Board. If election officials across the state made mistakes and rejected legal absentee ballots they shouldn't have, well, tough luck. They were "not within the scope of errors subject to correction," Meyer wrote for the slim majority.

On the other hand, the same majority of three wrote that, if county election officials and representatives of the two candidates all agreed as to which individual ballots had been wrongly rejected, those ballots *should* be opened and counted by the Canvassing Board. In this recount, in which the scientific identification and tracking of voters was already underway, mostly by the Franken side, the Supreme Court was allowing the campaigns to pick and choose which absentee ballots were acceptable. That seemed astonishing.

"The legislature has created processes for correction by county canvassing boards of 'obvious errors in the counting and recording of the votes,'" the majority wrote. "We conclude that improper rejection of an absentee ballot envelope is not within the scope of errors subject to correction . . . and therefore county canvassing boards lack statutory authority to count such ballots and submit amended reports on that basis." Chalk that up as a win for Coleman. "But where the local election officials and the parties agree that an absentee ballot envelope was improperly rejected, correction of that error should not be required to await an election contest in district court." Mark that down as a loss for Coleman.

The majority then ordered "candidates Norm Coleman and Al Franken and their campaign representatives, the Secretary of State, and all county auditors and canvassing boards to establish and implement a process, as expeditiously as practicable, for the purpose of identifying all absentee ballot envelopes that the local election officials and the candidates agree were rejected in error." The deal: if both campaigns and county auditors agreed on the legality of an absentee ballot, it should be counted. If there's not agreement, that voter is screwed. All the amended returns had to be to Ritchie's office by December 31.

It was enough to make Justice Page flip out. He was mad as hell and couldn't take it anymore. His written dissent began, "Josef Stalin is alleged to have once said, 'I consider it completely unimportant who . . . will vote, or how; but what is extraordinarily important is this—who will count the votes, and how.'" Page then went on to methodically blast the majority. In his blunt view, validly cast ballots should be counted and recorded by local canvassing boards, and errors should be corrected so that voters weren't disenfranchised.

He scolded the majority for not protecting people's right to vote. "The court's order may seek the peaceful way out by asking the campaigns to agree on improperly rejected ballots. But the order does not guarantee that the candidates and their political parties will agree on any rejected ballot. Instead, the court's order will arbitrarily disqualify enfranchised voters on the whim of the candidates and political parties," Page wrote. "It is a perverse result, indeed, for political parties and their candidates to determine whether a voter's absentee ballot was properly or improperly rejected. By making the acceptance of an improperly rejected ballot contingent on the candidates' agreement, the court has abdicated its role as the defender of the fundamental right to vote. Instead, it has made the candidates and their parties the gatekeepers—even though they are likely to be more concerned with their own election prospects than with protecting the absentee voter's right to vote."

Of all the orders and opinions that were written and were to be written in this saga, Page's December 18 screed took the most disgusted and least patient tone. It was also the most heartfelt and direct. Rather than evoke a mass murderer like Stalin, Paul Anderson quoted witty playwright Tom Stoppard in a mixed-bag concurrence with and dissent from the three-person majority.

"It's not the voting that's democracy, it's the counting," Stoppard wrote, and Anderson used that as a jumping off point. "I agree with the majority that we should direct the parties and local election officials to make every effort possible to agree as to those absentee ballots that were rejected in error in Minnesota's 2008 race for the United States Senate.

But I disagree with the majority's decision to enjoin county canvassing boards from including, in the absence of such an agreement, any previously rejected absentee ballots in the administrative recount now underway." He feared the Supreme Court was wading into a "legal thicket"—a description offered by his pal, Roger Magnuson. "In a democracy, the act of voting and having a validly cast vote accurately counted are inextricably linked. The right to have one's vote counted is as important as the act of voting itself."

Anderson attached to his opinion examples of two voters whose absentee ballots were rejected for not being registered when, in fact, they were registered and were diligent voters. He worried that their "trust and confidence in our voting system may well be significantly undermined once they learn that, as a result of an obvious error, their absentee ballots were not only rejected but that, once the error was discovered, Minnesota law as interpreted by the majority does not allow the county canvassing board to simply correct the error."

Anderson had been prescient in noting during the oral argument in this episode the day before, that "This is not Florida!" He proved himself to be prescient once more. This, after all, was December 18, 2008. No one knew then that a victor in this election wouldn't be determined for another six months, after a few more stops at the Supreme Court and two months of trial. If Page wrote to chastise, even embarrass, his colleagues, Anderson sent an almost avuncular note to Minnesota's citizens.

"It is important to keep in mind that this order is a result of a preliminary skirmish in what appears to be an extended legal contest regarding Minnesota's 2008 Senate election," he wrote. "Winston Churchill is reputed to have once said, in an admiring tone, that Americans ultimately do the right thing after they have exhausted all the other alternatives. Sometimes, the wheels of justice and due process take time to fully turn. While I believe that we have incorrectly exhausted one alternative today, I have complete confidence that ultimately the right thing will be done and all validly cast absentee ballots will be properly counted."

Today's enemy, he seemed to be saying, may be tomorrow's ally. He did not want to alienate his colleagues in the majority. Anderson was reaching out, waiting to fight another day for unanimity. He also seemed to be assuring Minnesotans that, at another time, in some other way, the Supreme Court would get this right. Just be patient, he seemed to be saying. Be patient.

Hamilton received the decision at Franken headquarters in Minneapolis and, in a high-pitched screech reminiscent of Gomer Pyle, exclaimed to Schriock, "What is this? I've never heard of anything like this before, counties identify errors and both sides have to agree!" The idea that the two parties could veto the acceptance of a voter's ballot was mind-blowing to him, and to just about everyone else. But Elias was OK with the decision. It was an order to count ballots. It had that December 31 deadline. That's what he wanted.

Within the Judicial Center, Supreme Court staffers walked around with grim faces. The Court had embarrassed itself with such an unorthodox order. It stood the Coleman "victory" on its head, with the conservative judges, perhaps unknowingly, snatching defeat from Coleman's jaws of victory. Legally speaking, Coleman's position prevailed; the Canvassing Board was not the place or body where improperly rejected absentee ballots should be evaluated and counted, the court said. But, in the long run, Coleman lost because the Court ordered a process for these absentee ballots to be opened, something Franken's team wanted. Elias et al. had an inkling these ballots could favor their candidate. Franken's legal machine, with the aid of advanced DFL voter lists, possessed a good feel for what was inside most of those absentee ballot envelopes. On the foundation of the Data Practices Act requests they had filed and the names those documents revealed, Franken's forces could project relatively well how their candidate might do once the envelopes were opened and the ballots counted.

Coleman's side, however, could not. To a person, members of the Coleman legal team and campaign effort said the Minnesota GOP's voter lists were old or inadequate. "It wasn't a category thing," one high-ranking Coleman campaign official said, meaning the absentee ballots couldn't be assessed by precinct or county or gender. "It was an individual voter thing and they [the Franken side] had the data."

Now, there were ways for Coleman and his lawyers to walk away from this ruling without opening a single absentee ballot, without enhancing Franken's lead. Indeed, the Franken lawyers expected them to do just that. Justice Page drew them a road map in his scathing dissent. One way to dodge the absentee-ballot bullet was for Coleman's side to make a noisy equal protection claim and invoke *Bush v. Gore*. As Page wrote, the court majority's scheme to allow the campaigns to participate in the acceptance of certain ballots could mean that valid ballots would be treated differently in the different counting locations, allowing "a distinction that can only be described as arbitrary." It was the equal protection claim Coleman sought.

There was another way for Coleman's lawyers to shut down the process. In its order, the majority threatened to sanction lawyers on either side who used shenanigans to improperly halt the inclusion of ballots. Frivolous rejections were a no-no. The sanctions would come at a future election contest, if there were one. It's part of Rule 11 of Minnesota's Rules of Civil Procedure. This warning was to keep the attorneys in line.

But Page himself scoffed at that purported disincentive, and suggested lawyers could finesse their way out of any sanctions. For one, he noted, the candidates themselves had no obligation to agree to any ballots, "whether reasonable or not. It does not appear to me that counsel for either campaign is in a position to control the outcome of that process, and I question our authority to sanction the attorneys or their clients for a decision that the attorneys' clients have every legal right to make."

Coleman's lawyers, overly fearful of the Rule 11 sanctions and flying blind on the potential outcomes of the ballots, chose to ignore Page's hints. Instead, they engaged too freely in the absentee-ballot approval exercise, one of their biggest blunders. Matt Haapoja, who worked with Trimble, said there was discussion about whether to participate in the fifth-pile procedure, but they viewed Rule 11 as "a sword of Damocles" hanging above them ready to strike. "We could have told our clients not to open a single one of those nine hundred and lost our licenses," Knaak said months later. "[Coleman] understood that dynamic." The final counting of the challenged ballots was to occur. As complicated as everything was, because of the careful and remarkably unbiased work of the Canvassing Board, this election was about to flip, and only the Franken side knew for sure which way.

CHAPTER SEVEN

THE SUPREMES THROW A CURVE

"We've never been able to figure out how they do their calculating."

The first blizzard of the recount arrived on Saturday, December 20, producing a white landscape of empty streets and bundled humans trudging through drifts. It was what most people envision when they think "Minnesota." Outside the frosted windows of the Franken campaign headquarters on University Avenue, where Minneapolis and St. Paul meet, this definitely was not Florida, even though seventy-two hours earlier Roger Magnuson implied that Minnesota was headed toward becoming the first post–*Bush v. Gore* electoral laughingstock and, a day later, the Supreme Court contributed to such a perception.

No matter the weather, Elias and Andy Barr called a news conference because they wanted to share something and they wanted it to hit the widely circulated Sunday newspapers, assuming any paper deliverer could navigate his station wagon through the Twin Cities streets the next morning. Two intrepid reporters braved the snow to attend Elias's announcement, while a few others were on a conference-call line, likely yawning while presuming another campaign spin. That was not the case.

The data was in. The challenged-ballots analysis was completed. Elias, with the twinkle in his eye of a magician about to pull a rabbit out of his hat and a dove from his sleeve, was bursting to announce that in three days, when the state Canvassing Board was set to meet to resolve the final challenges, he had no doubt that, "Al Franken will have more votes than Norm Coleman...We believe firmly that margin will be between thirty-five and fifty...At some point not long after that, Al Franken will stand before you as the senator-elect from Minnesota."

127

His words were filled with confidence and certitude, even a slight tinge of smugness. This was no spin. It was, in retrospect, history. There was no crowd, no cheering, no banners, no band, just Elias in a yellow-and-gray striped dress shirt and khakis, standing at that same lectern where he'd entered this drama five weeks earlier. Now, to an almost empty room, Elias declared numerical victory for Franken. Sautter's regimen to count the election judges' decisions at the tables across the state, Schriock's leadership to discipline the entire Franken army of two thousand volunteers, the speed and reliability of Trice's Pony Express, and the careful analysis of which challenges would survive the Canvassing Board's scrutiny later in the month had brought the campaign to a bottom line that it was sure meant that Franken would replace Coleman in the U.S. Senate.

Ever since the *Star Tribune* had projected indisputable defeat for Franken on December 1, Elias, fighting back, had tossed out intermittent running counts like M&M's to the hungry reporters. One day Franken was ahead by twenty-two, one day by one, depending on how the Franken team evaluated the progress of the recount. One day the margin was four. But on this snow-bound Minnesota winter day, Elias said firmly, "Our internal count has no uncertainty as to what will happen on Tuesday."

A few weeks earlier, when Elias began announcing Franken table-count numbers because of that damaging *Star Tribune* story, Coleman lawyer Knaak reacted with sarcastic disbelief. "We've never been able to figure out how they do their calculating," Knaak said, and labeled Elias's numbers "empty rhetoric" and "fictitious. . . . Our volunteers haven't seen any evidence of that kind of note taking or that kind of information gathering being done" by Franken observers, Knaak said. When Franken staffers saw Knaak's comments in the news media, they gasped. They figured that if Coleman's legal team didn't believe Franken was tracking the call at the table, then Coleman's side must not be doing it. Team Coleman must not know where they stood in this recount.

On that snowy Saturday, Coleman's spokesman, Mark Drake, scoffed at Elias's numbers. "This is just more bluster and hot air from a campaign that has been trailing for two years," Drake said. "While we can understand their need to latch onto their temporary lead, the reality is there's a long way to go in this process. We have no doubt that once this recount is fully completed, Senator Coleman will be in the lead and will be reelected to the Senate."

Three days later, the state Canvassing Board completed the recount. As Elias promised, Franken led by forty-six votes. A few days later, when the secretary of state's staff conducted some housekeeping with both campaigns, the margin grew to forty-nine. Elias joked that he was glad it wasn't fifty-one—one more than his prediction of thirty-five to fifty votes—because then no one would trust his numbers again, but his credibility had been fully rehabilitated since his debut news conference about the non-existent eighty-four-year-old woman from Beltrami County.

As for the Coleman forces, months after the recount ended, there remained confusion as to what had happened. For sure, their side didn't consistently keep track at the recount sites. Instead, lawyers back at Coleman headquarters evaluated the challenged ballots and made their own calls without the benefit of knowing how nonpartisan judges saw the ballots.

Once the case ended, Trimble admitted he knew that his client was falling behind during the recount, even though all of the Coleman campaign's public statements said that wasn't the case. "Did we know we were slipping and sliding? The answer is yes. Were we surprised by the forty-nine? No. Did we express surprise and denial? Absolutely," Trimble admitted. "Politics is not a game where expressing or acknowledging defeat or slippage on a continuing basis does you a lot of good."

Coleman campaign manager Cullen Sheehan said that when his team completed its analysis before the final Canvassing Board sessions, he believed, "We could be up as much as eighty or down by as much as eighty. It was going to be within that window." Of Elias's thirty-five to fifty prediction, Sheehan thought it was a good guess.

Knaak, Coleman's other recount lawyer, said he was surprised when Franken won the recount. "I thought we were ahead," he said. "We felt confident we had a good solid number. I never saw a count internally that put us behind. We were wrong." Knaak believed that Elias was making up his numbers for the media. But in a Coleman team conference call the day after Elias's prediction, lower-level staffers were told that Franken was, in fact, headed toward a fifty-vote victory.

Whatever anyone's presumptions or recollections in the Coleman camp, those absentee ballots should have been handled differently. The effect of not knowing exactly where they stood in the regular recount phase was devastating for Coleman. Or, if in fact Trimble knew the lead was slipping away, he should have more aggressively or creatively tried to block the counting of more Franken votes. He should have taken Justice Page's lead and returned to the Supreme Court to seek uniform standards for evaluating those ballots wrongly rejected. On the other hand, because Coleman's forces believed he would win, they never fully explored the opportunities—if there were any—of the unknown absentee ballots until it was too late. "If we had known early enough that we were going to be upside down [on the recount]," Knaak said, "we would have let go of the rope on the issue of absentee ballots."

By the time they got to thinking about that, the Coleman side had lost the numbers game, as well as the political, public relations, and legal games. Another knee to the midsection was coming. Just as they did with the calls at the tables, Team Franken had far better intelligence on the absentee voters than did Team Coleman.

Not only was Franken now officially ahead in the recount, but the Pandora's box of wrongly rejected absentee ballots was about to open. All that work with the Canvassing Board, all that backdoor help from the Supreme Court, all that optimistic patience had gotten Elias where he wanted to be. Coleman's side never wanted to be here. They had fought doggedly since November 5 to keep out any additional votes they could. Inexplicably, that was about to change.

In response to the Supreme Court's ruling of December 18, the two campaigns, the secretary of state's office, and election officials in counties with a fifth pile were required to devise a system to examine the improperly rejected absentee ballot envelopes that were set aside, and do it fast. The Court wanted all eligible ballots determined by December 31. All of these apparent mistakes had been previously identified by local election officials of both major political parties, who, by now, had examined each ballot envelope at least twice. Election officials across the eighty-seven counties concluded they had erroneously rejected 1,346 ballots. The names of the voters were known to each campaign since Franken won his Data Practices Act request case in St. Paul in November. Under the terms of the Supreme Court ruling, both candidates had to agree to count each of the 1,346 ballots, or they wouldn't be opened by the Canvassing Board and included in the count. It was an ugly way to exercise democracy, but when the Supreme Court speaks, people have to listen.

Franken's legal team did some quickie calculations. The analysis was based on the geographics of these ballots, not the demographics. (The X-ray-like, drilled-down demographic analysis would come later.) The theory was that the ballots would follow the trends in the cities, counties, and precincts of the voter; that is, if Precinct Z voted 55 percent Franken and 45 percent for Coleman, chances were the individual voter was more likely a Franken voter. In their calculations, the Franken team also assumed that slightly less than 1 percent of the 1,346 ballots, about 0.08 percent, would include some with undervotes, that is, no vote for the Senate race but a vote for president. Thus, in this exercise, their universe was artificially reduced to 1,335 ballots.

Doing the numbers on this pro rata basis, they projected that those 1,335 previously rejected ballots would break like this: 582 votes (44 percent) for Franken, 534 (40 percent) for Coleman, and 219 (16 percent) for Barkley or others. In this simplistic, but logical scenario, Franken would pick up a net of 48 votes. Add that to his lead from the Canvassing Board's count a few days earlier, and Franken would own an approximate hundred-vote victory come January. Not bad at all for a guy who had trailed since Election Day.

Their comfort level was even higher because of real information they had acquired from various national voter-information organizations, including one called Catalist. That's a company that provides massive voter data about geographic regions and demographic slices. Through results of a giant poll, it's possible to specifically identify a voter's leanings or, more likely, the leanings of a composite citizen: for example, she is white, forty-two, lives in the suburbs, has a household income of ninety thousand dollars, finished college, sends her children to public schools, and subscribes to *Newsweek*. Some Franken staffers believed they knew, almost for certain, how approximately 20 percent to 30 percent of the absentee ballots were going to go, based on all the data they had at their disposal. The Franken team scored the others based on the profile of the precincts in which the voters lived.

With that knowledge, the Franken lawyers told the Coleman side and Ritchie's office on Saturday morning, December 27, that they would gladly accept the opening and counting of all 1,346 wrongly rejected ballots. Not a problem and, politically, that was consistent with Elias's position from the start: count every legally cast vote. Coleman's side rejected that option. At this point, without any in-depth voter data and now behind in the recount, Coleman's lawyers probably should have agreed to count all 1,346. They needed votes now. These were the only ones remaining.

Instead, Trimble and Knaak decided to turn aside some ballots, particularly a bunch in heavily DFL-leaning St. Louis County. A day earlier, they had attempted to add another 654 ballots in the mix, this after county election officials already fixed on the 1,346. Exactly why Trimble and Knaak believed these 654 were valid ballots was unclear, but this much was clear; they came from precincts that favored Coleman. The secretary of state's office rejected that last-minute attempt because the Coleman lawyers missed a deadline, meaning the universe of the fifth pile stood firmly at 1,346. The Franken team, as ever, was prepared and concerned that Coleman's lawyers would employ "sharp elbows" and scientifically reject envelopes that seemed Franken-leaning. Now, that would have required solid data on voters, and the Republicans lacked that. True to form, Team Franken had a plan. True to form, Team Coleman miscalculated.

On Sunday, before the ballots were opened, a series of e-mails bounced between Elias, Hamilton, Lillehaug, and Schriock as they developed a defensive scheme in case those sharp Coleman elbows emerged. The Franken squad was particularly conscious of about 130 envelopes in St. Louis County, a good locale for Franken, that were a bit imperfect. In many cases, they either lacked a date or the voter's and witness's dates didn't match. By law, goofy dates were not reasons to reject ballots, but, under the Supreme Court's everybody-must-agree ruling, the Coleman side could make a stink over it and claim the ballot was improper and should be discarded. The Franken leadership feared the Coleman team pinpointing objections to Franken-friendly envelopes and, if they did, Elias told his comrades, "We need to blow it all up and go to court." That is, return to the Supreme Court and complain that the Coleman lawyers were up to shenanigans, should be sanctioned, and this phase of the recount halted. After all, if the Coleman lawyers strategically removed some Franken absentee votes from the 1,346, that tenuous forty-nine-vote Franken recount margin could slip away.

In preparation for that, Lillehaug, the writer of just about every aggressive letter to every court and administrative body in the case, composed what the Franken team referred to as the Red Button Letter. In that letter, to be sent to local voting officials conducting this fifth-pile examination, the Franken team was poised to shut down this critical phase of the recount if Coleman's side targeted Franken ballots. It was a risky political move, to be sure. If Coleman's forces started throwing elbows, the letter was ready to go.

The first test of Coleman's tactics came in Duluth on Tuesday, December 30. How rough would Coleman play? With Knaak reviewing ballots for Coleman and Minneapolis lawyer Charlie Nauen reviewing ballots for Franken, Nauen e-mailed Lillehaug at 12:31 p.m. to report that Knaak rejected only 46 of 122 ballots they had reviewed, not nearly the number of rejections Elias and others feared, and not enough to dramatically reduce Franken's margin. The Red Button Letter never saw the light of day.

The fifth-pile agreement sessions, such as the Knaak–Nauen meeting, occurred in central locations around the state. Election officials watched as Franken lawyers sometimes consulted with aides on laptops before accepting or rejecting some envelopes. An envelope came up for approval. The four statutory thresholds for acceptance were discussed: proper name and address on the application and ballot envelope; signature matches that on the ballot application; certified registered voter; and didn't vote on-site on Election Day. The local election judge explained that she believed it was a properly offered absentee ballot envelope. Each side then pondered its own reasons for striking the envelope, or allowing it to trickle down to the Canvassing Board to be counted. If it were Michael Kienley from St. Paul, Coleman's lawyer might ding the ballot because his precinct went overwhelmingly for Franken and chances were good that he did too. But if it were Dennis Anderson of Scott County, the Franken side probably rejected the ballot because it had solid information he was not a DFLer. More than once, voting officials and Coleman reps witnessed Franken lawyers check with staff members—"computer geeks" as Knaak called them—who sorted through voter data information on their laptops. In a few cases, the staffer with the computer gave a thumbs-up or a thumbs-down to the Franken lawyer, and a decision was made.

Coleman's side was not nearly as data rich and blocked some ballots that were actually Coleman votes based on hunches or simple geography. Nauen remembered Knaak striking the ballot envelope of a well-known Republican volunteer in Duluth because of a date issue—the voter's witness didn't sign the envelope on the same day the voter did. Again, that was not a proper reason to reject an absentee ballot. But Knaak blocked it. "I actually tried to talk him out of it," Nauen said, keeping with the

Franken policy of letting votes in. "It fit his pattern." But now that they were behind, Coleman's team should have embraced the Sautter mantra, to expand the pool when you're trailing. They did not.

When, on December 30, everyone's work was completed, 933 of the 1,346 previously rejected absentee ballots were sent to the Canvassing Board to be opened and counted, more than Elias and his colleagues expected and with better geographics and demographics than they ever could have dreamed. Twenty-seven percent of the 933 ballots came from Hennepin County, a Franken stronghold; Hennepin County accounted for only 23 percent of Minnesota's electorate. Eleven percent of the 933 came from St. Louis County, even though that county accounted for only 4 percent of the Senate race voters on Election Day. The 933 surely would favor Franken.

Coleman loyalists argued that DFL-leaning elections officials in those counties were more likely to reconsider rejected absentee ballots once the Supreme Court ordered them to reexamine them. But Franken data experts noted that larger counties, with more voters and more professional staff, have a tendency to actually reject more absentee ballots than smaller jurisdictions do. In Minnesota, the most populous counties tend to vote Democratic. It makes sense that more of the rejected absentee ballots, including those that were originally rejected wrongly, would lean Democratic.

Trimble and Knaak said months later that they believed they would fall victim to sanctions from the Supreme Court if they unreasonably blocked envelopes from being opened, and the Franken campaign was surely poised to make such accusations. But others, including conservative legal pundit Scott Johnson, who made his mark as one of the creators of the influential Minneapolis-based Power Line blog, slammed Coleman's lawyers in a National Review Online article for engaging at all in the fifth-pile exercise — even though it was Coleman's legal team that triggered the whole mess by taking the matter to the Supreme Court in the first place.

"The Coleman campaign was caught flatfooted by the Minnesota Supreme Court's December decision. Coleman should not have agreed to the inclusion of a single one of these ballots until he secured some agreement on the uniform treatment of absentee ballots," Johnson wrote, adding, "The attorneys who publicly led Coleman's team through the recount (local lawyers Fritz Knaak and Tony Trimble) appeared like Pop Warner players going up against an NFL team." If Coleman's lawyers had fought to block the 933 ballots, claiming there were no uniform standards from county to county, could Ritchie and the Canvassing Board have even attempted to open them? Unlikely, at least not without another visit to the Supreme Court and, perhaps, a more rational ruling by the justices.

Instead, as 2008 came to a close, those 933 ballot envelopes — all agreed to by Coleman's lawyers — sat in the Secretary of State's office unopened. Inside of them was Coleman's political demise.

New year, same election. On the first Saturday of 2009, January 3, there was an air of curiosity and hours of tedium in store in room 10 of the State Office Building, the Canvassing Board's regular meeting space. It all began at 9 a.m. The major task was to protect the privacy of the 933 absentee voters whose ballots were to be counted. Ritchie staffers carefully opened the outside envelopes, and set them aside. They opened the secrecy envelopes, and set them aside. They removed the ballots from the secrecy envelopes, and set them aside. Lawyers from both campaigns watched and examined the ballots to make sure each voter's intent was clear. A surprisingly sparse crowd of about forty recount junkies and reporters was on hand. That exacting and transparent process, extremely Minnesotan, took six hours, with a lunch break. Something else happened in there. At 11 a.m., Minnesota time, Norm Coleman's term ended. Minnesota's lone senator was Amy Klobuchar.

By the time Minnesota Elections Director Gary Poser began declaring what was inside the 933 ballots it was 4:50 p.m. He sat in the front of the room, where the members of the Canvassing Board usually sat, and he lifted the ballots from their pile, looked at them, and began declaring which candidate won each vote. It turned monotonous. It became hypnotic.

"Franken, Franken, Franken, Franken, Barkley, Barkley, Franken, Franken . . . Coleman, undervote, Franken, Franken, Franken . . ." the officious Poser, a college math major if ever there was one, called out, almost as if he were chanting a mantra. And he said Franken 481 times, an exotic chant, to be sure. From the back of the room, Schriock, sitting with Barr, couldn't believe it. The Franken team had its data and felt good about it, but not this good. Even Elias was surprised. "We were showered in Franken votes," said Sautter, who was stunned by the margin. "It was like raining money." Dan Cramer, who worked with Sautter, listened and said, "We expected it to be good, but not *that* good." From the right side of room 10, Knaak and Trimble heard Poser's chant, and their shoulders drooped.

"Franken, Franken, Franken." By the time the chant ended, Franken had pummeled Coleman, 481 to 305, with Dean Barkley collecting only 11 percent, or far less than on Election Day; actually, 37 of the ballots opened and counted, a full 4 percent, didn't vote for any Senate candidate. While 45 percent of the 933 ballots came from counties that Coleman won, the incumbent managed only 33 percent of the votes in Poser's count. Bottom line: the people who voted absentee, and especially those whose outside envelopes were a little bit goofy, were disproportionately Franken supporters. With his 176-vote trouncing of Coleman, Franken's lead surged to 225 votes, a nearly thousand-vote swing since the earliest returns in the hours after the polls closed in November.

"Obviously, I've had better days, and so have we," said Knaak in the hallway outside of room 10. Elias, as noticeably gleeful as he allowed himself to get, said boldly, "We are confident since there are no ballots left to count that the final margin will stand with Al Franken having won the election . . . It is not a large margin, but a comfortable margin . . . 225 votes is a real victory. One vote is a real victory, but 225 votes is a close election but it is a fairly clear victory." Elias instantly began calling Coleman "former Senator Coleman," just to rub it in.

The savvy of Franken's data on the absentees became crystal clear. According to the simplistic analysis of precinct tendencies that Team Franken had developed on December 26, Franken should have won 44 percent of the original 1,346 rejected ballots. Once the Franken data magic occurred, once the pool was reduced by Franken and Coleman reps to 933, Franken captured more than 51 percent of the fifth pile, a 7 percentage point premium for a net of 176 votes. Coleman got handed a big math problem, a huge political problem, and a tough legal problem.

Knaak and Trimble declared that Coleman had no other choice but to take the election to court, but even looking around under every rock, it was going to be nearly impossible to overcome a 225-vote deficit. Knaak and Trimble said again there was double counting of an unknown number of ballots statewide, but the Canvassing Board and Supreme Court didn't bite on that assertion earlier. The Canvassing Board had included the 132 Minneapolis "missing votes" in its count, and removing them now would be a Herculean legal task for Coleman. A trial would follow and judges would see a relatively comfortable 225-vote gap, not the smaller

49-vote lead of the first round of the recount. It would be difficult for judges to overturn a 225-vote victory. There was a cushion now for Franken, not a sliver. Counting the wrongly rejected absentee ballots—adding the fifth pile—lent numerical and political legitimacy to Franken's increasing lead.

This recount and its election contest would extend for a mind-numbing six more months of testimony, exhibits, and appeals. But this election was won and lost at the state Canvassing Board, with legal finesse on the part of Franken's team, with admirable fairness by the members of the board, and with fortuitous help from the Supreme Court.

There was poetic justice, too. One of the "Franken" votes Poser sang out belonged to Clare Bohmann, the college student from Seattle whose mother made the call to David Lillehaug on the day after Election Day that launched the absentee ballot chase, intensified the hunt, and ended with a bountiful harvest.

Two days later, as afternoon rush hour began on the Monday after the Poser chant, Franken stood in front of a dozen microphones outside his downtown Minneapolis townhouse. Earlier in the day, the Canvassing Board, comprising Justices Magnuson and Anderson, Judges Gearin and Cleary, and Secretary of State Ritchie certified that Franken received the most votes. They couldn't grant him the election certificate, the pass he needed to become a U.S. senator. Only Ritchie and Governor Tim Pawlenty could do that. Still, it was Franken's turn to declare victory, two months to the day after Coleman did. With the vapors of the frigid air popping from his mouth, with the dark overcoat making him look senatorial, Franken told reporters, "For our state, today marked the end of a long process that will forever be a part of Minnesota history. But today is also a beginning . . . The history of our country will be forever altered by what we do together to address the challenges we face together. So, with tremendous gratitude for the victory we have won, I'm ready to get to work."

With Franni to his right, it fit the mold of every televised victory (or resignation) seen on CNN. He made a statement but wouldn't answer questions. If anyone wondered if Franken could be reflective, that was put to rest. "I . . . know this was a hard-fought victory," he said, "and that I didn't win the support of every Minnesotan. I'm going to have to earn it by being a senator who fights for every Minnesotan, whether you voted for me or not." He reached out to Coleman. It wasn't a full, frontal, let's-hug-Norm moment, but it was as generous as could be expected from a slugger like Franken after the campaign, after the recount, with a court challenge looming. "I know this is not an easy day for Norm Coleman and his family, and I know that because Franni and I and the kids have had plenty of time over the past two months to contemplate the possibility that this election would turn out differently."

Time for healing? Not yet.

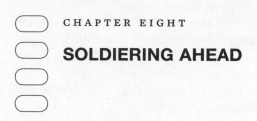

CHAPTER EIGHT

SOLDIERING AHEAD

"We need to get this right."

"Norm, Norm, Norm! Norm, Norm, Norm!"

The room was overfilled and overheated. The recount was over. The Canvassing Board had spoken. Norm Coleman was unemployed. Al Franken was packing for Washington. The swearing-in of new members of Congress was set for this day, January 6. Franken and his wife, Franni, were poised to jet off to their new home away from home. But room 181 in the State Office Building, the site of many Mark Ritchie news conferences, located up the stairs from where the Canvassing Board deliberated, didn't appear to be a concession venue. Instead, it was a stage of defiance and denial.

Despite the declaration by the Canvassing Board that Franken received 225 more votes than Coleman, the former senator and his supporters believed the war needed to continue to be waged, and in a noisy way. Barely twenty-four hours after the board's certification of Franken's vote margin, a couple hundred Coleman supporters crammed into room 181. They turned what could have been—nay, should have been—a postmortem into a never-say-die rally. It was a good old-fashioned, made-for-TV, staged event, and it came a full two months after Election Day. The campaign mentality and bitterness lingered and drove the next phase: an election contest. The contest is a full-blown trial to determine if the Canvassing Board acted correctly and if, indeed, Franken won more legally cast votes than Coleman. It was an effort to overturn all the work already done by the counties, Ritchie's office, the board, and, in the case of the absentee ballots, both candidates. Coleman wasn't going to give up. This former assistant attorney general was carrying his case to

Minnesota's courts; in this case, a still-to-be-named three-judge panel of district court judges from around the state. That's how the law read.

Coleman had a right to his day in court. No one could take that away from him. But the question was whether this move was about the law or about politics, about being wronged or about blocking Franken and the Democrats from controlling the U.S. Senate and aiding the new president on his agenda for change. GOP Senate leaders, most notably Texas Senator John Cornyn, said any attempt by the Democrats to seat Franken before the election contest trial verdict and before a formal election certificate was signed by Ritchie and Republican Governor Tim Pawlenty would trigger an ugly Republican filibuster. That meant Minnesota's second U.S. Senate seat would remain empty. Coleman lawyer Fritz Knaak predicted the trial would take a month; it wouldn't begin, under state law, until January 26, in twenty days. Still, that was absurdly swift for a trial to get under way, for pretrial discovery and depositions to be conducted, for witnesses to be subpoenaed, and for judges to get up to speed on the issues and the law. All while the nation watched and Washington waited.

Without question, the election contest would push Franken's entrance into the Senate back, perhaps as far as March — or maybe later. Some Minnesota law professors opined that the entire trial and series of potential appeals could mean no final decision until the summer of 2009. In most states, a seat in question is filled by the presumptive victor. Provisional election certificates catapult the apparent winner — in this case, Franken — into the Senate. Under those conditions in those other states, any subsequent legal flip by a court would promptly replace Franken with Coleman. People like Kevin Hamilton and Chris Sautter were familiar with such guidelines. When Hamilton represented Washington State Governor Christine Gregoire in her recount, the governor retained her seat as her victory was challenged. In 1962, during Minnesota's last great recount between sitting governor Elmer Andersen and challenger Karl Rolvaag, Andersen remained in office while the recount stumbled on. But not in this statewide federal office recount in Minnesota, where fairness, patience, process, and niceness prevail and where out-of-towners like Marc Elias couldn't believe what they were seeing. In Elias's mind, Franken should have been headed to Washington, D.C., on this day. The state of Minnesota was guaranteed by the U.S. Constitution to have two senators, not one, he reasoned. Franken won the recount, game over, was Elias's view. Had Elias been in room 181, he would have been all alone in thinking such thoughts.

Coleman backers waved signs reading One Person One Vote and repeated chants of "Norm, Norm, Norm!" rang out as Coleman entered the room, candidate style, not loser style. The boosters spilled into the corridor, which happened to be adjacent to Ritchie's office. Coleman seemed tired, but, performer that he is, he delivered for his audience. "A six-year term is a long, long time," he said. "Crucial decisions will be made during that period on the economy, national security, and the rights of all Americans. Minnesotans deserve a 100 percent confidence that their senator was fairly elected by the people . . . We need to get this right for all of us."

The crowd of Coleman faithful cheered and added, "Blame the media!" or, challenging the horde of reporters in the room, "Look at Ritchie!" as if the secretary of state had somehow managed the Canvassing Board or fiddled with a recount in more than one hundred venues overseen by officials from both political parties.

The crowd's noise provided the background to a rambling ten-page election contest petition, accompanied by nearly two hundred pages of supporting documents and ballots in question, filed that day in Ramsey County District Court in St. Paul. After the Canvassing Board's ruling, Coleman had seven days to file such an election contest, but Trimble filed it quickly, within one day. It was a throw-everything-against-the-wall complaint, all of which Coleman's lawyers would need to prove before a three-judge panel at a trial that, according to Minnesota statutes, had to begin in twenty days. The complaint re-alleged what Trimble and Knaak had been charging since early November, charges that had fallen on deaf ears at the Canvassing Board and the Minnesota Supreme Court.

Among the allegations in their election contest complaint were that 654 valid absentee ballots remained unopened and uncounted, ballots they identified as likely Coleman friendly. In late December, the Coleman lawyers missed a deadline to bring these into the count with the 1,346 ballots that election officials established from the fifth pile. Coleman's side wanted these 654 ballots to be revived. Furthermore, they said that the 132 votes from Minneapolis should not be included in the Canvassing Board's total. "The utter lack of uniformity in the treatment of rejected absentee ballots," was yet another issue, Trimble alleged. Similar ballots were treated differently by different counties, creating an equal protection violation. Knaak went out of his way to promise the appearance of at least one witness who would testify to having seen votes counted twice. "The other side was calling this a fiction," Knaak said. "It's not."

They claimed that there were illegal ballots among the 933 counted on January 3, although they approved that group. They added that "a material number of persons voted more than once," a felony, if true. Bottom line: Knaak and Trimble said enough votes had gone uncounted or were miscounted to swing the election from Franken's 225-vote Canvassing Board–sanctioned victory.

If Coleman's lawyers seemed buoyed by the chance to take on Elias, Hamilton, and Lillehaug in court, Elias looked as sober as he'd made himself appear over two months. His client had just flipped election results, slam-dunked an absentee-ballot chase, and edged the Democrats closer to control of the U.S. Senate. After eight weeks of victories, an uneasy feeling set in among Franken's legal and political team. What is this all about, this election contest, this trial? Now Elias, so good at being on the offensive, would have to move to the other side and play defense. He reacted to the filing of the election contest petition with disdain, understanding that he was about to spend another month or two in Minnesota, where the temperatures were dipping even as he continued his refusal to wear a topcoat.

An hour or so after Coleman's rally, Elias stood alone in the lobby of DFL headquarters, tucked amid warehouses south of downtown St. Paul. It was the Franken team's new home after leaving an unneeded and expensive campaign headquarters. A photo of Hubert Humphrey hung behind him as Elias labeled Coleman's election contest assertions "the same thin gruel warmed over, leftovers, meals that we've all been served over the last few weeks . . . When you lose by 225 votes, you have to go mining for votes somewhere . . . Desperate times call for desperate measures." If Elias's patience began in small supply, it was now completely spent. He and Hamilton had plane tickets home and visions of time away from all this.

"I believe I'm going to win," Coleman said hours earlier. "I believe I won the election [on] Election Night . . . As Americans, we believe that every valid vote should count and that everybody's vote is equal to everyone else's . . . At this moment, I may not have a working office in D.C. or in St. Paul, but I still have my voice in Minnesota, and I certainly plan to use it."

For the Franken side, it felt as if time stood still. So much had happened so quickly between November 4 and January 5 — an election, charges of ballots in trunks, a recount, the Canvassing Board, the Pony Express, the trips to the Minnesota Supreme Court, bursting the absentee-ballot barrier, tear-jerking DVD propaganda, the giddy counting of ballots—and the result was victory. Now, a trial wasn't set to begin until January 26. Who knew how long it would last?

Late in the afternoon of January 8, the phone rang in Denise Reilly's chambers on the sixth floor of the Hennepin County Government Center. Alan Page was on the other end. Reilly, a former assistant U.S. attorney and veteran state judge in Minnesota's most urban and crime-filled court, sat straight up in her chair. She was friendly, or at least acquainted, with most of the members of the state Supreme Court, what with judges always mingling and her office a quick nine miles from the Minnesota Judicial Center, home base of the Supremes and the Court of Appeals, but Page wasn't calling about some run-of-the-mill wine-sipping gathering. He had a direct question and firm request: would Reilly like to be on the three-judge panel of the Franken–Coleman election contest trial?

"I was stunned," Reilly remembered. She was intrigued. "There's going to be a lot of publicity," Page told her. "Is there anything we should know about why you can't be on the panel?" Reilly, who had been appointed to the bench by Republican Governor Arne Carlson in 1997, needed some time to think it over. A dozen years earlier, Reilly had been the chief of the narcotics and firearms unit in the U.S. attorney's office. It was her then boss Lillehaug, now Franken's lawyer, who promoted her to that position, but she didn't view that as a conflict. So, on her drive home to suburban Orono, she called Page back. She accepted. It was just two days after Coleman's decision to take the recount to a trial. Minnesota's Supreme Court wasn't wasting any time in filling the spots on the election contest panel. The law was clear. "The case must be heard and determined in Ramsey County by three judges assigned by the chief justice of the Supreme Court." Chief Justice Eric Magnuson, fresh off his Canvassing Board stint, continued to recuse himself from the contest. Page continued as the acting chief. He may have telephoned Reilly, but his colleagues aided him in selecting the panel members. They signed off on the judges to be considered. As divided as the Supreme Court had been three weeks before over the absentee ballot matter, the robed Gang of Five understood the importance of naming an experienced, geographically and politically diverse three-judge panel. They understood the importance, too, of coming back together as a unit after such a divisive ruling on the fifth pile. Later, Justice Paul Anderson told students at Duke

University Law School that he and his colleagues conferred about possible names of trial judges for "about two weeks"; that is, before Coleman even announced for sure that he was going to force the recount to a trial.

A day after Reilly got her call, the phone jingled in the St. Cloud chambers of Judge Elizabeth Hayden, sixty-three, chief judge of Stearns County, and among the most senior women judges in the state. She was appointed by Democratic Governor Rudy Perpich in 1986. Well connected to various statewide judicial committees, Hayden had more concerns than Reilly. She and Page chatted for about ten minutes. His staff quickly e-mailed to her a list of lawyers involved in the case for her to ponder any conflicts. Hayden called Page back. She was on board. "By the way," Page said, as they prepared to hang up, "It's Minnesota Statute 209." That's the state's election law. Hayden had never read it. She reached to her shelf for the Minnesota Statutes.

On Monday, January 12, Judge Kurt Marben was on the bench in Crookston, when a court employee told him there was an urgent call from the state Supreme Court. Crookston is one of the cities in his massive Ninth Judicial District circuit, with Thief River Falls his home base. Unknown to most lawyers in the Twin Cities, Marben was well-known to members of the Supreme Court, including Paul Anderson and Lorie Gildea, who is the court's liaison to the Ninth District. Marben, fifty-seven, worried about how his cases would be covered if he agreed to serve. A series of phone calls followed to resolve that. Within an hour, he agreed to the assignment. Before the end of the business day, an order was signed and an announcement was made. Somehow, organically, miraculously, thankfully, the three would become interchangeable, a unit, the "ThreeJudgePanel," as they would be dubbed by Eric Black, the political commentator for the Twin Cities Web site MinnPost. (Later, Justice Paul Anderson said in a lecture at Duke University Law School that, before picking Hayden, Marben, and Reilly, "We eliminated a number of [other] judges," after first calling them and asking if there were any issues that might affect their sitting on the case. Apparently, some bowed out.)

Before they became inseparable and before their minds entered into a sort of unified warp to create three months' worth of unanimous decisions, Hayden, Marben, and Reilly had not known each other and wouldn't have recognized each other on a street had they bumped into each other. When they did come together just four days after being appointed, Reilly arrived at the Minnesota Judicial Center and wasn't sure where she and the other judges were to meet with Franken's and Coleman's lawyers. "There's this young-looking guy standing there and I thought he was one of Ramsey County's fine clerks," she said later. She asked him for directions. The fellow was lost too. It was Marben, whom Reilly later labeled the "boy judge."

It was as if the Supreme Court's selection process had sought assistance from central casting. There was Reilly, the energetic, almost perky, former prosecutor whose values were framed by her years as a religion major at Ohio's College of Wooster. Her independent project there focused on Leviticus 25, an Old Testament passage of justice about the "year of jubilee." Coming from Hennepin County District Court, Reilly had seen it all. She was patient, but not overly so; at fifty-five, she was the youngest of the three.

Hayden, the soon-to-retire aunt-like figure, was a former social worker with the demeanor of your favorite seventh-grade teacher. She seemed stern, but she had a biting sense of humor and a knack for good-natured teasing. It was no surprise that she and Canvassing Board member Kathy Gearin were pals, veteran women in an occupation dominated by men. Hayden brought that Gearin-like down-to-earth twinkle, even while coming from one of the state's most conservative jurisdictions.

And then Marben: a guy who was born in Grand Forks, North Dakota, grew up as the son of the high school principal in Tracy, Minnesota, population two thousand, went off to Bemidji State University, then to the big city to the University of Minnesota Law School. Coincidentally, he was a pal and classmate of Canvassing Board member Ed Cleary. Marben went off to work in a law office in Thief River Falls and, by 2000, was appointed to his judgeship by Independence Party Governor Jesse Ventura. Wacky Ventura was known for his offbeat interviews of judicial appointments. Strict and substantial compliance, equal protection, and due process brain twisters were not on Ventura's agenda. No, the standard question Ventura asked judge candidates in their final interview with him went something like this: If you had a free day or two and unlimited resources, What would you do? Where would you go?

Others, more prepared than Marben, had heard of Ventura's trick question and spoke of wanting to go golfing at an elite course or travel to Scotland or take all of their friends to an Eric Clapton concert in London. "If you had one day to do whatever you wanted, what would it be?" Ventura asked Marben eight years before he ascended to the recount case. Marben had not known the question was coming. "Well," he told the edgy Ventura, "you know, I just had a day like that, and I spent it in Walker [Minnesota] on Leech Lake and did some hiking and had a friend with a sailboat, a pretty simple day." Undoubtedly, Marben said it softly and sincerely.

The three fit together as if designed to be one. Their mission seemed simple enough, as dictated by Minnesota law: "When a contest relates to the office of senator... of the United States, the only question to be decided by the court is which party to the contest received the highest number of votes legally cast at the election and is therefore entitled to receive the certificate of election." But from the moment they were joined at the hip, they had a lot of catching up to do with Minnesota election law and with the past. They worked in the echoes of history: a 1962 Minnesota gubernatorial election recount on one shoulder and a 2000 U.S. presidential election recount on the other.

While some nostalgia buffs during the Franken–Coleman recount longed for "the good old days" of 1960s civility, there was nothing polite at all about that confrontation between incumbent Republican Governor Elmer Andersen and Democratic challenger Karl Rolvaag in 1962.[1] As in the 2008 campaign, there was a third-party candidate, William Braatz of the Industrial Government Party, a socialist group. Braatz didn't garner the support that Dean Barkley did, but his 7,300 votes meant that Andersen and Rolvaag tied with 49 percent of the vote.

After the first returns, Rolvaag was ahead by 58 votes, but a politically partisan and divided state Canvassing Board refused to certify the election. As in 2008, the state Supreme Court intervened. With most of its members appointed by Andersen, the Court allowed ten counties to adjust "obvious errors" in their original counts. That decision caused the election to flip to Andersen by 142 votes, and thus gain the Republican-leaning Canvassing Board's certification.[2] In 1962, there was no trigger for an automatic recount, as in 2008, and there was no law establishing a three-judge panel appointed by the Supreme Court to oversee an election contest. Rolvaag sought and gained a statewide hand recount only after filing an election contest petition. Of the 1.25 million votes, 63 percent were originally cast by hand—not by machine—in a state that was still largely rural. When the recount got underway, volunteers for both candidates, encouraged by their respective political parties to be picky, challenged the validity of 104,000 ballots—including 7,000 absentee ballots—a far higher challenge percentage than in the 2008 recount.

To avoid the appearance of political bias, Supreme Court Chief Justice Oscar Knutson allowed the two campaigns to jointly select a three-judge panel to rule on the challenges and conduct the election contest trial. This laid the groundwork for the later enactment of a law that made way for the statutory creation of three-judge election contest panels. After months of legal spats and feisty counting across the state, the three district court judges, now hearing the case in 1963, ruled on a pared-down total of about four thousand challenged ballots. After determining voter intent on each ballot, the judges declared Rolvaag the winner by 91 votes. That process took 139 days, extending to March 25, 1963.

One procedure aided the judges in ruling on the legality of the challenged Andersen and Rolvaag ballots. As a way to examine them, lawyers for both candidates divided the ballots into twenty-six categories, including potentially double-counted votes, errant marks on ballots, and oddball write-in votes. The judges encouraged such categorization. "Category 26" was labeled "Absentee Ballots Claimed to be Valid Votes but not Included in the Recount." They were, in 2008 verbiage, improperly rejected absentee ballots.

As the 1962 election contest wound down, eleven unopened and, apparently, inexplicably rejected absentee ballots remained that DFL lawyer Clayton Taylor wanted included. Taylor nervously joked that he wasn't sure what was inside the envelopes; that is, which candidate won those votes. But authors Ronald F. Stinnett and Charles H. Backstrom expressed skepticism in their book *Recount* (1964). They wrote, "Very thorough research and tracking down of absentee voters were carried on to be assured that the voter cast his ballot for the proper candidate," proving that, despite the creativity and nifty high-tech data gathering of Franken's legal team, there were few new election tricks under the sun in 2008.

The 2000 Florida recount was the other slice of history and law floating above Hayden, Marben, and Reilly as they prepared for the spotlight. Anyone with a rudimentary knowledge of election law had read the U.S. Supreme Court's *Bush v. Gore* decision handing the election to George W. Bush and knew that the ruling was not "precedential"; that is, the U.S. Supreme Court's majority wanted the meaning of *Bush v. Gore*'s holding to be limited to the facts of the 2000 Florida presidential recount because of this sentence written on December 12, 2000: "Our consideration is limited to the present circumstances, for the problem of equal protection in election processes generally presents many complexities."

Eight years later, there were few apparent similarities between the way the Florida recount had played out and the way the Minnesota recount and Canvassing Board drama had so far unfolded, but there were definitely many complexities. Generally speaking, in Florida the Bush side argued that there wasn't uniformity in the standards that local election officials used in determining voter intent as they examined ballots. The terms *hanging chad* and *dimpled chad,* referring to the squares that voters pushed out of the punch-card ballots to indicate their votes, became part of the American political lexicon. If the punch wasn't sufficient, the chad — that tiny piece of paper next to a candidate's name — didn't come totally undone and instead appeared to be hanging or dimpled or even "pregnant." Because of those incomplete punches, the ballot became controversial. Another issue in Florida: only four counties underwent recounts, and they were, arguably, Gore-leaning counties. That wasn't fair, the Republicans argued, or legal. These and other problems were rolled by Bush lawyers into the category of equal protection violations of the Fourteenth Amendment of the United States Constitution and eventually upheld by the U.S. Supreme Court.[3] Exact comparisons to the Minnesota recount didn't exist, but the Coleman forces asserted in documents filed early with the election contest court that different standards were used in evaluating the acceptance of absentee ballots. But before the recount began, Coleman lawyers, along with the Franken crew, hammered out and signed on to the complete "Proposed Administrative Procedures" of sixteen recount rules. In addition, Ritchie's office provided a detailed, eighteen-page recount guide for all statewide election officials and the public soon after Election Day. Months earlier, there was also uniform training provided to election officials statewide.

At the absentee-ballot stage, Minnesota's laws and standards were clear about what rules a voter had to follow, what was a valid envelope and what wasn't. Some absentee-ballot boards and poll workers may have fudged on those standards when accepting or rejecting ballot envelopes, but a uniform statewide system of evaluation did exist on Election Night 2008, and Franken's forces were about to argue that. This was not Florida 2000.

As for any quirks in evaluating voter intent of the wrongly rejected absentee ballots, that wasn't an issue; no election judge knew what was inside the envelopes. All they could see was the voter's name and address, and the name of his or her witness. Perhaps, based on the data it possessed, the Franken campaign had a good idea of the votes inside the envelopes. Perhaps, the Coleman side should have had a better idea of the leanings of the voters. But no arbitrary judgments about the voter's intent were made by election officials on the basis of the outside envelope.

In some ways, the deeper relationship between *Bush v. Gore* and *Coleman v. Franken* was the public script that both sides used during the recount, the Canvassing Board phase and, as the ThreeJudgePanel would soon discover, even during the trial. For instance, in Florida, the Democrats kept declaring that all votes should be counted, just as Elias did in Minnesota in November and December. In Florida, the Republicans' position was to halt the recount, as in Minnesota it was their position to block the counting of the absentee ballots. When the Republicans thought they were being treated unfairly by the Democratic-leaning Florida Supreme Court during the recount, an exasperated James Baker, who was Bush's public representative, said, "It is simply not fair . . . to change the rules, either in the middle of the game, or after the game has been played." Those same words would soon be uttered by Coleman lawyers in St. Paul at the Minnesota election contest trial. But, as the Coleman case unfolded, Coleman's legal team had the task of proving, using the civil standard of the "preponderance of the evidence," that, in fact, there had been constitutional violations in this Minnesota recount, and that either there was no way to tell which candidate received the most legally cast votes or that Coleman was the recipient of more votes than Franken. By all measures, election law experts agreed, *Coleman v. Franken* was bound to become the most significant test of *Bush v. Gore* since the U.S. Supreme Court ruled in 2000 in favor of the Republican, who, a year later, helped to handpick Norm Coleman to be the 2002 GOP candidate for U.S. Senate, a symbiotic relationship that made Coleman such a vulnerable incumbent in 2008 and someone whom Elias wanted to replace as quickly as possible.

From the moment he arrived in Minnesota and became the face of the Franken recount unit, Elias publicly insisted that he was in the business of "taking one step at a time." Frequently, a reporter asked a breathless, hypothetical question that could only be answered in days or weeks hence, such as, If you lose this or that, if they do that or they do this, are you going to appeal to the U.S. Supreme Court? Are you? If not, why not?

Elias tried not to chuckle, and consistently replied, his right arm moving this way, his left arm moving that way, "Look, we're going to take this one step at a time." He said that a bunch, trying to mean it, but in the cubicles of Franken headquarters, in which he paced like a caged animal, Elias continually thought of taking giant steps that could leapfrog Franken to Washington as quickly as possible. Elias hauled around impatience like most lawyers tote briefcases and breath mints.

On November 26, when the state Canvassing Board initially declared its opposition to counting the wrongly rejected absentee ballots, Elias slyly threatened to take the entire case to the U.S. Senate to see if his pal Harry Reid would handle it. He didn't do that, and it turned out swell for Franken. The board changed its mind weeks later, the Minnesota Supreme Court intervened, and those 933 ballots got counted. So far, so good on keeping one's powder dry.

On January 5, when the state Canvassing Board certified that Franken had won the most legally cast votes and held a 225-vote margin over Coleman, Elias had another urge to take the recount to Washington. With the 2008 Election Day winners in other states getting their desks, offices, and committee assignments on Capitol Hill, Elias believed it was time to close the deal, and to do it before Coleman had a chance to extend the game. Why not take the Canvassing Board's decision that Franken had won to the Democrat-controlled U.S. Senate before Coleman could file his election contest petition? Franken's official election certificate had not been approved by Secretary of State Ritchie and Governor Pawlenty, but it was worth a try. In his deepest constitutional interpretations, Elias truly felt Franken should be seated in the Senate before the election contest played out, even if Minnesota law seemed to read otherwise.

Elias privately took this option to Franken in early January. Franken shot it down immediately. With very little discussion, the putative senator-elect rejected that tactic, understanding Minnesotans would rebel at the idea and trusting his faith in the Minnesota courts system. Besides, if he actually won this thing, he figured he might want to run again in 2014. Making a grab at the seat now would not endear him to Minnesotans. The Franken kibosh was, by everyone's memory, his only veto of an Elias notion during the entire recount and trial process. It also ran counter to Franken's impetuous image.

There might be still another way, Elias thought. Now that Coleman had filed his petition for an election contest, now that the trial wouldn't start until January 26 and wouldn't end for weeks, if not months, Elias had yet another plan. It emerged on January 12, hours before the announcement of the appointment of the ThreeJudgePanel. In the end, it would unfold as the start of Elias's biggest mistake of the recount, not a fatal one, to be sure, but one that could only be attributed to his constant state of being antsy and his disconnect with Minnesota sensibilities. This move was a bit too cute.

The law was, in fact, a bit squishy.[4] One subdivision said that, "In an election for United States senator, the governor shall prepare an original certificate of election, countersigned by the secretary of state, and deliver it to the secretary of the United States Senate . . . if a recount is undertaken by a canvassing board . . . no certificate of election shall be prepared or delivered until after the recount is completed." Well, the recount was completed with Franken ahead. Franken's side was arguing that the governor "shall" sign the certificate, with "shall" being an instruction or command.

But the very next subdivision of the statute read: "No certificate of election shall be issued until seven days after the canvassing board has declared the result of the election. In case of a contest, an election certificate shall not be issued until a court of proper jurisdiction has finally determined the contest." Of course, the trial had not begun.

Most states seat their elected officials provisionally; that is, if there is a contest or a disputed recount, the apparent victor takes his or her seat, only to be removed from office if it so happens they lose at the eventual trial. In Minnesota recount history, Governor Elmer Andersen, who wound up conceding after a lengthy recount after the 1962 election, remained in office until March 25, 1963. The governor's office was not left vacant.

The attempt to get Mr. Franken to Washington sooner rather than later began quietly enough with a letter on January 12 from Lillehaug to Ritchie and Pawlenty informing them that, as Team Franken saw it, the U.S. Constitution and Minnesota state law "requires" them to certify the election "by the close of business today." After all, Article I, Section 3, of the U.S. Constitution states that "The Senate of the United States shall be composed of two Senators from each State." It was a typically crisp Lillehaug-written missive, thoughtfully sent by the local Franken lawyer and not pushy East Coast guy, Elias.

In less than an hour after Elias told reporters of the Lillehaug letter, Ritchie, branded by the GOP as a flaming liberal, issued a statement unequivocally declaring he wouldn't sign a certificate until the election contest ended, and that "Even if the governor issues a certificate of election prior to the conclusion of the contest phase, I will not sign it." Minutes later, Pawlenty, who otherwise historically disagreed with Ritchie on all matters having to do with election law, seconded the secretary of state's motion and announced he would "follow state law" and wait until the matter was resolved "in the courts." *Courts*—plural—opened the door to waiting until various appeals could be waged, even beyond the ongoing trial.

Undeterred, Elias, Hamilton, and Lillehaug, with Franken's approval, opted to take the matter to the next level. The next day they filed a petition with the Minnesota Supreme Court, the same five-judge panel that had authored the oddball decision on the absentee ballots three weeks earlier. They sought an order "requiring Governor Pawlenty and Secretary Ritchie to promptly prepare and countersign a certificate of election and deliver the certificate to the President of the United States Senate." Perhaps the high court would agree that Minnesota deserved to have two senators now and not months from now. "Each day of delay is a further breach of [Pawlenty's and Ritchie's], and Minnesota's, constitutional duty," the Franken lawyers opined.

In a conference call with journalists announcing the Supreme Court move, Elias found himself under attack. It was reminiscent of the feisty news conference two months earlier about the nonexistent eighty-four-year-old voter from Beltrami County. He turned uncharacteristically agitated, and more lawyerly and parsing than usual. The questions came quickly and skeptically, led by Eric Eskola, the respected veteran reporter for WCCO radio, the state's fifty thousand–watt traditional AM station. Eskola understood Minnesota's political sensibilities as well as anyone. "Mr. Elias," Eskola asked, "does Mr. Franken run the risk of looking greedy and in losing ground in the court of public opinion in grasping for this at this point?"

To the contrary, Elias responded, "I think many Minnesotans, if not most, would be dismayed to learn that they don't have full representation in the United States Senate . . . Right now, every other state has two United States senators . . . What we are seeking to insure is that Minnesota has a full voice, not a half voice, during the pendency of this contest."

It sounded democratically correct, but after months of cynical campaigning and a razor-thin 225-vote victory out of nearly three million votes cast, it also sounded presumptuous and self-serving. Ruffled by the gall of Eskola's question and others in the same vein afterward, Elias lectured, "Your readers and your listeners face a very, very uncertain economic world out there, with a new president with a bold set of initiatives. Should the people of Minnesota be deprived full representation because former Senator Coleman wishes to have his day in court to try to scrounge up more votes to drag this process along? . . . He has a right to his day in court. That's one of the great things about our country, that even people without meritorious claims get to bring them to court. Now, they don't get to win them, just bring them."

With Obama taking office and his agenda full, the Democrats needed as many votes as possible. The Georgia Senate runoff in December resulted in the Republican Saxby Chambliss retaining his seat and denying the Democrats a possible sixtieth vote.

The Coleman campaign jumped on the chance to bash Elias and Franken, with Knaak issuing a screeching statement, calling the move "a publicity stunt" and framing it thus: "Al Franken knows he can't win in court, abiding by the rules of Minnesota election law. So he's coming up with every desperate move he can, and his Washington legal team as well, to take this out of the hands of the law here and not to have to go to trial against our election contest." In Washington, Texas Senator John Cornyn, the new head of the National Republican Senatorial Committee, threatened to launch a filibuster against any attempt by Reid to seat Franken without final resolution in Minnesota of the election contest. In the U.S. Senate, the minority party can block actions by the majority party if there aren't sixty votes — a so-called super-majority — to shut down such a filibuster. Franken, of course, was poised to become that sixtieth Democratic senator.

Minnesota having just one senator was cause for concern, but there was an even more serious scenario that Kevin Hamilton imagined. To establish a precedent of a state having just one senator because of protracted election litigation could create a constitutional crisis. What if the country were at a crossroads on policy, or at war? What if we were being invaded and life-and-death decisions had to be made by the Senate? What if there were five, ten, or twenty states in lengthy recount modes, dragging out their elections? "You've got to be done with recounts by the time the Senate is seated," Hamilton said. It was a highly unlikely possibility, but so was the notion that a former *Saturday Night Live* writer could become a senator. Besides, as Elias had noted, everyone is entitled to his day in court, whether the case was meritorious or not.

Already, Franken had missed the first week of the Congress's session. His committee assignments awaited him. Reid shut down Coleman's office in D.C., and Coleman's St. Paul office was shuttered. The Minnesota Supreme Court set a hearing on Franken's petition for three weeks hence. That wasn't Coleman or the Republicans slowing the process, but Minnesota's high court. When Elias appeared before them, he would learn that smart Washington lawyers working in Minnesota should refrain from getting too cocky.

CHAPTER NINE

REINFORCEMENTS ARRIVE

"I have been brought in apparently as the pretty face."

While Elias schemed to get Franken to Washington quickly, Coleman worried about who was going to be his lead trial attorney and spokesman as the recount moved to the courtroom and to the trial known as the election contest. The newly ex-senator had watched as, with Trimble and Knaak out front, he lost the recount. The reality seemed to be that Franken actually received more votes, but the Canvassing Board's flipflop on the absentees, the related goof-up on the handling of counting 933 absentee ballots, the inability to convince the board and the Minnesota Supreme Court that there was double counting, and flying blind on the calls at the tables all added up to defeat. So far. Even worse, Elias out-quoted Knaak in the national media, which was where fundraising was stirred up. Coleman needed to shake up his troops.

Minnesota law says that the election contest has to begin twenty days after the contest petition is filed. This trial was set to begin on January 26. Most lawsuits of this magnitude, with this many documents and potential witnesses, usually take months, if not years, to get to trial. When Kevin Hamilton tried the Gregoire gubernatorial election contest in Washington State, he had five months to prepare. In Minnesota, for all the whining among Franken supporters that things were moving slowly, the process, by most legal standards, moved at a head-spinning pace. Coleman needed to make major personnel decisions, and fast.

It was January 13. The first pretrial scheduling conference was three days away. The first pretrial oral arguments were eight days away. Coleman's lead trial lawyer had not yet been hired. Trimble and Knaak knew by now it wouldn't be one of them, but they didn't know who was going to jump into that role at this very last minute. Knaak figured it would be someone from the prestigious Dorsey & Whitney firm, home to Roger Magnuson. A Magnuson partner, James Langdon, had been working behind the scenes on the case for weeks now. Magnuson himself was unavailable. Some in the Coleman camp were happy about that. They blamed the erudite lawyer for blowing the absentee-ballot argument in December by ticking off Justice Paul Anderson with the Florida reference. Magnuson would love to have been in the middle of such a high-profile and politically charged case, but he was committed to a prolonged international arbitration case in Los Angeles that kept him from the recount matter.

Maybe it was Coleman's inability to take a step back and to refrain from thinking as if he were his own lawyer. He had been known as a solid attorney during his seventeen years in the Minnesota attorney general's office, working for a while under Hubert H. "Skip" Humphrey III, the son of the Happy Warrior and DFL icon, former vice president Hubert Humphrey. Maybe it was Coleman's reluctance, and the reluctance of others around him, to bring in national-level litigators, believing Minnesota judges would appreciate local faces rather than hired guns from D.C. When Coleman selected his lead counsel, it came late, and it came oddly, but it was Coleman's decision alone. "Norm got more into the decision-making mode," Knaak said of this post–Canvassing Board, pre-trial period.

On January 13, David Lillehaug's Minneapolis law firm played host to a continuing legal education seminar for local attorneys featuring a couple of federal judges. Lillehaug was too busy preparing for the election contest trial to attend the training sessions, but opted to schmooze afterward with the judges and other participants at a reception. Who should he bump into there, but one of Minneapolis's best known and most respected criminal defense lawyers, Joseph Friedberg, a seventy-one-year-old former traveling encyclopedia salesman, who was born in New York, had the physique of a fireplug, and the charm of everyone's favorite Uncle Morty, the one who always pinched your cheek too hard. Always dapper, often with a colorful silk handkerchief in his left jacket pocket, Friedberg, who had about three hundred cases under his belt, looked the part of a riverboat gambler, even if his true love was horse racing. He had represented alleged (and even sometimes convicted) murderers, drug dealers, crooked bankers, serial shoplifters, and hit-and-run drivers.

As U.S. attorney, Lillehaug had seen plenty of Friedberg and his clients. Lillehaug and Friedberg weren't exactly pals. Friedberg resented what he viewed as Lillehaug's aloofness and unbearable Harvardness. "He's a Harvard guy," Friedberg said. "I grew up hating Harvard. I always grew up knowing I wouldn't get in." Friedberg received his law degree from the University of North Carolina in 1963, six years before Marc Elias was born.

At this Tuesday reception at the Fredrikson & Byron office, thirteen days before the trial was to start, Friedberg said to Lillehaug, "You're not going to believe this, but I'm going to be interviewed tonight to be Norm Coleman's trial counsel."

"Really," Lillehaug replied, with much curiosity. "Who are you going to interview with?"

"Ben Ginsberg," Friedberg replied, meaning the well-known Republican elections lawyer from Washington, D.C., who was a key honcho in George W. Bush's Florida recount in 2000 and who had been advising Trimble, Knaak, and Coleman on recount matters the past few months. He had been Coleman's elections law and campaign lawyer for years too.

"So, what's this all about?" Friedberg asked Lillehaug.

"Ah, what do you mean?" answered Lillehaug, a bit startled. He was, of course, a lawyer on the other side of this matter.

"I mean, how does it work?" Friedberg asked.

"Well, Joe, Coleman has filed an election contest and, under Minnesota law, we're going to trial in twenty days," Lillehaug tutored Friedberg.

"Nah, come on, really?" Friedberg said, incredulous that the trial would start that quickly. "What kind of complaint is it?"

"It's got a lot of allegations," Lillehaug informed him. "It's kind of a scatter gun case."

"Well," Friedberg grumbled, "that's not the way I like to try a case."

Amused and amazed, Lillehaug returned to his office down the hall and zipped off an e-mail to others on the Franken legal team telling them of this strange encounter. Lillehaug didn't believe Friedberg would get the job. Yes, Coleman and Friedberg were old pals, having met thirty years before when Coleman was a prosecutor and Friedberg a defense attorney, two New York-born-and-raised Jewish lawyers in white-bread-and-mayonnaise Minnesota. Their paths crossed frequently, and after his two terms as St. Paul's mayor, Coleman joined the Minneapolis law firm of Winthrop & Weinstine, with which Friedberg was loosely affiliated. Friedberg had been co-counsel for Coleman's eighty-one-year-old father when he was caught having sex with a thirty-eight-year-old woman in a pizza parlor's parking lot in 2006.[1] Coleman trusted Friedberg.

There was a more prickly issue. Friedberg also represented Coleman's pal and gift-giver Nasser Kazeminy, who was named in the lawsuit that turned the campaign sideways in October. In a news story reporting he was hired by Kazeminy, Friedberg told the St. Paul *Pioneer Press,* "Over the years, my position is I would do anything for Norm—except vote for him—and I've told him that."[2]

The first meeting of the lawyers for both sides occurred three days after Lillehaug and Friedberg's chat. At the Minnesota Judicial Center, home to the Supreme Court, the conference to work out the schedule for the election contest trial took place in room 210, a pint-sized tax courtroom down a flight of marbled stairs from where Roger Magnuson made his "invitation . . . to Florida" boo-boo. Judges Hayden, Marben, and Reilly— coworkers for the first time—turned their initial event into an in-chambers session. No journalists were permitted to watch and no transcript was recorded.

In the privacy of that session, Lillehaug did a double take when he saw Friedberg walk in with Trimble, Knaak, and Langdon. Denise Reilly was also shocked. When she was an assistant U.S. attorney, she had opposed Friedberg in court, going back twenty years. She considered him a genial adversary and a top-notch criminal defense lawyer, but she and everyone else in the Twin Cities legal community knew Friedberg's strength was his ability to woo jurors. There would be none in this case. His strength was finding holes in a prosecutor's case; in this trial, Friedberg would have to present the case. He was skilled in cross-examination. This Coleman case Friedberg was about to present would rely on direct examination, and most lawyers will tell you direct is tougher than cross. Friedberg had his politics—pretty much Democratic nationally, independent locally, an admitted Franken voter—but he was not a political lawyer. "There's nothing complicated about me or what I do," he told an interviewer in 1992. "I don't have causes, just clients."[3]

A pack of reporters waited outside room 210, along with some Coleman staffers, and when the doors opened, who, to the surprise of the reporters, should emerge but stubby, sartorially resplendent Friedberg, who moseyed on up to the microphones and cameras as if he were actor Joe Pesci making a guest appearance on a *Law & Order* episode.

"What would you like to know?" Friedberg asked the reporters, without even identifying himself. He proceeded to declare that, yes, the Coleman side preferred that the trial start later than January 26, but, no, the judges were going to stick to the letter of the law. Yes, it seemed as if the judges were going to allow the case to be televised, the first fully televised trial in the history of Minnesota, even though, no, that wasn't his idea.

"And you are Joe Friedberg?" a journalist asked, wanting to get the ID correct.

"Still," he said, without missing beat and with a delivery worthy of a Las Vegas lounge act. He explained how he got here. Coleman asked him. "He called me," Friedberg said. "He's obviously at a very important place in his life. He asked me if I would help. He's a friend. What am I going to do — say no?"

Blackberries and iPhones of select Twin Cities reporters vibrated with an incoming e-mail message from Franken communications ruffian Eric Schultz. He was back in Washington, D.C., about to take a job with the Democratic Senatorial Campaign Committee. The idea that Friedberg was Coleman's lawyer was too much for him. "it can't be true," read the lowercase subject of Schultz's e-mail. "now i'm sad i'm gone ... the kazeminy piece is STUNNING. out of all the lawyers in the country coleman picks him??? people are gonna start to wonder if kazeminy is paying for him."

Off to the side and behind Friedberg stood Coleman's other, now-demoted, lawyers, Knaak and Trimble. Knaak's role as the face and voice of the recount was about to be eliminated. Trimble was to be "second chair," the details guy and assistant to Friedberg, who was not known as a details guy. Trimble was also there to emphasize the Republican Party line with the Democrat Friedberg, who was now representing the Republican Coleman.

When Trimble and Friedberg met for the first time, the night before Friedberg emerged from room 210, Friedberg asked Trimble, "What are our chances?" Trimble replied, "Very, very tough."

Also standing behind Friedberg, facing the cameras and digital voice recorders, was James Langdon, the Dorsey & Whitney partner who worked with Roger Magnuson on the *Bush v. Gore* trial in Florida. Langdon was a financial services litigation expert. He delivered some early oral arguments once the trial started, but mostly he was responsible for all the evidence and massive brief writing back at the Dorsey & Whitney offices. As the clock ticked toward the start of the trial, the Coleman team was re-forming with new people and new roles.

As to who was in charge of the legal strategy and team, Langdon and Friedberg said afterward they were not ever quite sure. Early on Knaak believed he was the leader, but so did Trimble. A few months after the case ended, Langdon was asked who Coleman's lead legal decision maker was. "At what point in time are we talking?" Langdon replied. He paused briefly and continued, "Actually the answer doesn't depend on the point in time, because the answer is no one. As best I can tell, at some point it became very clear to me that the senator was in charge and was making the calls, but that didn't become apparent—it may have been true all along—but that didn't become apparent to me until very late in the trial."

As Friedberg completed his first news conference on his first day of his first election law case, someone asked what the difference was between one of his typical criminal cases and an election contest. "Well, nobody goes to jail at the end of it," he said, "unless it's one of the lawyers." Everybody laughed. However, this was to be Friedberg's last news conference for a while. Coleman had made another decision. A new spokesman was coming to town, the Republicans' best and most biting, a real major leaguer. Off-the-cuff comments from avuncular Friedberg were instant history. From here on in, talking points would be targeted like darts.

It sounds like a cliché, but it was tangible. There was an air of excitement in courtroom 300 as the first pretrial hearing of the election contest grew nigh. The nation's political eyes were mostly turned to the East, where Barack Obama had been inaugurated a day earlier and expectations were off the charts. But many knowing political eyes were focused on this modern but reverential venue, built of Kasota limestone and furnished in stained oak, with translucent Vermont-marble windows sending beams of light from behind the judges' bench. Ben Ginsberg, who approved the Friedberg hiring for Coleman and who was about to become Friedberg's election law tutor, mingled with journalists in the front rows of the court's gallery, laughing and smiling, kibitzing and chitchatting as they all waited for the judges to appear. If Friedberg was an election law rookie, Ginsberg was a suave veteran, practically a Hall of Famer. His recount résumé challenged Sautter's. Sautter and Ginsberg met in

1984 in the Indiana Eighth Congressional District recount—that one also flipped in the Democrat's favor—and they had encountered each other in dozens of recounts for the next quarter century. Sautter and Elias had an enemy's respect for Ginsberg, but they wondered what he had done to help Coleman during the recount. Either he wasn't listened to by Coleman's local troops or he wasn't fully engaged. There were a few Ginsberg sightings in the fall, but no public pronouncements, which is his stock in trade.

Ginsberg's Patton Boggs associate, William McGinley, was on-site for the recount and Canvassing Board meetings. Ginsberg was on conference calls and was on the ground in Minnesota during recount training sessions for volunteers, but Trimble remained the election lawyer and Knaak the spokesman. Now, Ginsberg was suddenly the new sheriff of spin. "We had to create a separate identity in this phase of the process," Knaak said. "We needed Ginsberg talking through the locals to the national audience." During the recount phase, Elias could pick up the phone and score with key Washington media, such as *Politico* or influential *Washington Post* blogger Chris Cillizza, who writes the insiders' must-read Web column "The Fix." Knaak could not. One Coleman staffer said when they tried to linkup Knaak with D.C. media types, "the reaction was as if Knaak was 'Farmer Dave.'" Ginsberg was no Farmer Dave. Ginsberg was Elias's buzz-creating equal; he was Coleman's first visible outsider and signaled the belated recognition of the Washington Republicans that it was crunch time. For Democrats, Ginsberg was a sort of traveling Republican bogeyman, an ultraconservative Darth Vader in pin-striped suits and psychedelic ties, moving from one tough GOP cause to another, charmingly stabbing here and poking there, always on message. Upon his arrival in Minnesota, he was instantly dubbed the Democrats' "prince of darkness" in a blog item by the St. Paul *Pioneer Press*. Elias, Barr, and Franken's press secretary, Jess McIntosh, took instant notice of his presence and knew the game was on.

The son of a world-renowned microbiologist father and immigration lawyer mother, Ginsberg grew up as a suburban Philadelphia liberal. As a student at the University of Pennsylvania, he rose to be editor of the campus newspaper. He spent a summer working with gang kids in Philadelphia as part of a federal jobs program. That transformed him because he came to believe that this do-good project was nothing more than a big government boondoggle. His liberal idealism evaporated further as a young *Boston Globe* reporter covering that city's school bus-ing controversies. Before long, he turned to election law and federal redistricting matters, and began to move from recount to recount in the 1980s and '90s, for the Republicans. He splashed onto the cable TV and Sunday talk-show circuit as a lawyer for the Bush-Cheney campaigns in 2000 and 2004, and was a major character in the 2000 Florida recount, working closely with Bush's personal recount emissary, James Baker. Ginsberg was so effective at his job that he won the 2001 Pollie Award, the political consultants' Oscar, for Most Valuable Player in a Campaign. Sautter, his rival, nominated him.

Ginsberg said all the other Coleman lawyers would have their hands full during the trial so he was invited to Minnesota to handle the media. "I have been brought in apparently as the pretty face," Ginsberg said. By the looks of things, it was far more likely the bald-headed, salt-and-red-pepper-bearded Ginsberg was brought in to do what he does best, and that is stir things up.

In contrast, Franken's choices were made months earlier. He knew days after the election that Elias, Hamilton, and Lillehaug were his lawyers. With the exception of some key arguments to the judges, Elias delegated the meat-and-potatoes of the trial to Hamilton, who was thinking about its possibilities from the moment he landed in Minnesota on November 10. Perkins Coie, Elias and Hamilton's firm, and Fredrikson & Byron, Lillehaug's shop, provided a strong bench of talent to support the trial lawyers.

Among those designated as contributors, sometimes in Minnesota and other times back at the Perkins Coie offices on each coast, were two rising stars, Lisa Marshall Manheim in Seattle and Kate Andrias in Washing-ton, D.C. Both were Yale College and Yale Law School grads, both were former clerks for U.S. Supreme Court justices, Manheim for Anthony Kennedy and Andrias for Ruth Bader Ginsberg, and both were U.S. Court of Appeals clerks before that. Manheim, easily mistakable for a high school senior (she turned twenty-nine years old during the trial), had been the managing editor of the *Yale Law Journal*. Andrias, increasingly pregnant during the entire recount process, was hired by Perkins Coie recruiters years earlier when they received a personal note from a cir-cuit court judge she'd clerked for describing Andrias as "the smartest person I've ever worked with."[4]

Besides adding rare female insight to an otherwise all-male legal team, Manheim and Andrias paired up to become a round-the-clock, Web-based, e-mail-driven, brief-writing relay duo. Once the trial began, as issues developed, the two collaborated cross-country on briefs and memos. One of them was always in the courtroom in St. Paul, the other in her office in Seattle or Washington, D.C. Ideas flowed from the legal team in court and flew to Andrias or Manheim, who picked up the ball in the evening. Drafts of briefs zoomed in the wee hours from St. Paul to Seattle to the nation's capital, with Andrias and Manheim often writing until the crack of dawn. Another Seattle Perkins Coie partner, Will Rava, came on board to oversee day-to-day trial preparation issues. With the first pretrial scheduling meeting with the judges set for Friday, January 16, the Franken legal team was an increasingly well-oiled machine. Any early tensions between Elias and Lillehaug appeared settled. The Minnesotan proved himself to Elias and Hamilton through the Canvassing Board phase, as did others at his law firm, Fredrikson & Byron.

Elias couldn't sit still. His legal strategy in advance of the trial included a new wrinkle that demanded the retention of another Twin Cities attorney, Charlie Nauen. Nauen was a valuable behind-the-scenes lawyer during the recount phase. In 2006, he had represented the St. Louis County auditor during a recount in that DFL stronghold. He knew the Duluth and Iron Range ropes. On Election Night 2008, Lillehaug e-mailed Nauen to ask if, based on that experience, he would join the Franken recount unit in Duluth to monitor the situation. Duluth was sure to be a ballot battleground, and Franken territory. Lillehaug's electronic missive was not out of the blue; Lillehaug and Nauen had known each other since junior high school in Sioux Falls, where both were debate champions. They had remained friends for forty years. Nauen agreed to join the show and became a sort of regional manager for the Franken legal team in Northern Minnesota all the way through the fifth-pile exercise. In internal meetings, Nauen impressed Elias with a certain steely insight. Plus, Nauen's law firm—Lockridge Grindal Nauen—owned a pedigree that tickled Elias; the founding partner of the firm was Vance Opperman, one of the nation's leading Democratic donors and former president of West Publishing, the legal online and print publishing company.

Early in January, Schriock asked Nauen to a meeting at Franken headquarters. Elias had an idea developed, really, out of fear. As the countdown to the trial wore on, Elias imagined what he would do if he were Coleman's lawyer. At trial, Coleman was the plaintiff and had to present his case and prove—with the preponderance of the evidence—that it was he who garnered the most legally cast votes on November 4, 2008. Coleman was behind now. Coleman would need to be aggressive and begin finding votes to overcome Franken's 225-vote lead. What would Coleman's team do now that the game had changed? Elias figured, and worried, that Trimble, Knaak, and the folks at Dorsey & Whitney would begin their own voter chase now, using a Minnesota statute that allowed individuals to petition to correct "errors and omissions" in the election. These would have to be voters whose absentee ballots had been denied by election judges or Franken's observers and that hadn't survived the review to become one of the crucial 933 ballots opened. But if a voter had done everything right, wouldn't a trial court allow that ballot to be opened?

To counter this presumed offensive play by the Coleman side, Elias suggested to Schriock that Team Franken open another front. Like Coleman's original post–Election Night margin, Franken's cushion could easily slip away if his lawyers weren't diligent in protecting it. Enter Nauen, who was selected to lead the charge to find individual citizens—some of whom were eliminated by Coleman in the reduction from 1,346 to 933 ballots that the Canvassing Board counted—who were Franken voters. The campaign needed an attorney not working on Franken's trial to represent these people. Schriock agreed to pay Nauen's fees as he represented voters.

Nauen's approach was to use Minnesota Statutes § 204B.44 that said, "Any individual may file a petition . . . for the correction of any of the following errors, omissions, or wrongful acts which have occurred or are about to occur." The wrongful act, omission, or error could have been made by "any election judge, municipal clerk, county auditor, canvassing board or any of its members, the secretary of state, or any other individual charged with any duty concerning an election."

The law went on, "The petition shall describe the error, omission, or wrongful act and the correction sought by the petitioner. The petition shall be filed with any judge of the Supreme Court in the case of an election for state or federal office . . ."

For Nauen, it was ethically tricky. He couldn't seek out clients, becoming a sort of election law version of an ambulance chaser. But the Franken campaign could and it did. The campaign had all the data, data of ballots blocked, of the names on the ballots, of the leanings of the voters named on those outside envelopes. It had lists of voters who contacted the campaign complaining their votes hadn't been counted. They were all Nauen clients in waiting. So, once a Franken campaign representative reached a voter, permission was received for Nauen's office to contact the voter.

Within days, Nauen and his partners Bill Gengler and David Zoll had written their petition and memo and, with the help of the Franken campaign, acquired sixty-four affidavits of voters whose ballots had not been counted, even though it seemed as if they had followed the law. (Quickly, that number was reduced to sixty-one after it was discovered that, in fact, three of the petitioners' votes had been counted.) The "Nauen sixty-one" was born on January 13, the same day Friedberg was first interviewed. The Supreme Court instantly sent the matter to the trial court to include it in the election contest.

The Nauen group was a profound addition to the Franken case. It revealed just how many ways a vote could be turned down and how, even if an election official tried his or her best, there could be errors and omissions. A county worker, who accepted one voter's ballot in person, wrote in the man's voter registration number where his address should have gone. That ballot was rejected for not having a proper address. An older woman with debilitating Lou Gehrig's disease insisted on signing her absentee ballot envelope after her daughter signed the application for the ballot. The mismatch caused an election judge to stop the vote. Voters were registered, but poll workers didn't see their names on lists. Those ballots were denied. Anecdotes like this laid the groundwork for the notion that, in order to understand why a vote was turned down, each and every ballot had to be examined individually. Nauen's clients' affidavits and ballot envelopes proved that every ballot told a story. This "defensive" move by Elias would go on to deeply affect the ThreeJudgePanel, all of whom were new to election law. The Nauen mission was one they could get their arms and heads around. While the Coleman lawyers wanted to argue about "categories" of votes that were turned down by elections officials across the state during the recount, the Nauen sixty-one created a framework to understand that this case was about individual voters, and about hard evidence that showed their votes had been legally cast.

The Nauen effort signaled something else: Kevin Hamilton's litigation modus operandi. "Any military strategist will tell you want to triangulate into a kill zone, if you can," Hamilton said. "You want a cross fire going. You want to pin down the other side. You want somebody on one hill and somebody down here shooting in every direction." Elias and Nauen were on the hill. Hamilton and Lillehaug were about to march into court and commence the cross fire.

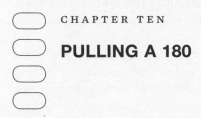

CHAPTER TEN

PULLING A 180

"I'm somewhat speechless and amazed."

The gavel banged. Pennington County District Court Judge Kurt Marben, looking remarkably accountant-like, read from a piece of paper in his hand. "The Court calls 'In the matter of the contest of General Election held on November 4, 2008, for the purpose of electing a United States Senator from the State of Minnesota, Cullen Sheehan and Norm Coleman, contestants, versus Al Franken, contestee.' This matter is on the calendar to argue the contestee's motion to dismiss. Is the contestee ready to proceed?"

With those formal words, at 2:30 p.m., on January 21, 2009, the day of Ben Ginsberg's arrival, the first pretrial hearing of the Coleman–Franken trial began. Marben sat on a high-backed brown leather chair in the courtroom normally used by Minnesota's Supreme Court justices, and the site of earlier Canvassing Board–related recount legal skirmishes. To his right was Stearns County District Court Judge Elizabeth Hayden. To his left was Judge Denise Reilly, a Hennepin County jurist. The previously anonymous judges gazed out onto two counsel tables filled with high-priced lawyers from Washington, D.C., Seattle, and the Twin Cities. The judges were aware of the scrutiny about to be placed on them, but couldn't have known that, as they sat in St. Paul, Senate Majority Leader Harry Reid was telling reporters in Washington, "We're going to try to seat Al Franken. There's no way that Coleman can win this. The numbers aren't there." And soon Reid would meet with Franken at the Capitol. There were many arenas in this ongoing game, but courtroom 300 was about to take center stage for longer than anyone had ever anticipated.

From the snazzy suits alone, Marben, who served as the presiding judge on this day, had to know he wasn't in Thief River Falls anymore. There were enough attorneys to turn the courtroom, with the long chandelier hanging from the skylight forty feet above, into a dandy basketball court. On this day, Franken had five lawyers on his side, Coleman, six. The three rows of courtroom benches were filled to capacity with journalists, campaign staffs, a school class, and curiosity seekers. This first argument was the result of Franken's motion to dismiss the entire case, which, of course, was not going to happen.

As part of Coleman's election contest petition, his side, represented at this hearing by Dorsey & Whitney's Langdon, essentially proposed to redo the recount and reopen the issue of all of the absentee ballots that had been rejected over and above those that were counted. The Franken team, with David Burman, a Seattle-based Perkins Coie lawyer, speaking, said Coleman's position was mere delay and it was time to make Al Franken the senator. The three judges took what was at issue under advisement, but all the players knew there was zero chance this case was not going to trial.

After these introductory arguments, Ginsberg wasted no time in cranking up the rhetoric outside the courtroom. He began what would become a daily, and often twice daily, ritual with Elias. Once the trial moved into full swing, there would be news briefings every day at the noon lunch break, and then again at 4:30 p.m., when the court day ended. In a corner of the corridor just outside the courtroom doors, tripods and TV lights stood permanently, and, at those appointed times, the two spokesmen from Washington, D.C., both used to staring into cameras, recited their talking points in front of them. Ginsberg didn't need any batting practice. On this first day of pretrial hearings, he swiftly went after the Franken side for arguing that no more votes should be counted, charging that the Franken legal team wanted to "short-circuit Minnesota law, Minnesota processes, and Minnesota votes." This from the man who, eight years earlier in Florida, doggedly fought to shut down a recount desired by Al Gore and, in early November, fought for a Coleman team that hadn't wanted any absentee ballots counted. Ginsberg trashed the Franken side for "boldly asserted legal sophistries." He said if the ThreeJudgePanel would just allow a reexamination of absentee ballots, it would mean "a significant increase of votes for Senator Coleman."

Speaking of any effort to circumvent a trial and take the matter directly to the U.S. Senate, Ginsberg growled, "It is something like a sand castle waiting for the next tide to come in, and what they're trying to do is to buck the case to the United States Senate . . . It's a fairly crass partisan maneuver on their part. It really is kind of an insult to Minnesota law and Minnesota courts." It was an entertaining maiden mouthful from him, and an earful for the reporters. After eleven weeks of Knaak and Elias, Ginsberg breathed new life into the recount theater.

While there was national attention shining on the trial, the media corps was fundamentally local. The two mainstream newspapers—the Minneapolis *Star Tribune* and the St. Paul *Pioneer Press*—Minnesota Public Radio, WCCO radio, Twin Cities news Web site MinnPost,[1] the Fargo (N.D.) Forum, and, some days, the commercial TV stations were fed party lines, grabbing quotes and, from time to time, asking pointed questions. The Associated Press's Twin Cities bureau, and sometimes CNN, covered for the nation. There was an even more significant outlet for Ginsberg and Elias, the Web channel the UpTake, a sort of psychedelic C-SPAN. The UpTake's political correspondent Noah Kunin was in the corner to the left of the courtroom's front door every day at noon and 4:30, sending raw video onto the Web, around the world, but more important, to Washington, D.C., where backers of both Franken and Coleman could watch. Coleman's local media relations aides viewed the UpTake as "a liberal blog" and had actually barred Kunin from all news conferences during the election campaign. Ginsberg couldn't have cared less about the biases of any outlet. His job was to send messages to donors and the Republican base, and the UpTake was a channel for them too. Kunin was a little slice of CNN, Fox News, and MSNBC right there in little ol' St. Paul. Ginsberg knew all too well how the twenty-four-hour news cycle had superimposed itself on this recount. Both sides were maddened by it and driven by it. Both exploited it and rode it.

The flattening of the news media landscape was apparent during the process. In the months of the election campaign and then the recount and election contest, Minnesota's largest newspaper, the *Star Tribune*, declared bankruptcy. Its local competitor, the St. Paul *Pioneer Press*, was part of a chain that also was on the brink of bankruptcy. Meanwhile, the national big-foot outlets that normally would have covered such a critical political story—the *New York Times, Los Angeles Times, Chicago Tribune,* and *Wall Street Journal*—rarely positioned reporters in Minnesota to produce firsthand reports, as they were cutting back too.

Small local and national Web sites took to competing with the newspapers, and they were treated with respect by the campaigns. If a new and small outlet in Minnesota, such as the fledgling news Web site Minn-Post, wrote a recount story, it had a solid chance of being linked to Google News, a *New York Times* blog, the Daily Kos site or, on a good day, the Huffington Post, and all before anything appeared in the next morning's newspapers. The campaigns and their PR staffs were supersensitive to this quick turnaround and the power of the Web's echo chamber, especially since many remote bloggers watched the trial via the UpTake. Some local reporters used the micro-blogging Twitter platform to send quick news items, although the judges did not allow reporters to use laptops or smartphones in the courtroom.

As the days wore on, Ginsberg's pithy comments intensified. The Three-JudgePanel had almost no face-to-face contact with him, but through friends, spouses, their clerks, and their own Web browsing, the panel members heard and read what he was saying out there in the hallway. Elias was always respectful of the judges, never commenting on their actions. Lawyers who spent time with Hayden, Marben, and Reilly said the judges seemed bothered by Ginsberg's pronouncements. The judges themselves said in interviews after the trial that they were not. But later in February, they sent a message to Ginsberg that indicated they were, at least, paying attention.

Two days after his rival Ginsberg splashed onto the scene, Elias showed his own stuff in the courtroom. For two months, members of the news media had witnessed his monologues, his staccato repeating of phrases for emphasis, his dramatic use of his big hands to form an imagined globe to describe the size of the "universe" of absentee ballots, or his long arms sweeping the air as if to swat away flies when denigrating Coleman legal arguments.

The scheduled event for January 23 was the hearing for summary judgment, an effort from both sides to convince the judges there was no material dispute about facts in their initial petitions or pleadings. The goal was to get the judges to simply rule in their favor and not take certain facts and issues to trial. Langdon argued for the Coleman side, Elias for Franken.

This was the day it became known, in open court nonetheless, that the Coleman side was in the midst of a tectonic pivot on the notion of counting absentee ballots and now wanted to do so in some new, never-before-conceived categories. Once against the opening of previously rejected absentee ballots, now, it seemed, Coleman was for opening them all, legal or illegal. Elias was altering his own stance too. Now that Franken was ahead, Elias was playing defense. Part of his task in this hearing was to begin to build trust with the three judges, he the inside-the-Beltway interloper, they salt-of-the-earth robe-wearing Minnesota judges. They also needed to be schooled. None of them had read the Minnesota election law statutes until a few days before, when they had received those life-changing phone calls from the Supreme Court.

Langdon, who had worked beside Roger Magnuson in Florida in 2000, told the judges that Coleman's lawyers now believed there were at least 4,500 previously rejected absentee ballots that needed to be examined and likely opened and counted. Langdon also declared there had been "widespread, pervasive, inconsistent application of the standard" in counting absentee ballots, which went to the critical issue of equal protection. If the judges believed that different voters' ballots were handled differently from others in different locations across the state, that could raise a constitutional issue. It was unclear whether that meant a new election was needed, but Langdon said that the number of ballots wasn't limited to 4,500. "The universe [of potential ballots to examine] isn't done yet," he said. It was changing in its form.

Langdon unveiled sixteen newly created categories for rejected absentee ballot envelopes. They were new to everyone in Minnesota. The law, Minnesota Statutes § 203B.12, subdivision 2, said there were four criteria that had to be met for a ballot to be accepted, but Langdon wanted the court to consider the validity of thousands more ballots using these sixteen new criteria. He needed to stretch the limits of acceptability. In this hearing, Langdon was seeking an order to include all of the previously rejected ballots, or "every rejected absentee ballot that substantially complied" with the Minnesota law, rather than keeping with past cases in which strict compliance was the standard. Langdon proceeded to explain some categories of ballots that should be counted, even though, for instance, a voter's application for the ballot couldn't be found, there was an obvious signature mismatch between an application and the ballot envelope, there was no address of the ballot witness, or a voter wasn't registered. It was a long list, and the evidence, of course, for all of Langdon's examples would have to be fleshed out at trial. Just because Coleman's lawyers pointed to one flaw in a ballot didn't mean there wasn't another one or two associated with the same ballot. While new to the topic, the judges expressed great skepticism from the start of Langdon's presentation.

Marben: "Of these 4,500 absentee ballots, how many of those did you ask the Canvassing Board to open?"

Hayden: "These votes that we're referencing right now, you said that they were such that you were unaware of them until you got into this proceeding. Why was that?"

Reilly: "Did you dispute [these new ballots] in front of the Canvassing Board? . . . The local officials didn't flag these 4,500 that you now are saying should be counted?"

Marben was troubled by Langdon's argument that there were ballots in this new universe of 4,500 that should be counted and opened because similar ballots were part of the 933 ballots that the Supreme Court ordered to be opened. The Coleman side didn't complain about the opening of those 933 in January; indeed, it was Coleman who had gone to the Court to establish a standard, and the justices responded with their divided, hybrid order.

No wonder Elias, sitting to Langdon's left, stared incredulously at the presentation with his jaw open, as if he were watching a high-wire act between two Minneapolis skyscrapers. He couldn't believe what he was hearing. He was almost pale. Upon Langdon's completion, Elias strode to the lectern and said, "I'm somewhat speechless and amazed . . . While I have read much of deathbed conversions, this is quite dramatic in its completeness." It was hard for the judges not to smile and more difficult for those in the courtroom's gallery not to laugh.

Revving up his emotions, Elias walked the judges through a lengthy, historical trip down memory lane, contrasting the Coleman side's strict compliance stance during the recount to its flip-flop now. "What they are asking you to do today is to declare unconstitutional the process that the high court in this state put in place," Elias said. "I would submit that not only isn't it an equal protection problem, but that . . . it is not within the authority of this court to declare the acts of the state Supreme Court unconstitutional."

Elias got more riled up about the 4,500 new ballots Langdon wanted considered. Or was it all 11,000 rejected ballots, legal or illegal? He noted that the Coleman lawyers sought the reexamination of only 654 ballots in their January 6 election contest petition. Now, seventeen days later, they wanted multiples of that many ballots opened. "That the State

Canvassing Board, that the county canvassing boards, that the county absentee-ballot boards, they were off not by fifty ballots, not by . . . ninety or hundred . . . they were off by a staggering number. These county officials got it wrong and they must have gotten it wrong big time . . . It's extraordinary . . . We have four piles plus the fifth pile. It turns out we were eleven piles short . . . I would argue it is too late, it is too late for them to change on the eve of the trial what their theory is regarding this case."

He spoke rhythmically, heading for crescendos to emphasize his points of view. It was tiring just listening to him as his motor kept charging and his outrage kept building. Mild-mannered Judge Marben interrupted. "Mr. Elias, in the sixteen categories, are there any of those categories that you feel summary judgment would be appropriate for?"

"Not one, not one," Elias said. ". . . If there are specific ballots that they believe were wrongfully rejected, then let them prove it at trial." Let them prove it one ballot at a time, he said, and that's how the Three-JudgePanel first got to know Marc Elias.

Something else baffled Elias on this day, just three days before the formal start of the election contest trial. The Coleman side proposed that all the voters whose absentee ballots had been rejected—whether properly or not—should be allowed to join the case just like the sixty-one voters represented by lawyer Charlie Nauen were joining the case. The difference in the Coleman approach was to make it a class action of all the allegedly aggrieved voters in the state, all 11,000 whose rejected ballots remained uncounted. This sweeping effort, which was quickly denied, proved Elias wrong, but to his great pleasure. Creating the Nauen sixty-one was an effort to counter what Elias presumed would be a gathering of individual voters by Coleman's lawyers. By throwing all 11,000 voters en masse into a group, Coleman's lawyers revealed they had no plans to engage in the difficult task of seeking voters one-by-one and to bring to the court via detailed affidavits or live testimony the reasons their specific ballots should be counted as Nauen was going to do for Franken. Instead, Coleman's side was focused on these odd, made-up categories. The Coleman lawyers must have misread or ignored the ruling from the Minnesota Supreme Court a few days earlier. When the justices sent the Nauen case to the trial court to include in the full election contest, the Supreme Court order read, "The relief sought in the petition requires a determination whether the absentee ballot submitted by each petitioner complied with the legal requirements for such ballots and was therefore improperly rejected by local election officials." Each petitioner, each voter was about to become the important factor in the trial. To organize such a specific voter campaign, and to analyze each voter's ballot and whether it fulfilled legal requirements, demanded impeccable data and aggressive hunters, something Franken had and Coleman apparently did not.

Norm Coleman was in the house—the courthouse. This was his case, and Friedberg, as a criminal defense lawyer, liked having his client there for the judges to see. They did notice him. Coleman was a former prosec'utor, so this was familiar territory, and the start of frequent appearances by the erstwhile senator. By being there regularly, it made it seem as if he had nothing else to do. Looking around the courtroom, he didn't see Franken on this first day, or ever. Franken decided he could use his time more wisely, preparing for what he thought would be his victory, but frequently checking in on the UpTake's video feed. His communications staff preferred Franken not be in a position to comment on the courtroom events either. Franken was briefed nightly by his lawyers and campaign manager Stephanie Schriock, who served as his sort of client surrogate. Over time, being absent from the trial seemed more senatorial than being present.

As Coleman looked around the courtroom, he should have noticed something more troubling than a missing Al Franken. Franken's counsel table was filled with three laptops, all fitted with wireless Internet antennae. Elias, Hamilton, and Lillehaug were wired to each other, to Franken headquarters, and to the Perkins Coie and Fredrikson & Byron offices. Through e-mails and instant messaging, the lawyers at the table received and sent suggestions. At Coleman's legal table, only twentieth-century yellow legal pads were in use where Friedberg, Trimble, and Coleman sat. It was a precursor of a technological deficit that was going to turn day one of this trial into a disaster for Coleman and his lawyers.

Opening arguments framed each side's positions and showcased the styles of each lead lawyer for the trial, Kevin Hamilton for Franken and Joe Friedberg for Coleman. Friedberg's self-deprecating approach jumped right out of the box when the cannonball of a man said, "May it please the court—everybody else—we've very fortunate that we have this methodology for settling the winner of an election that is a statistical tie. Were we in another country, we would settle it a different way, probably with guns and knives." He went on, "Our issues are simple, once they've been dumbed down for me."

His case was based on those categories of ballots that had been rejected, rightly or wrongly, echoing Langdon's deathbed conversion a few days earlier. Other ballots, uncounted, should now be included by the three judges, he said, because ballots like them had been counted on Election Night. This was their equal protection argument. Then there was a claim of double counting of votes, and the missing Minneapolis 132. He asserted that different standards were used by election officials in different counties when accepting or rejecting absentee ballots, and that too was a constitutional problem. "We don't have smart-people counties and dumb-people counties," Friedberg said. "This court can take judicial notice of the fact that people in one county are just as smart as people in another. That only leaves the variance coming from one thing, the eyes that look at these unopened ballots." Election officials screwed up, and that wasn't fair.

Friedberg minimized the differences between a right and a privilege, although case law—especially *Bell v. Gannaway*—had established absentee voting as a privilege in Minnesota. It also stood for the notion of strict compliance to state election law, not the "substantial compliance," the sneak-around-the-rules compliance, that the Coleman side now wanted. Absentee voters were required to follow the law, providing a proper address, a proper signature, a proper witness, and proper voter registration. Friedberg called those laws "guideposts," which they clearly were not. He attacked *Bell v. Gannaway,* and then he raised *Bush v. Gore,* noting the language of the U.S. Supreme Court stating that "each of the counties used varying standards to determine what was a legal vote." He said, "Exactly what we've got here."

His goal was to introduce somewhere between 4,500 and 5,000 ballots to the judges for their examination. Friedberg explained that to launch his case he planned to directly examine a witness from the Coleman legal team who would help him offer into evidence, one by one, the 5,000 rejected ballots now sorted into binders according to the new categories. "I remarked to somebody that that's going to take a number of days while I stand here and do a job that a trained monkey could do, but there's no other way," Friedberg told the judges. "It's going to be boring. It's going to be difficult, but that's the way we got to do it." The award-winning encyclopedia salesman in him shined through. He was likable, the epitome of common sense.

There was a structural problem to the Coleman argument on equal protection, which is guaranteed by the Fourteenth Amendment of the United States Constitution. The crux of the Coleman argument was that election officials applied the absentee ballot statute differently in different precincts or counties, and that the more lenient officials happened to be in more Democratic areas. This may have been true, but it wasn't *Bush v. Gore*–like. In Florida, election officials during a limited recount determined voter intent differently. The Coleman–Franken election involved decisions on Election Night on the legality of absentee ballot envelopes, not on voter intent. Minnesota had a statute detailing the four reasons that left absentee ballot envelopes open to rejection. Florida didn't have a clear standard.

Kevin Hamilton was the opposite of Joe Friedberg in almost every way. At five foot ten, he was inches taller. At 140 pounds or so, he was a string bean to Friedberg's apple. And Hamilton wasn't selling anything, Hamilton was explaining. "If you're looking at the lawyer and thinking he's slick, he could sell you anything, then he's not effective," Elias said of Hamilton. "Kevin comes across as genuine."

Fun-loving away from court, Hamilton was deadly serious on this day and, if they had not already realized it, he informed the judges that their responsibility was awesome. "Overturning the results of the recount, the hard work of the local and state canvassing boards, and the state Canvassing Board's certification of the results would be a breathtaking exercise of judicial power that should be undertaken only in the rarest of cases and only on the most powerful of evidentiary records," Hamilton said. "In an election contest, the contestant has the burden of showing that an election is invalid and that if the errors occurred, they were sufficiently serious to change the outcome of the election. The law doesn't require that such errors could change the outcome or might change the outcome or it could be statistically possible . . . The law requires proof that an error did in fact change the outcome of the election."

Hamilton went on to acknowledge that "this democracy of ours is not a perfect system . . . In every election errors occur." And if they did in this election, Hamilton told the judges, "Those aren't limited to precincts where Al Franken prevails or precincts where Norm Coleman won. Those kind of errors typically wash out across the state."

Unlike Friedberg, who rarely looked at his yellow handwritten legal pad, Hamilton frequently read carefully from his laptop-produced monologue, looking up to engage with the judges or to indicate something his legal assistant projected onto a screen, such as the Canvassing Board's certification of Franken's victory. In his deliberate style, Hamilton was, as Franni Franken came to call him, "the surgeon." From his opening argument on, he elegantly sliced the opposition.

Take, for example, his description of the Coleman side's flip-flop on absentee ballots. He called it, "perfect symmetry, perfect inconsistency, and a perfect contradiction." In mocking the possibility that Coleman wanted the judges to review 11,000 ballots, or 5,000, or 4,500, he said the trial "will likely extend until long after the snows of Minnesota have melted, the ice-fishing season is over, and our children are out of school for the summer." He proceeded to shoot down every claim that Coleman's petition made, stating that the hunt for the missing Minneapolis 132 votes "might indeed compete for the best-documented investigation in history." He wondered where the evidence was for double counting of votes.

"At the conclusion of the contestants' case, these claims should be dismissed summarily for what can only be described as a complete failure of proof," Hamilton said, making each syllable count, never cracking a smile or giving an inch.

For all the weeks he had been in Minnesota, all the work he had done on the absentee-ballot chase, the preparation he had undertaken for this moment, and all the direction he had given others, Kevin Hamilton had been pretty much behind the scenes. Elias was out front and center. Lillehaug was the local voice, and had made appearances in court and at canvassing boards. Chris Sautter was active and visible in examining the recounting of votes. Fifty-one-year-old Hamilton, arguably, had spent more time on the ground in the Twin Cities than any other outsider, having arrived on the Monday after Election Day and returned to his home in Seattle for only a handful of days before January 5, when Franken's victory was certified by the Canvassing Board.

A native of Edmonds, Washington, the son of an insurance broker and a French teacher, he attended the University of Washington as a political science major. His mother was born in France, and Hamilton is fluent in French. His grandfather was a prisoner of war in both World War I and World War II. By the time Hamilton graduated from college, he was already politically active and interned for a Democratic congressman in Washington, D.C. Before long, he attended Georgetown University Law School (a couple of years behind Ben Ginsberg) and became editor-in-chief of Georgetown's prestigious law review. With his Georgetown connections, Hamilton was hired to be a clerk to one of the nation's most progressive federal judges, J. Skelly Wright of the U.S. Court of Appeals for the District of Columbia. Wright was an activist desegregationist despite his New Orleans roots. After that gig, Hamilton went international as a law clerk for the Iran–United States Claims Tribunal, an agency that grew out of the 1970s hostage crisis at the U.S. embassy in Teheran and is headquartered in The Hague (Netherlands).

By 1988, married, with children, it was time to get back to Seattle, where this free-spirited Democrat joined the law firm of Perkins Coie, "Legal Counsel to Great Companies," as its logo states. The venerable Perkins Coie firm incorporated Seattle-based Boeing in 1916, and was off and running. In 2008, Perkins Coie represented such behemoths as Intel, Amazon, and Starbucks, the latter a client whose business Hamilton supervised. He led a unit of more than 160 consumer product lawyers at Perkins Coie. The other side of Perkins Coie was its election law shop in Washington, D.C., run by Bob Bauer, with Elias at his side. For Hamilton, the corporate–political marriage was perfect. "I like doing big cases," he said, and generally that meant taking on unions, or aggrieved employees on sexual harassment or race discrimination cases against his clients, or working on legal projects such as this, as listed on his résumé: "enforcement of noncompetition agreement involving silicone injection technology for buried power cable life extension." No wonder politics seemed so exciting.

In 1992, he left Perkins Coie to work for Bill Clinton's presidential campaign and by 1996, back in the firm's fold, he tackled his first recount, a congressional tussle in which the Democrat lost. The Republicans gained ground during that recount on the strength of absentee ballots. By 2000, Hamilton had crossed paths with Elias working on the Maria Cantwell U.S. Senate recount, in which she upset incumbent Slade Gorton without having to go to trial. And then Hamilton was one of the lead litigators in the protracted recount trial for the governor's office in Washington State in 2004. He won that one for Christine Gregoire. Absentee ballots were part of that mix. Hamilton was equipped for this election contest in St. Paul like no other lawyer in the courtroom. He had never met Franken, Schriock, or Lillehaug, but Elias made Hamilton the "air traffic controller" for all things courtroom.

His dual legal personality—corporate lawyer extraordinaire at times and Democratic election law soldier at others—was matched by the two-sided nature of Hamilton's demeanor. In court, as he displayed in his first public performance during opening arguments, he was as stern as a New England private school headmaster. Out of court, he became the Franken team's social director. He, Schriock, Elias, and other out-of-town Perkins Coie lawyers, along with press secretary Jess McIntosh, lived at the University Radisson Hotel on the University of Minnesota campus throughout the recount and trial. It was a nice enough hotel, but got old fast. With their work schedules, dinner often came near 10 p.m. While someone like Elias was happy to eat fried cheese curds at some local campus haunt, that didn't make it for Hamilton. Because they were regulars, the one restaurant in the hotel responded to a list of Hamilton's gastronomic and enological demands: better grade of steak, better wine list, preferably from Washington State or Oregon, and later hours. Most nights, the Franken legal team—with Lillehaug sometimes joining them before driving home to Edina—was the only dining party at the Radisson restaurant. Amid the wine, there were strategy sessions. Early on, Hamilton realized that Friedberg, not known for his meticulous attention to detail, was about to get outgunned. With thousands of exhibits about to be introduced, this was Hamilton's sort of case. "My litigation strategy is to be very polite, very professional, and very calm," he said. "Then I like to overwhelm the other side so they have no opportunity to deal with anything. I want them asking, 'What's next? A plague of locusts?'"

Friedberg's first plague of locusts was not Hamilton's doing. It was self-inflicted by the Coleman campaign. It began with his very first witness on the very first day of the biggest political trial in Minnesota history, and it was, to put it mildly, an embarrassment of the highest order for the veteran lawyer. It was also a shocker to the judges, who did not need a controversy in the first minutes of one of the most important cases of their careers either. On the other hand, it was a wonderful moment for Elias, Hamilton, and Lillehaug, who set their incredulousness aside long enough to giggle at the woes of their opponent.

As Friedberg had explained in his opening argument, it was his intention to walk a witness through the various categories of ballots that Coleman's legal team wanted to add to the universe of votes the judges might consider. In order to do that, he had to admit into evidence every ballot. To lay the foundation for this effort, Friedberg called as his first witness Kristen Fuzer, the political director of the Norm Coleman for Senate campaign. She testified that in November, pursuant to the Data Practices Act requests that both campaigns filed, Coleman headquarters received copies of absentee ballot envelopes from county officials statewide. Most of the copies of the ballots came via e-mail, Fuzer told Friedberg, but some came as hard copies, others via fax.

Friedberg: "Now, have you in the course of these events made recopies?"

Fuzer: "We tried not to . . . If they were e-mailed, we printed them off. If they were given to us, we hand . . . you know, filed them away." He asked her if the ballot envelope copies had been in her custody and control. She said yes, and he had no further questions. Elias had plenty, and he was ready to pounce. Elias posted on an easel a series of side-by-side enlarged copies of the same absentee ballot, but there were differences in these copies.

Elias: "Tell us for identification purposes whose absentee ballot this is."

Fuzer: "Elizabeth Stuart."

Elias: "OK, what are the differences as far as you can see between the two copies of the envelope?"

Fuzer: "It looks like a copy error. The bottom portion . . . where it says, 'Application ballot, signatures do not match' is cut off."

Elias: "Right, and that would have been the reason for rejection, right?"

He kept coming with ballot after ballot. The Coleman campaign had not taken good care of its evidence. It seemed as if they had never considered ballots as potential evidence. Hamilton, on the Franken side, had been thinking that since the moment he landed. Now the Coleman team was attempting to introduce the ballots, but with critical parts of the evidence tainted, or poorly copied, or even, in some cases, with Post-it notes from election officials redacted. Franken's campaign, which was data driven, scanned in every document it received, creating thousands of PDF files. It then set aside paper copies of all documents. It was, according to someone like Hamilton, who was an expert on complex litigation cases, common practice. If evidence was fiddled with by anyone, it was called "spoliation of evidence," and that's enough to get many cases tossed out of court.

Franken's lawyers warned the Coleman team at the summary judgment hearing three days earlier that the documents they were using as evidence were tainted. Over the weekend, Dorsey & Whitney lawyers frantically tried to redact any markings campaign staffers had placed on the ballots. The campaign had just this one, muddled set of ballots. It was a mess.

When Elias finished with Fuzer, Friedberg then moved to his next step with the evidence. He put a Dorsey & Whitney lawyer named Gloria Sonnen on the stand. She was the witness who was going to help him admit ballot after ballot into evidence by category. Before he could get going, Elias objected, telling the judges that the notebook Sonnen was using to introduce the evidence was filled with uncertified copies of ballots. "There is no reason to believe these are accurate records," he said.

Judge Marben, who was the presiding judge in what would become an unpredictable rotation among the three, overruled Elias's objection. Friedberg and Sonnen continued, reading off the name of a voter, his or her county, and placing that person in one of the categories the Coleman legal team had contrived. There was nothing more specific about the ballot, no details about the rejection of it, just the simple introduction of a person's name and the alleged reason his or her ballot had been turned down.

Elias, standing, and baffled: "Objection, your honor . . . I don't understand the process we're undergoing."

The judges didn't understand either. They began questioning Friedberg about markings on the ballots, and what they meant. Reilly wondered about an *A* that was circled on the top of a ballot.

Reilly to Friedberg: "Who put that on there?"

Friedberg: "I don't know."

Reilly: "Do you know what that means?"

Friedberg didn't, but Sonnen did and her answer was a bombshell. "These ballots were received by the Coleman campaign," Sonnen said, "and the people who worked for the Coleman campaign may have made notations on them, which is why we redacted information from these ballots before they were submitted to the court. In redacting, some of the redactors got a little overzealous."

Reilly: "So as I look at these exhibits, how do I know what was put on by the voter, the witness, or the election judge, or someone else?"

Elias: "Your honor, I renew my objection."

With that the judges took a recess, walked out the back of the courtroom, and headed down the hall to the conference room that was usually the home for conferences of the Minnesota Court of Appeals. They simply could not believe what they were seeing and hearing. The three of them were still getting to know each other, but they quickly came to their first unanimous decision. They were shocked at the way Coleman's side handled the evidence. Hayden, in particular, was thinking to herself, "This can't possibly be what it appears to be." At first, they thought, perhaps, a page or two, a ballot or three, had been poorly copied, but as Friedberg continued to question Sonnen, and different ballots didn't fit into categories and he wasn't sure of the markings, the judges had to call the whole thing off.

Back in the courtroom, Marben sustained Elias's objection "of best evidence" and told Friedberg that he was going to have to obtain and then offer originals into evidence. There went Friedberg's plan for the next week or so of the trial. Coleman's selection of his lead trial attorney so late in the process had not helped either. Friedberg thought the exhibits had been acquired by Dorsey & Whitney via subpoena. He assumed they were in the condition they had received them from the counties. He said months after the trial that he wasn't aware the campaign had marked them up. Knaak, who became less engaged once the trial started, admitted that he should have been more attentive to the ballots as evidence when he was among the lead lawyers in November. "That is the most nonplussed I have ever been in a courtroom in my life," Friedberg said. "Here are three judges in front of the world and they're not about to relax evidentiary rules ... After that first day, we never ever caught up." Also, in all his years, he had never seen five thousand "best evidence" objections upheld all at once.

The next day, the Coleman lawyers, without clean evidence to introduce in their category effort, trotted in a parade of voters whose absentee ballots had been rejected. At almost every turn, during cross-examination, Hamilton found some marking, some data, some problem with their ballots, whether it was a signature or an election judge's note that meant something that the voter-witness couldn't explain. Hamilton called them "pop bottle" witnesses because he blew them up. It didn't seem as if any of Coleman's witnesses would see their votes counted based on the evidence presented in court.

During a break, Friedberg, still recovering from day one, wandered over to chitchat with some reporters. He told them of an exchange he had with his wife of nearly fifty years the night before. "I went home late, hopped in bed, and thought Carolyn was asleep. She opened one eye and said to me, 'You got an ass-whoopin' didn't you?'"

For the next two weeks, as Friedberg called voters, county auditors, and officials from Ritchie's office to explain their ballot envelopes, what happened Election Night, and how election judges were trained, the trial took on a tedious sameness in court and out of court.

Every morning, Elias, Hamilton, Schriock, and McIntosh wandered down to the Starbucks in the Radisson lobby for coffee and a pastry. Lillehaug drove to St. Paul from Edina. Schriock usually embedded herself in the DFL headquarters not far from the courthouse, watching the trial on the UpTake and overseeing fundraising and media operations. The round-the-clock brief-writing operation was under way coast-to-coast, often with Kate Andrias in Washington, D.C., or Lisa Manheim in Seattle. Elias was on the phone with them constantly, or e-mailing them.

Friedberg rose early at his Minneapolis home, got to downtown Minneapolis, and met Ginsberg at the Marriott City Center around the corner from the Dorsey & Whitney offices. They sipped coffee and prepared for the day's events. Ginsberg served as Friedberg's election law tutor. Langdon worked nights, writing briefs in the Dorsey & Whitney offices. They met up with Trimble at the courthouse.

The judges had their *Groundhog Day* moments too. Hayden and Marben stayed in furnished apartments at a nearby high-rise in downtown St. Paul. Reilly drove daily from her home in the Minneapolis suburb of Orono. They were all at the Minnesota Judicial Center no later than 8:30 a.m. All of them worked at night on cases hanging over from their regular judge responsibilities.

For those first ten days of trial, the judges seemed a bit frozen in time. They wanted to give Coleman a fair shake, but they weren't seeing anything substantial coming their way. On February 4, on the eighth day of the trial but a full two weeks since pretrial hearings had begun, Judge

Reilly, who the lawyers believed to be the one pushing the other two, said something jarring from the bench. She blurted out: "The panel is going to make sure that every legally cast and wrongfully rejected ballot is opened and counted." It suggested that after these initial days of reading and figuring out election law, the judges had bought Elias's summary judgment stance and Hamilton's opening argument emphasis. Somebody would have to prove to her and her robed partners which ballots were legally cast or wrongfully rejected. As Elias and Hamilton liked to say, "Not could be," "not may be," but proved.

Reilly also spoke to the lawyers occasionally in chambers about Elijah. Unlike many of the lawyers in this case, she was not Jewish, but she knew of the role that Elijah plays at Passover. Elijah is a sort of imaginary spirit or unknown guest for whom a glass of wine is kept on the Passover seder table. At some point in the seder, the family's front door is opened for Elijah to "join" the feast. It is a symbol that strangers are welcomed at the table. The judges worried that in their chambers were lawyers, but no voters. In Reilly's view, the judges kept a place for Elijah in their conference room, a place for the voters in their decisions.

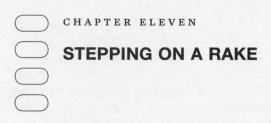

CHAPTER ELEVEN

STEPPING ON A RAKE

"I'm not familiar with all of the details."

> The times, places and manner of holding elections for Senators and
> Representatives, shall be prescribed in each state by the legislature
> thereof; but the Congress may at any time by law make or alter such
> regulations, except as to the places of choosing Senators.
> —U.S. Constitution, Article I, Section IV

Erudite Roger Magnuson had been decked by Supreme Court Justice
Paul Anderson's verbal punch in December when he mentioned his fantasy "trip to Florida." Marc Elias was about to take a Supreme hit on
his pet project: getting Franken his election certificate before the snow
melted. It was Elias's deepest belief, and not just a lawyerly fetish, that if
the Canvassing Board had concluded that Franken got more votes, then
the guy should be sent to Washington and seated in the Senate. The
Republicans might freak, but those fellows Reid and Schumer would
have something to say about Franken's status, even if it were provisional.
Elias believed Minnesota should not be represented by just one senator when the second senator-elect showed he had enough votes to be
seated.

No matter how nastily the Minnesota media and Republicans reacted
to the letters and petition Elias and Lillehaug filed on January 12, no
matter how clearly it seemed the state statute read that Franken wasn't
entitled to his certificate yet, Elias was psyched to make his case to the
Minnesota Supreme Court. The trial was recessed and the spotlight
shifted across the street to the State Capitol and the historic Supreme
Court courtroom there. He had argued in front of U.S. courts of appeals

and federal boards, but his appearance on February 5 was Elias's first in front of a Supreme Court at any level. His experience began in a Minnesota-enough way.

In late January, flying back from a short trip home to Washington, Elias read *Making Your Case: The Art of Persuading Judges,* a book by U.S. Supreme Court Justice Antonin Scalia and writer Bryan A. Garner. One of the tips in this primer on appellate practice is to prepare assiduously for oral argument, including scouting out the courtroom for items such as the adjustability of the microphone at the lectern. At six foot five, this was critical for Elias. During the trial's lunch break on Wednesday, February 4, in advance of his scheduled argument the next day, Elias decided to follow Scalia's instructions. Elias had never been to the Supreme Court's ceremonial courtroom on the east side of the Capitol. He didn't know where in the building to go or how to get there.

During the Canvassing Board hearings of December, Elias had the occasion, with an escort at his side, to traverse the twisting, turning tunnels that connect the State Office Building to the Capitol and then to the Judicial Center. As do many newcomers, he found the tunnel system to be maze-like, dark, and daunting. Getting to and from the judicial building required security-card access that was reserved for employees and media members. How would Elias, the man without a winter coat or gloves in Minnesota in February, get to the Capitol courtroom?

Elias wandered down the three flights of marble steps from the trial courtroom to the Judicial Center's lobby to find out. He approached a friendly Minnesota state trooper who was working a security detail in the courts building. "What's the best way to go over to the old Supreme Court chamber?" Elias asked the officer. "Oh, through the tunnels," the officer said. Go here, go there, turn there, twist here. "To be honest with you," Elias said impatiently, "thanks, but I think I'll just go outside and get there. I did this tunnel thing once before, it's complicated and I don't have an ID."

"You know what?" the trooper stated. "Hang on, just follow me." He escorted Elias out the side door of the Judicial Center and opened the back door to a black sedan. Elias hopped in and they drove the 200 yards or so to the Capitol's entrance, where the trooper parked the vehicle. It was an impressive event for Elias who was used to stone-faced Washington, D.C., security guards and cars being restricted by barriers set at extended distances from important government buildings. The two entered the Capitol and headed up to the old chamber, which was locked.

The officer nonchalantly produced a key and opened the courtroom for Elias, who was thinking to himself, "This is helluva good service." Elias entered the regal courtroom, scoped out the proximity of his lectern to the justices, figured out its adjustable nature, and got the general feel that Scalia suggested he should. The trooper wasn't heading back to the Judicial Center, so Elias thanked him and walked as fast as he could through single-digit temperatures, shaking his head about this display of Minnesota nice. He was so impressed that he would later share it with the ThreeJudgePanel as a way to endear himself to them and attempt to show that, no, all things Minnesotan did not confound him. Elias was always concerned that the ThreeJudgePanel didn't like him.

What Elias didn't know was that Knaak and Trimble were eating lunch that day in the third-floor Judicial Center anteroom they used for conferences and trial prep. From their window, they happened to see Elias hop into the sedan of a state trooper. They thought it was the car and driver of Governor Tim Pawlenty, one of the men whose signature Franken needed on that certificate. It got them wondering what that ride was all about. Later, Knaak and Trimble said they carried no deep fears Pawlenty was going rogue on them, but they did nervously ask Elias about the excursion and wondered why he didn't simply use the tunnels. Elias looked at them quizzically. He wasn't a tunnel kind of guy. Why not get a Minnesota-nice ride from a friendly trooper? The unfriendly piece came a day later.

Four justices sat before him. Eric Magnuson and G. Barry Anderson remained recused because of their Canvassing Board duties, and this time Helen Meyer, she of the controversial absentee ballot opinion, was missing because of a skiing accident; she watched the argument via video. As the hearing got underway, Elias was quickly shoved into a series of legal tunnels from which he couldn't escape. Elias told the panel that Franken was entitled to his election certificate under "federal law, under the United States Constitution and under state law...We are here in short because the governor and the secretary of state have failed to fulfill their legal duties."

Soon an interruption came from Justice Paul Anderson, the same fellow who had scolded Roger Magnuson. He wondered if Elias was simply asking the Court to abide by U.S. Senate rules, not state statute or the Constitution. Next, Justice Christopher Dietzen wondered where in Minnesota law did Elias see even the possibility of the granting of a provisional certificate that could be revoked, if and when the election contest flipped the victory back to Coleman. "It seems to me that this court lacks the authority to issue a provisional certificate of election," Dietzen stated.

Countered Elias: "The fact is the state of Minnesota has an obligation to participate in the federal scheme that has been set up under the Constitution, under federal law and to not opt itself out and leave this seat unfilled . . ." His passion shined through, but, no matter how closely he had read Scalia's book, there was nary a sympathetic question coming from the four justices before him. About twelve minutes into the argument, Justice Lorie Gildea, somewhat peeved and totally unconvinced, said, "Fine, then let's look at what the South Dakota Supreme Court did in *Thorsness v. Daschle*. I don't know if you're familiar with that case."

Elias shifted his balance. His shoulders tightened. He placed his hands on the table before him. He looked down at his notebook on the raised adjustable lectern. Elias prided himself in preparation. The Franken legal team prided itself on its research operation, with Kate Andrias in Washington, D.C., and Lisa Manheim in Seattle working around the clock to produce brilliant papers to wow judges. But Elias had never heard of *Thorsness v. Daschle*. He sort of knew where South Dakota was. He personally loved former senator Tom Daschle, who had served as a mentor to him during Elias's early years as counsel to the Democratic Senatorial Campaign Committee. Elias was thinking, "Senator Daschle means the world to me, but . . ." Neither he nor his super associate Manheim had read the case. Elias punted.

"I'm familiar with it, generally," Elias said nervously to Justice Gildea. "I'm not familiar with all of the details."

It turned out that Gildea had a personal interest in recount cases. In September 2008, just about four months earlier, her opponent in her Supreme Court reelection campaign had been, coincidentally enough, determined by a statewide recount, the first statewide recount since the Rolvaag–Anderson recount—until this Senate exercise. Gildea went on to explain that *Thorsness v. Daschle* stood for principles that were exactly on point to Elias's argument. "Who won? That's up to the states to decide," she said of the South Dakota case. "Who sits [in the U.S. Senate] is up to the United States Congress to decide. Why is that not exactly the right way to analyze this issue?"

Elias had little ammo on that one. As if he were talking with reporters in a hallway or at a staged news conference, he resorted to talking points, about how the state of Minnesota can't opt out of the federal family, about how the nation has important business to conduct. He sipped a glass of water. Why hadn't he known the *Daschle* case? More questions came from other justices, but it was time for Elias to sit down.

He was followed by Coleman lawyer James Langdon, his opponent in the earlier summary judgment argument in the trial court. Langdon needed no deathbed conversions here. Justice Alan Page, who had sat silently, with his right hand supporting his chin, during Elias's presentation, wondered why January 6, already past, wasn't a deadline for the state of Minnesota to send a senator to Washington. Langdon said, simply, because no statute says that to be the case. "Minnesota has chosen a two-tiered process to make absolutely sure that it gets it right, as to who has won," Langdon said.

To pile on, Alan Gilbert, the lawyer from the Minnesota Attorney General's office who helped write the second fifth-pile opinion to the Canvassing Board, stood up and said the state law is clear: the secretary of state and governor can't sign a petition until the election contest is over. Gilbert went one step further. In response to a Gildea question, he opined that a certificate couldn't be issued until the end of the appeals process. Franken could be waiting a long time.

Elias returned to the center of courtroom for his rebuttal and cranked down his bluster. "What we are asking for then," he said, in a cute pivot of his previous argument, "is actually something quite judicially modest, which is that the State of Minnesota opt in, not out, of the federal system of choosing senators."

The sideshow was over. The trial would reconvene across the street minutes later and continue to head toward determining the winner. Elias soon recovered, and also remembered. In her tripping up of Elias, Gildea handed him a lifeline that he wouldn't forget. Months later, *Thorsness v. Daschle* would raise its head again, and Elias would run with it.

As the trial's third week was about to begin, courtroom 300 looked like the disorganized warehouse of a chain of office supply stores. White and blue three-ring binders climbed higher on the judges' bench, on the clerks' tables, in the foyer entering the courtroom, and outside the doors of the private meeting rooms for each legal team in the back of the courtroom. As the piles of binders and documents grew higher, the trial grew flatter. As much as the Franken team pushed the Coleman squad to prove specific ballots were worthy of counting, there was little of that.

Mostly, it was county election officials and secretary of state staffers explaining their procedures. It was Lillehaug who said the trial wasn't like watching paint dry, it was like waiting for paint to peel. The Franken lawyers wanted to get this show on the road.

On February 9, Lillehaug complained in court about how "inefficient" the Coleman lawyers had been, and about how they had not answered written interrogatories, or legal questionnaires, that Franken's lawyers had been seeking since this election contest was first filed. Absent those interrogatories, Lillehaug said, Franken's lawyers couldn't adequately prepare for the witnesses Coleman's side was putting on the stand. It was as if Lillehaug's overt frustration poked the judges into action. In rapid succession, the trial became a series of decisions, scenes, and verbal skirmishes, all of which Coleman lost.

The next day, the judges came back with their first ruling that revealed the direction they would take on including more ballots to the universe. Their ruling came for the clients of Charlie Nauen, the Franken-linked lawyer who, with the help of the Franken campaign, had gathered up sixty-one petitioners, developed sixty-one specific affidavits, and presented to the court real evidence about each ballot. On February 10, Hayden, Marben, and Reilly ordered that twenty-four of those sixty-one Nauen petitioners should have their ballots opened. "Having reviewed all of the evidence provided by Petitioners in support of their motion, the Court determines that the Petitioners . . . have provided unrebutted evidence that their absentee ballots were legally cast and should be counted," the judges wrote.

In one case, that of Roxanna Saad, Nauen and Saad told the judges that Saad's voter registration card was inside the secrecy envelope of her absentee ballot package. This was the case for many voters in the election. The judges wrote that at a future date, when her envelope would be opened, if the registration card was in there, her vote would count. They also rejected counting many of the Nauen petitioners because there wasn't enough evidence to prove they strictly complied with state law. The first outlines of a road map were being drawn by the judges. "The strike zone became clear," Nauen said later. "If you want to win the case you've got to comply with the strike zone." If either side wanted to have more ballots included, this sort of nitty-gritty evidence must be supplied, the judges indicated. In one fell swoop, it sure looked as if Franken had just picked up twenty-four votes because of Nauen's motivated petitioners. If so, that was a 10 percent increase over the 225-vote lead Franken took into the trial. His lead was now up to 249. Could Coleman find 250 votes somewhere to overcome that margin?

On February 12, the judges conducted a hearing to make decisions about Coleman's proposed categories, and it was another down day for the Coleman forces. The judges, having shown allegiance to strict compliance of the law on Nauen's group of ballots, had established guidelines that didn't bode well for Coleman. This hearing was set to help the judges narrow the universe of ballots. Langdon attempted to loosen up the judges as they prepared to reduce the possible evidence and, thus, the scope and, ideally, length of the trial. He pointed to testimony in the first weeks of the trial that some counties accepted absentee ballots without checking whether witnesses were registered while others checked fastidiously. Some counties diligently compared the signatures on ballot applications and the ballot envelopes while others didn't have the time or inclination for such a review. In the documents Langdon filed before the hearing, he listed more than a dozen categories of ballots that should be accepted for counting, even if the voter didn't follow basic rules, because sometimes those illegal ballots were created "through no fault of their own." For instance, if a voter didn't sign his application for a ballot, his vote should count; after all, he still received a ballot and voted. Or, if a person sent her absentee ballot to the wrong precinct, her votes for statewide offices should be counted. Or, if an absentee ballot was cast by someone for whom there is not an absentee ballot application, his vote should be accepted. In this latter case, Langdon tried to explain that there could be a situation in which an absentee voter received an application in person at city hall, filled it out, handed it to an election official at the city hall counter, received a ballot in exchange, voted, but never signed her application. Days later, that lack of signature on the application is discovered and her vote is thrown out. That ballot should be counted, Langdon said, because of official error and because the voter substantially complied with the law, even if she didn't follow it in its entirety. "It's a gotcha game," he said.

As he spoke on and on, there was a collective eye glazing underway in the courtroom. The judges appeared busy taking notes. Elias watched the judges to gauge their interest in Langdon's ramblings. Hamilton appeared to be checking his e-mails at the counsel table. Langdon paused. There was silence. No snoring, just silence.

"I see you are not buying this, Judge Reilly," Langdon interjected, triggering laughter in the almost empty courtroom, and a blush and a hearty laugh from Reilly. "I thought I had a poker face," she replied, with a wide grin. "Nope, I don't think so," Langdon said. She kept laughing. "What can I tell you that will help you to buy it?" Langdon said. "Your concern is that there's a need for an application . . ."

Still with a smile, Reilly said, "My concern is that the legislature passed a statute, and I took an oath to uphold the law."

"And how are you not upholding the law, may I ask?" Langdon said, digging a deeper hole, even as the judge continued to politely spar with him.

"You know, typically, judges ask questions, and lawyers answer," she told him.

Other lawyers in the courtroom and the judges themselves had never seen or heard a lawyer admit defeat like that, and then playfully challenge a judge. A certain barrier was violated with his "you are not buying this," comment. He had, more or less, thrown in the towel.

When the court day ended, Hamilton and Langdon were packing up their respective documents at their tables, just a few steps apart from each other. Hamilton, a collegial sort who charms his opponents while slowly strangling them, turned to Langdon and said, sympathetically, "That was kind of interesting Jim, just from a trial advocacy point of view. I don't know if I've ever seen that done before. I don't know that I would have done that."

Langdon replied, "I don't think I'd do that either. I wasn't planning on doing that, but I was channeling Paul Newman."

"Jim," Hamilton countered, "you're not Paul Newman."

Langdon even had his movie stars mixed up. It was Robert Redford in a barely watchable 1986 movie, *Legal Eagles,* who told a jury in opening arguments of a convoluted murder case, "You're not buying this, are you? You're not listening to a word I'm saying. Guess what? I don't blame you."

Months later, in an interview, Langdon reported that he had never said that in court before and probably would never say it again. "It was just a snap judgment," he said. "I could read her face. She clearly wasn't buying it. Either I got stupid for a moment, or I thought this was my only chance to find out what she was thinking." The next day he and the rest of Coleman's legal team found out exactly what Reilly and her colleagues were thinking.

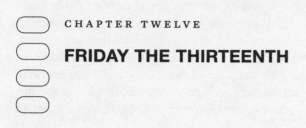

CHAPTER TWELVE

FRIDAY THE THIRTEENTH

"Welcome to the quagmire."

When they finally put their minds to it, Hayden, Marben, and Reilly knew exactly what they wanted to say. On Friday, February 13, the judges delivered a ruling that reduced Coleman's ballot universe by about a thousand but, more important, made seismic legal and political declarations that got the Coleman lawyers to thinking about an appeal, not a victory in this trial court. This first major opinion was more about substance than numbers, and Langdon was right: Reilly and her cohorts weren't buying his wares. They were, instead, eating up whatever Elias, Hamilton, and Lillehaug were selling.

Composing over a period of days and with relentless editing by all three (but especially Marben), the judges wrote: "Citizens of Minnesota should be proud of their election system, a system which has one of the highest voter-participation rates in the country...The facts presented thus far do not show a wholesale disenfranchisement of absentee voters in the 2008 general election...The Court is confident that although it may discover certain additional ballots that were legally cast under relevant law, there is no systemic problem of disenfranchisement in the state's election system, including in its absentee-balloting procedures."

While writing that they did not like the whole category idea, they did allow that some categories might be good guidelines for accepting validly cast ballots. They trimmed away some of the categories that the Coleman squad had created and kept only a handful in play. The judges were not impressed by Team Coleman's efforts to point out all the reasons that ballots were rejected. They wanted to see more of the proof that would enable ballots to be accepted. "Proving that the reason given by election officials for rejecting a ballot was invalid is not tantamount to proving that it was legally cast," they wrote. At first reading that sounded like a convoluted theory of physics, but that sentence went to the heart of the fallacy of Coleman's approach: just because any idiot could see that an absentee ballot was turned away incorrectly does not necessarily mean that ballot was statutorily legal. No, it came back to what Reilly said on February 4, and what the judges sculpted in the Nauen decision: Don't tell us about the rejections, tell us why each vote is acceptable. When you do, we will count it. In this Court of Dreams, if you prove it, we will count it.

Picking up on the road map first drawn with the Nauen decision, Ginsberg reacted relatively calmly in the early hours after the opinion was first released. "I view this opinion to say that they want testimony by ballot," said Ginsberg, "ballot by ballot. There are still many ballots very much in play." Knaak, in one of his final public statements, even said that the Coleman team was "very pleased . . . This is good news for the vast majority of Minnesotans." Going forward, however, the Coleman lawyers didn't take heed. Langdon said later that their early strategy of presenting groups of ballots by categories made it difficult to turn the proverbial battleship when the judges insisted on proving individual ballots. They simply didn't have the required resources either.

Nauen, who had become the king of hitting that so-called strike zone for Franken, never understood why Coleman's lawyers didn't begin to do a better job of proving ballots. "You're trying to win a trial, you're not trying to prove an ultimate truth," Nauen said. "The judges said to us, 'Bring it on.' Coleman didn't react."

Ginsberg did.

Maybe Ben Ginsberg realized he and Norm Coleman had lost and so decided to yell at the referees. Maybe he figured it was the only way to keep the fundraising going. After the February 13 ruling, the Coleman lawyers asked the judges to reconsider their decision. The claim was that some of the Nauen petitioners' votes would have been denied under some of the categories the judges erased in their February 13 ruling. (In response, the ThreeJudgePanel changed its mind on one of the Nauen petitioners and ruled his vote illegal after first including it in the count.) The bigger claim in Coleman's reconsideration motion was that many votes counted on Election Night and in the 933 ballots under the Supreme

Court process would have been rendered illegal had the February 13 ruling been in place. That was true, but it was too late for that now. Those votes had been counted. There was no way to know which votes belonged to which absentee ballot envelope. No one could uncount votes already counted, could they?

Beginning on February 18, after the judges refused to reconsider their ruling, Ginsberg freaked and started blasting away at the panel. He issued statements, he talked in the hallway outside the courtroom, he poetically dubbed it the "Friday the thirteenth" ruling, as if more a horror movie than a judges' opinion, and he launched the Coleman effort of questioning the legitimacy of the election and the competency of the judges.

He said, in a bold written statement,

> This fatal inconsistency [of the Friday the thirteenth ruling] serves to disenfranchise some voters while allowing others with the same ballots to have their votes counted. The judges will need to certify at the conclusion of the trial the number of "legally cast ballots" in the U.S. Senate election for each candidate. However, their ruling, as well as testimony in the trial, shows that they cannot do this as a matter of law since illegally cast ballots under their definition are included in the counts.
>
> The net effect of the court's February thirteenth ruling, and their decision to not reconsider this ruling, is a legal quagmire that makes ascertaining a final, legitimate result to this election even more difficult.

The next morning, the six lawyers made their daily chambers appearance before the three judges. They took their appointed seats on one side of the long, polished table. The judges had put on their robes in the room nearby and entered, with Langdon, Trimble, and Friedberg rising alongside Lillehaug, Elias, and Hamilton, as the judges approached their seats on the other side of the table. "Well, gentlemen, welcome to the quagmire," said Judge Hayden, in her best, acerbic vice principal voice. If anyone felt the judges were living in a bubble, reading and writing briefs and not following Ginsberg's and Elias's hallway shenanigans, they were wrong. Ginsberg's comments, as Langdon put it in military terms, "had taken us to DEFCON 1, threat level red." Mr. Ginsberg was in the doghouse.

Friedberg had been uncomfortable with Ginsberg going after the judges. It wasn't a Minnesota thing to do, and the statement about a quagmire and questioning a "legitimate result" came on a particularly odd day. While he had been in St. Paul for a month and in the courtroom almost daily, Ginsberg never was formally admitted to participate in the trial. So, at some point in mid-February, it was decided he should file what is known as a pro hac vice petition. Pro hac vice is Latin for "this occasion" or "this event," and it's a way for licensed attorneys from other jurisdictions to practice law in a state in which they have not passed the bar exam. Elias and Hamilton, for instance, had been admitted pro hac vice at the beginning of the case. It is considered a routine deal. Ginsberg happened to file his petition on February 18, the day he made the quagmire statement. The judges never ruled on it. It just sat there like a dead fish on their piles of motions and briefs.

The hits just kept on coming. On February 19, Elias pulled a reporter aside and said, "You watch, they said before they don't want to uncount votes, but they do. You watch." As he sat in one of the back benches of the courtroom before the start of the day's events, he was steaming. Elias had a policy never to discuss what went on in chambers. That was a zone of confidentiality. It's where he was his most aggressive in pushing the judges toward action and decisions. He sometimes viewed what was going on in courtroom 300—with voters testifying and county auditors droning through documents—as "the show trial." The court of appeals conference room down the hallway, with the six lawyers, the three judges, and their law clerks, was where the real pushing and shoving occurred. And it was in a chambers session that the Coleman team hinted it was poised to pull out of a major agreement that it entered into twice since December. That agreement—a stipulation, in legalese—was that the 933 votes counted in response to the Supreme Court ruling were part of the overall tally, and Coleman was OK with that. Coleman's lawyers had agreed to that late in 2008 and again at the beginning of the trial.

But on February 20, in a storm of brief filing, the Coleman lawyers, fulfilling Elias's prediction, filed a motion to undo the 933 absentee ballots that were counted on January 3 under the theory that the February 13 ruling turned some of those ballots illegal. Coleman's forces also sought a temporary injunction to halt the secretary of state's office from removing some privacy information from those ballots counted six weeks earlier. On January 3, the day when Poser broke into his "Franken, Franken, Franken" mantra, Mark Ritchie's troops, at Trimble's insistence, had meticulously marked the ballot envelopes and ballots of each voter. That was done so that, if necessary at some future date, a court could, in fact, attach a vote to a ballot and see if it was valid. Numbers were placed on the outer envelopes and ballots. All of the material was held by Ritchie's office. At some point, it was assumed the numbers would be erased so that no one in the future could match up the envelopes with the ballots and violate voters' privacy.

On February 3, when the trial was about a week old, and as the Three-JudgePanel was mowing down some details, the Coleman side formally stipulated to the results of those 933 ballots in the total recount. On that day, the judges ordered Ritchie's office to begin redacting those numbers from the envelopes and ballots. After all, the judges believed, those votes were immutably now part of the tally. That's what a stipulation meant, until now, that is. Now, Coleman's guys wanted out of it.

When Lillehaug, the typically zipped-up one, heard that Coleman's lawyers were seeking to renege, he almost popped his Brooks Brothers buttons. On the afternoon of February 20, he approached the lectern in courtroom 300. He waved a copy of the stipulation in the air, so the judges could see it. He read the full stipulation into the record, so the journalists in the gallery could get its full meaning. He noted that all of Coleman's lawyers had signed it. He glanced to his right to make sure they all remembered. Lillehaug's voice was cracking with anger.

> This was a settlement of a disputed claim in a case and the settlement was approved and ordered by the court . . . It doesn't make any difference whether you're in small claims court, conciliation court or whether you're a former United States senator . . . I think I know what's going on here . . . this is the next step in an attack on the integrity of Minnesota's election system and I believe a step toward attacking the legitimacy of this proceeding.

It was as much a wow moment as any in the recount. David Lillehaug, the coolest of Minnesota cucumbers, was turning into Marc Elias.

The judges agreed to keep the stipulation in place. Meanwhile, Coleman's lawyers began making "offers of proof," a legal maneuver to begin offering evidence into a trial in preparation for appeal to a higher court. The Coleman forces kept losing ground at every turn. On February 25, Coleman's supposed star witness, Republican election judge Pamela Howell from Minneapolis, was put on the stand to testify about alleged double counting in her precinct. She never saw it. She just heard about it. Under questioning from Lillehaug, she admitted she had been coached by the Coleman team, and that e-mails between her and a member of the Coleman team existed that had not been disclosed to Franken's lawyers. The double counting issue went nowhere.

On February 26, the issue of the 132 Minneapolis ballots missing from a Lutheran church went away too. The Coleman side continued to insist that the votes never existed and, if they did, no one knew how many. Lillehaug, the one-time chair of the Crosstown Conference of the Minneapolis Synod of the Evangelical Lutheran Church in America and a former member of the Church Council of the Edina Community Lutheran Church, had a Johnnie Cochrane moment. "If it doesn't fit, you must acquit," was Cochrane's legendary line to the jury about O. J. Simpson's alleged murder gloves. The only thing Lillehaug and Cochrane would ever have had in common was their law degrees, but with the trial a month old, Lillehaug produced a similarly demonstrative fit-or-acquit example. Minneapolis elections chief Cindy Reichert was on the stand discussing that missing white Tyvek envelope, the one supposedly marked "1 of 5," but that was never found.

"Your honor, I would like to approach the witness and give her a couple of Tyvek envelopes," Lillehaug said. "These are not from the city of Minneapolis. They are merely for illustrative purposes . . . I would represent that these Tyvek envelopes were purchased this morning and they are manufactured by a local company, Quality Park Products in St. Paul, Minnesota," Lillehaug said, turning to the judges, who were impressed and smiling. "And, by the way, Tyvek is the registered trademark of the DuPont Corporation." As he approached witness Reichert, about 15 feet away, he passed Friedberg, who was asked by Judge Reilly if he had any objection. "I would feel unpatriotic if I were to object," Friedberg said.

Lillehaug asked Reichert about her familiarity with such envelopes. Yes, she said. But the ones that were missing might have been bigger.

"The material is the same, yes?" Yes, she said. "Now, Ms. Reichert, I'd like you to take the two envelopes and put your hand on one side of them and one hand on the other and rub them together," Lillehaug said. She did so, the shhh-shhh-shh-shhing sound of the rubbing coming through her microphone. The recount had been reduced to an election official rubbing two envelopes together.

"How would you characterize the interface between the two envelopes?" Lillehaug asked robotically. "They are slippery," she said, with a grin. "They are slippery envelopes?" he repeated, raising the possibility that it was perfectly possible that someone carrying five Tyvek envelopes under his or her arm from one place to another might have had the misfortune of one slipping away from the others.

Later during the cross-examination, Lillehaug raised suspicion as to what exactly might have happened to that slippery envelope. He asked her about the post–Election Night tactics by the Coleman campaign to guard ballots, from Ritchie's office to the woman from Washington, D.C., at Mansky's office to, she testified, someone who began staking out the Minneapolis ballot warehouse. Lillehaug was implying that maybe it was those Coleman ballot guards who did something fishy.

Friedberg rose and said, for the first time, that the Coleman side was no longer saying those ballots never existed. "There were some ballots there. They were in an envelope. They're gone." So was another Coleman trial issue. Mark that up as forty-six votes for Franken. Even Ginsberg enjoyed it. "I think there are many things that are slippery," he said. "Envelopes might as well be among them."

On that same day, very quietly, Friedberg withdrew the pro hac vice petition for Ginsberg. The Coleman team got the chilly hint that the judges had no interest in seeing Ginsberg argue in their court or their chambers. On March 2, after five weeks of putting on its case, the Coleman legal team rested. They had proved nothing. They had lost ground. They were 0-for-February. The Franken legal team was poised to pile on.

CHAPTER THIRTEEN

MASTERING THE DATA

"This is a major lift ... This is a lot of bodies."

Once the Coleman team rested its case, Hamilton and Lillehaug ran up the score. The Franken organization called it Voterpalooza, and it was as lockstep an operation as everything else Team Franken had executed. It was their turn to put on their case, and they had votes to count. Not just the Nauen crew, which was up to forty-one votes for Franken out of Nauen's original group of sixty-one. Now, with all of the data Bechhoefer and Schlough and the other absentee-ballot hunters had acquired along the way, Hamilton and Lillehaug had more votes to prove. The procession began.

Each witness was met at the courthouse's side door. An aide for the legal team handed the witnesses rolls of quarters for the parking meters. Two lawyers were there to interview and prepare the witnesses; a file folder had been prepared for each witness. If the volunteers and lawyers had swarmed the recount tables in November with an approach reminiscent of a North Korean army maneuver, the Franken team was now a Ferrari, lean, fast, efficient. They subpoenaed, they followed up, they got voters to the courthouse, they interviewed them. If the voter was going to be a problem, they sent her back home, with a few quarters left over.

The routine went like this in court. Hamilton called a witness. He asked him the basics—name, age, address—and then went to the four statutory requirements of a legal ballot. Was the voter registered? Yes. Is that your true signature on the application and ballot envelope? Yes. Did you have a witness who was registered? Yes. And, then, as he did with a fellow named Chad Olson of Minneapolis, Hamilton asked if Olson had voted in person too.

"Didn't go down to the polls?'"

"No."

"Didn't vote another absentee ballot?

"No."

"And if we don't count it, then your vote doesn't count?"

"My understanding, yes."

Bam. Sliced, diced, scalpel bloodless. Hamilton kept proving that ballots should be counted, and doing it significantly better than Coleman's team, which needed more votes. It went on for a week, mechanical and repetitive, but productive. One day, with the head of elections in St. Louis County as the witness, Hamilton proved the legality of thirty-five ballots from Duluth. Those were the ballots that Fritz Knaak had incorrectly rejected way back in December, ballots that Nauen warned him were legal. They had been rejected for not having the dates on them when voters and witnesses signed. But dates weren't required on absentee ballots.

The only Franken lawyer who suffered a defeat in early March was Elias. After a month of silence, the Minnesota Supreme Court agreed with everyone else who had listened to Elias's argument: Franken was not entitled to his certificate until this trial was over and Governor Pawlenty and Secretary of State Ritchie signed the sheet of paper. The Supremes did hand Elias and Franken a gift, however. In shooting down his gambit of getting Franken to Washington before the end of the trial, the justices wrote: "No election certificate can be issued in this Senate race until the state courts have finally decided the election contest." State courts, not federal courts. If Coleman had any inclination to take this case into the U.S. courts, the Minnesota Supreme Court was telling him not to.

The case was winding to a close, but Elias still had tons of energy. Like a fit marathoner in the final mile, Elias made a move to ensure his victory, arms up, tape breaking. His legal endorphins kicked in on the weekend of February 20, when Team Coleman was still attempting to recover from the Friday the thirteenth ruling and still stuck in the category-of-votes quicksand. This idea, hatched then, bore fruit at the trial's closing argument on March 13.

At a meeting at the University Radisson on February 20, Elias turned to Will Rava, the Perkins Coie partner who had been the behind-the-scenes guru of trial operations, and told him he had an idea. As Coleman's case had unfolded, it seemed as if his lawyers had proven very few of the ballots they had admitted. Indeed, they had tried to admit very few individual ballots, following instead a broad-brush strategy to admit categories of ballots. Elias was preparing for the end of the Coleman case when the Franken side would urge the judges to simply dismiss the case because Coleman had proven absolutely nothing. Elias wanted Rava to develop the mother of all spreadsheets.

He wanted to analyze every ballot Coleman's lawyers had introduced as evidence and show, using the statutory requirements and other guidelines established in all of the ThreeJudgePanel's rulings, exactly how Coleman had *failed* to prove the ballots were legal. Every ballot meant about four thousand of them. Rava, another Harvard guy in the mix, a guy who usually practiced intellectual property law for Perkins Coie, sighed. "Marc, this is a major lift," he said of the task. "This is not something I can get you the answer to tomorrow or in three days. This is a lot of bodies doing a lot of work."

This was a project that would display not only the Franken team's mastery of the documents but also its mastery of the testimony. Elias wanted to stand up in front of the court and point to a giant spreadsheet on a screen and say, "See! See, your Honors, these guys have proved squat!" Elias also wanted to lure the Coleman side into rebutting his spreadsheets. If they did, if they fell for this trap, their entire case based on broad categories would collapse on its foundation.

Rava got to work, calling on the help of other lawyers at Perkins Coie and at Fredrikson & Byron, Lillehaug's firm. Rava also gave the project a title: "Marc's Big Idea." At this point, in late February, the legal team didn't have full transcripts from all of the trial days. Perkins Coie associate Manheim and others had been keeping exacting notes, but there was no room for error in this data smart bomb.

The UpTake, that C-SPAN of and by the people, came into play. All of the trial was posted on the UpTake. The Franken team could access the site's archive. Now, it became a legal tool. Rava had Franken staffers and lawyers watch all the testimony that was in the UpTake's publicly available archive. Using this video, they were able to compile an exhibit for the judges at the March 13 closing argument. This was not, by the way, the only time the Franken team relied on the UpTake. During the trial, a partner of Kevin Hamilton's was watching the UpTake in Seattle. He noticed that Hamilton had forgotten to ask a key question in the cross-examination of a Coleman witness. The Seattle partner e-mailed Elias at the counsel table in courtroom 300. Elias leaned over and showed Hamilton the e-mail. The question was asked and answered. But for the UpTake, it would have never happened.

On March 6, when Elias moved to dismiss Coleman's case, he walked the judges through the spreadsheets. There were eight of them, some with nineteen different columns, highlighting the "deficiencies" in Coleman's evidence. After he addressed the judges with this shock-and-awe data, he concluded with this statement: "It appears the contestant has produced competent evidence for nine voters." Just nine, out of thousands. Could that be true?

The next day, Hamilton's exchange with Ramsey County elections manager Joe Mansky produced the eeriest and most chilling exchange of the recount and trial. It defined the totality of Franken's resources and confirmed that Hamilton knew no hurdles in search of a Franken vote. The ballot that Hamilton sought to prove should be included in the recount was labeled Exhibit F2232. It gave new meaning to Deputy Secretary of State Jim Gelbmann's oft-repeated aphorism that "every ballot tells a story." Coleman's lawyers had long ago given up on convincing the panel that ballots should be evaluated in categories. It was too difficult to know if a ballot discretely resided in one basket of acceptance or another. Was the address right and the signature wrong? Was the voter's registration good, but the witness's bad? In their rulings and comments from the bench, Hayden, Marben, and Reilly consistently declared they would examine each ballot offered to them, evaluate it individually, and then determine if the voter strictly followed the law and if election officials properly rejected the ballot.

Exhibit F2232 lived in a category by itself. The exhibit was the absentee ballot of Donald P. Simmons, cast on October 29, six days before Election Day. In as polite, but lawyerly, a way as he could, Hamilton performed a noticeably monotone direct examination of Mansky. Exactly why the exchange was so sober was soon evident.

"Mr. Simmons properly completed the absentee ballot application form?" Hamilton asked.

"Yes," Mansky said.

"And properly completed the absentee ballot outside envelope . . . the signatures match . . . and the address matches?"

"Yes," Mansky said.

"Now, Mr. Simmons, he was a properly registered voter at the time that he cast the ballot, was he not?" Hamilton asked.

Mansky paused. He looked at some documents.

Hamilton repeated: "Do you know if he was a properly registered voter at the time that he cast his ballot?"

Mansky took his time. "I don't know that," he said. "The reason I say that is I looked up the voter record here. He has deceased status. What we don't know is — since this was printed out recently — if he was eligible on Election Day."

Mansky was among the state's leading election officials. Now, Hamilton wanted to get the story straight about Exhibit F2232.

"What we do know is that registration was updated on May 2008," Hamilton said. "We also know he was alive on October 29, 2008, because that's the date of his absentee ballot envelope. You're raising the point that under status [in state records] it says, 'Deceased.' So, the question here is, did he die in that narrow window between October 29 and November 4?"

Mansky: "That is correct."

Hamilton: "If he passed away prior to November 4, then his ballot wouldn't be eligible to be counted?"

Mansky: "That's correct."

Hamilton: "Because you have to be alive on Election Day."

Mansky: "You do, yes."

Hamilton: "As long as you're alive at some point on Election Day, your ballot should count?"

Mansky: "Yes."

Hamilton: "So what we need to figure out is the time or date of death."

Mansky: "Correct."

The judges did not interrupt. Friedberg did not object.

Hamilton, being his surgical self, reviewed the criteria with Mansky for an acceptable vote, even that of a dead man: signatures match, address matches, witness registered, Simmons was registered, and he didn't vote at the polls. All good.

"So the only thing we're missing is the date of death," Hamilton said.

"Right," Mansky said.

"OK, let's move on to Exhibit F2233," Hamilton said, and the quest for other votes continued. Watching the trial on the UpTake, a member of Franken's rapid response team raced from DFL headquarters to the State

Department of Health, the custodian of death certificates. To get Simmons's vote to count, Hamilton needed to prove that he was breathing at some point during voting hours of November 4. When did Donald Simmons die? Would his vote count? Would democracy echo from his grave?

Donald Simmons died on Thanksgiving Day, November 27. He was sixty-five years old, a former security supervisor for a homeless shelter. He was awaiting a liver transplant. Simmons and his wife, Janet Troutman-Simmons, moved to St. Paul in 2006 from Springfield, Massachusetts. He was already ill and the couple wanted to be closer to their children, who lived in the Twin Cities. He was a jazz lover. On October 29, knowing he was too ill to get to the polls, Simmons voted via absentee ballot. The election was important to him. As an African-American, he wanted to vote for Obama.

Franken's thorough absentee ballot chase found its way to Simmons's home in St. Paul. The legal team examined his rejected ballot and saw no reason why it should not have been accepted. They mailed a subpoena to him in early March in hopes that he would testify at the trial. When he didn't respond, a Franken lawyer telephoned. His widow answered and informed the lawyers that her husband had died, but she wondered why his ballot was rejected by election officials. She thought he followed all the rules. As Mansky sat there in the courtroom, he couldn't, for the life of him, understand why Simmons's ballot wasn't counted either. It was a mistake.

After lunch, Mansky was back on the stand. Hamilton offered another exhibit into evidence, F3007, Simmons's just-acquired death certificate. Hamilton showed it to Mansky.

"Mr. Mansky, this is the same individual who we were discussing before the break, correct?"

"That is correct," Mansky replied.

"Can you read the name and the date of death of this voter?"

"The person's name is Donald Peter Simmons and the date of death was November twenty-seventh, twenty-oh-eight," Mansky read.

"OK, November twenty-seventh," Hamilton repeated. "So, he was alive on Election Day. His vote should count?"

"Yes," Mansky said.

A month later, when the three judges ordered properly cast ballots opened, Simmons's was included. Team Franken's ballot chase knew no boundaries. No ballot told a story as powerful as Donald Simmons's.

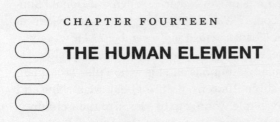

CHAPTER FOURTEEN

THE HUMAN ELEMENT

"You're going to have some errors in the process."

The trial ended, with closing statements from Hamilton and Friedberg on March 13, another Friday the thirteenth. In many ways, there was nothing new to be said, except that Hamilton's deliberate, concise indictment of Friedberg's and Coleman's case was devastating because it shot down everything in one place. He reprised "Marc's Big Idea," but with a new development: the Franken team believed it had established that 252 ballots were valid, plus there were the Nauen votes, now totaling forty-seven. So, "the Surgeon" said, about three hundred more votes should be counted.

"This court presided over what is undoubtedly the most comprehensive election contest in history," Hamilton said. "One hundred thirty-four witnesses testified, thirty-eight county and city officials appeared, and over 2,182 exhibits, in countless binders, have been admitted into evidence and piled up like snowdrifts on the bookshelves, tables, and floors of this courtroom. It's clear that contestants have utterly failed to prove their case ... This effort to overturn the result of the hand recount and the certified result of the recount canvass should be rejected ... Al Franken received the highest number of votes in this election. Al Franken is Minnesota's senator-elect. He is entitled to the Certificate of Election." It didn't get anymore concise than that.

Friedberg countered with Coleman's issues, but, by now, it was a fait accompli that an appeal was coming, that the missing Minneapolis votes were no longer an issue, that the double counting of votes hadn't been proved, that Nauen's forty-seven votes had increased the lead, that the judges hadn't bought any equal protection issues.

After a brief recess, however, something extremely Minnesotan occurred. They all stood for a group picture, judges Elizabeth Hayden, Kurt Marben, and Denise Reilly—robed and standing by their chairs—and the court clerks, the court reporter, and the two legal teams standing beneath them, everyone smiling for the history books. An employee of the state courts system took the photos. Noting that in forty-five years of lawyering, nothing like that had ever happened before, Friedberg, seventy-two, said, "This *must* have been an epic trial."

After that picture taking, there was still one final legal proceeding. It had to do with evidence that had been in dispute. The courtroom was empty save for the lawyers, the clerks, the judges, and some hangers-on. Franken lawyer David Lillehaug offered boxes and boxes of evidence. Friedberg, to make the event official, objected. Hayden looked over her red-framed reading glasses. "That will be overruled," she said, with a slight, tired, and final smile.

Many key rulings were issued in this case, but none was as scolding and belittling of the Coleman case as the ThreeJudgePanel's March 31 ruling. In this ruling, the judges ordered election officials statewide to deliver to them about four hundred ballots for examination and potential counting. What made the eighteen-page unanimous opinion powerful was that it indisputably knocked Norm Coleman out of any chance of winning the recount on the numbers. Of the four hundred ballots the judges ordered in from the counties for counting, 202 were from Hennepin, Ramsey, and St. Louis counties: Franken country. Included in those four hundred ballots were the forty-seven from Nauen-represented Franken voters that the judges had already ordered opened.

The judges wagged their fingers at Coleman's lawyers for not bringing in enough evidence. "Each party knew or should have known the scope of the Court's review... before [Coleman's lawyers] rested their case-in-chief... [Coleman's lawyers] must meet their burden of proof... The Court gave both parties every opportunity to meet their burden. The Court did not impose time limits on the length of the election contest nor did it limit either party's opportunity to call witnesses or introduce evidence."

On all of their rulings, Reilly was the ideas person, with a new view of things daily. Hayden was the overall crafter of most of the orders. Marben was the details editor. The goal, however, with the whole world watching, Hayden said later, was for their rulings to be based on "common sense and wanting to make sure it was always understandable."

But one reader didn't get it. "The court has reached an unprincipled decision," said relentless Ben Ginsberg. "The court was subsumed with its own logic . . . We believe the court is wrong in their entire standards of review . . . We just think they're wrong to sweep the problems of this election under the rug."

The last time the secretary of state's office counted votes, Gary Poser performed his "Franken, Franken, Franken," chant. It was time to clear his throat and deliver another rendition. April 7 arrived, the first time the two sides met in the spring, making it the third season of the year touched by the recount and election contest. Time to open the votes ordered a week earlier by the judges. Courtroom 300 was filled, sort of like graduation day. The judges invited some of their relatives — spouses and parents. Mark Ritchie was there. For the first time in the entire trial, there was enhanced security, with a metal detector for all those entering, an idea that came from the judges. Their concern grew from a comment that National Republican Senatorial Committee chairman John Cornyn made to *Politico* in Washington, threatening "World War III," if somehow the Democrats tried to seat Franken before Coleman got a chance to appeal. Maybe there was a nut out there who followed Cornyn's comments. Troopers and the magnetometer were there, just in case.

There sat Gary Poser again, the designated counter in this ongoing count, recount, absentee-ballot count, and absentee-ballot count 2.0. He sat at a table in front of and below where the ThreeJudgePanel sat during the trial. The mountain of loose-leaf binders was gone. The room looked back to its Supreme Court norm. With Elias and Trimble monitoring Poser's opening of the ballots, Franken kept putting more points on the scoreboard. In the end, 351 ballots were opened, and Franken won 198; Coleman, 111; all the long-forgotten others, 42. Six days later, the judges beat up Coleman even more. In their sixty-eight-page final opinion, they didn't agree with Coleman's case for even one sentence.

The judges: "The Court has received no evidence or testimony to support a finding of wholesale disenfranchisement of Minnesota's absentee voters . . ."

The judges again: "The Court did not hear testimony from any precinct election judge that they duplicated damaged ballots and failed to mark the duplicates or the originals." The missing 132 ballots were also "properly counted."

On Coleman's constitutional claim of equal protection, the three wrote: "Errors or irregularities identified by [Coleman] in the general election do not violate the mandates of equal protection." Later the judges acknowledged that some votes were handled differently in different counties and precincts, but, "Equal protection . . . cannot be interpreted as raising every error in an election to the level of a constitutional violation . . . Equal protection does not guarantee a perfect election . . . Equal protection does not demand rigid sameness." Finally, on this matter the judges went right at Coleman's assertion that some illegally cast ballots should be opened and counted now because some illegally cast ballots were opened and counted on Election Day. "Following Contestants' argument to its conclusion, the Court would be compelled to conclude that if one county mistakenly allowed felons to vote, then all counties would have to count the votes of felons." The judges called that "an absurd result."

For Hayden, Marben, and Reilly, it was the end of the road. For four months, they were unanimous in every decision. They meant it to be that way, and worked at it, but found they were of the same mind. "For me it was a sabbatical, being immersed in one project," Reilly said later. "It was like being on a little boat with two strangers at the very beginning. It didn't take long before the two strangers became dear and trusted friends and colleagues." The judges returned to their lives as daily jurists, with Marben riding his circuit from Thief River Falls to Crookston in northwestern Minnesota, Reilly returning to the grueling days of Hennepin County drug court, and Hayden deciding soon to retire. They had become deep friends, hugging when they greeted each other, legal soldiers in the recount foxhole.

The three judges may have been finished with their work, but Coleman was not. He took the case to its final resort, back to the Minnesota Supreme Court, and he filed his appeal on April 20. Franken kept raising money and preparing, but as health care reform, an issue important to him, began moving through the Senate, he had to stay on the sidelines. If it was frustrating to him, it was maddening to the Democratic leadership in Washington. On April 28, two weeks after the panel ruled, Pennsylvania Senator Arlen Specter announced he was jumping from the Republican caucus to the Democratic caucus. Franken became the sixtieth Democratic vote in waiting.

After six weeks of being away from courtroom 300, the same old gang reassembled for the Supreme Court argument, the final legal argument of the recount, a case that had now touched its eighth month. Friedberg argued for Coleman, and the five justices were not kind at all.

Friedberg began with the argument that votes should have been counted for "substantially" complying with state law. "What does substantial mean?" acting Chief Justice Page asked tartly. He was a strict compliance guy. Dietzen was all over Friedberg for the poor quality of the offers of proof the Coleman side presented once they decided to appeal. Gildea scolded Friedberg for not being more specific when he asserted that the ThreeJudgePanel ruled that all evidence of how election officials behaved on Election Night was excluded.

"Where did the contest court so rule?" Gildea asked.

"It ruled right from the beginning . . ." Friedberg tried to say.

Gildea, impatiently: "I apologize, when I say where I mean where, page, citation in the record."

Justice Helen Meyer dived in, again anxious for Friedberg to explain the lack of evidence in the court below. "Where is evidence from the overwhelming majority of counties and cities?" she asked. Friedberg countered that "twenty-six or twenty-seven" county auditors testified. "There are eighty-seven counties," Meyer snapped. "You didn't even call witnesses from a majority of Minnesota counties." There wasn't a sympathetic ear on the bench this day.

Elias was next. He was prepared, having undergone three rigorous moot court arguments in advance. The guy had it easy. He displayed a mastery of the topic area that even had Coleman spellbound, or stunned. The last time Elias had appeared before the Supreme Court, Justice Gildea tripped him up big-time with a case including former South Dakota Senator Tom Daschle, an Elias pal. As if doing Elias a favor, acting Chief Justice Page threw him a hanging curveball. Page wondered if the Supreme Court even had jurisdiction over who gets seated in the U.S. Senate. Elias embraced the moment.

"That is indeed the holding of a case from South Dakota of Senator Daschle, then Congressman Daschle's first election," Elias said, with glee, as he looked over to his left at Gildea. Their eyes met. He had finally read that darned case. She smiled. He said it was "no secret" he had spoken to the Court about this before and, as he said with a lilt in his voice, "The court spoke loud and clearly on that point," he looked at her again. Their point in March was they could decide who was the winner, but it would be the Senate that would decide who gets to Washington.

This time, Gildea was an ally. She wanted to know from him how she could know who received the most legally cast votes. This allowed him to talk of his "frustration with the appellants' case" and how "every ballot tells a story." This was not a case for "broad brushes" but for specifics.

Gildea: "So your point is: 'Look, it was his burden to prove it, he didn't prove it, he can't stand up here now and speculate.'"

Elias: "This is correct your honor."

Game over, with only Justice Paul Anderson to sum it up. Coleman saw "some chaos" in the absentee-ballot universe, Anderson opined. Franken saw some "intelligent design," a certain order. There may have been "aberrant stars," Anderson allowed, but, otherwise, all was right with this electoral world. Elias nodded.

On that first day of June, Franken, who never made one appearance at any proceeding, was back at his Minneapolis townhouse as Coleman sat in the courtroom and watched his case fade away. When would Franken get to be the sixtieth and decisive senator?

June was fading away, and still there was no word from the Minnesota Supreme Court. Election Day 2008 was a distant memory. Nearly a month had passed since Elias and Friedberg summed up their cases in courtroom 300, and those same five justices who seemed so divided in December remained mum. It was hard work. Justice Paul Anderson, the chattiest member of the court, privately joked to people around the Judicial Center that he and his colleagues would deliver something "by Canada Day." Only a trivia buff would know that was July 1. The most important aspect of why there was still no decision was this: "Some of us were absolutely sure we could make this unanimous," Anderson said, a sentiment that echoed the ThreeJudgePanel. "I love Minnesota . . . I didn't want to embarrass Minnesota."[1] The draft of the justices' opinion bounced back and forth from chamber to chamber for weeks.

Elias returned to his eighth-floor Perkins Coie office, the one with the photograph of Giants Stadium, the office within walking distance of the White House. Friedberg returned to his downtown Minneapolis office, short walks from the county and federal courthouses, taking calls from clients about the wisdom of plea deals. Franken prepared for what seemed to be his new job, having learned of the committees to which Senate Majority Leader Reid was to appoint him; among them the Judiciary Committee and its impending hearings for President Obama's Supreme Court nominee, Sonia Sotomayor. Coleman traveled a bit at his new job consulting for the Republican Jewish Coalition. He pondered running for governor in Minnesota in 2010, but didn't.

In an election, recount, and trial that relied on new media and the Internet for the rapid dissemination of much news and some misinformation, it was fitting that word of an impending Supreme Court decision came first on Twitter. On June 17, a writer for the conservative-leaning Politics in Minnesota tweeted, "Two sources: Supreme Court ruling on U.S. Senate race to arrive tomorrow." For a Court that relishes its secrecy, the leak was an annoying distraction. Court staffers scrambled to investigate. Other news organizations chased the rumor. The justices were furious. The ruling, in fact, wasn't completed. It wasn't even imminent.

Justice Anderson said that he was a subscriber to the old adage, "'My letter would have been shorter if I had more time.' We took the time to really narrow it, and make it precise," he said of the final opinion that once filled fifty pages, but was significantly trimmed when delivered. "There was some pressure to get it out," he said, "but there was pressure to get it right."

They beat Canada Day by a full eleven hours. At 1:03 p.m. on June 30, 2009, the Minnesota Supreme Court released its decision. Norm Coleman didn't win a syllable of it. The five justices—including Gildea and Dietzen, the two who had given campaign contributions to Coleman in years past—upheld everything the ThreeJudgePanel decided. It was signed per curiam, which in legalese and Latin means "by the court," or total agreement, one voice. The divided court of December had made up and unified.

"You are going to be frustrated in your attempts to figure out who wrote it," Anderson said later, "because it was written, really, by the whole court...We all came to our decision in different ways...This is the most per curiam opinion I've ever participated in."

The five justices shot down Coleman's five issues: whether the trial court violated Coleman's right to due process by forcing strict compliance to absentee ballots; whether his right to equal protection was violated because of some differences among counties in applying their absentee-ballot standards; whether the trial court excluded important evidence; whether the court made a mistake in refusing the precinct inspections that Trimble so badly wanted at the start of the trial; and whether Hayden, Marben, and Reilly were wrong when they included the 132 missing Minneapolis votes in the recount. The five justices emphatically ruled, "No, no, no, no and, furthermore, no."

On some fundamental issues, the justices were clear. "The distinction between errors by voters and errors by election officials is an important one," they wrote. Quoting an earlier Minnesota Supreme Court case, they declared that if a voter complies with the law, his vote should not be rejected because of the mistakes of an election official. There went the entire Coleman argument that somehow "the rules were changed in the middle of the game."

As to whether Coleman's right to equal protection was violated because different jurisdictions sometimes evaluated absentee ballots in differing ways, the high court, citing federal law, wrote that such discrimination must be "intentional or purposeful." There was no evidence of that in the trial.

Still, in a restrained scolding to election officials and to the Minnesota absentee balloting process, the Supreme Court wrote in a footnote:

> Although we affirm the trial court's conclusion that any differences in the application of the statutory standard by the trial court and by election officials on election day and during the manual recount are not of constitutional magnitude, we do not suggest that any such differences are inconsequential and need not be addressed. It is impossible to eliminate all variation in a process administered at thousands of locations around the state by thousands of people, many of them temporary volunteers. To the extent that this case has brought to light inconsistencies in the administration of absentee voting standards, we are confident that the appropriate officials in the other branches of government understand that efforts should be made to reduce those inconsistencies, even though they were not proven to be of constitutional magnitude.

In other words, as Anderson put it, "It's an election, it's a human institution . . . It is a human system and so you're going to have some errors in the process." In other words, legislature, take a look at this. We've got a problem, but it is not chaos.

The Minnesota Supreme Court also took on the *Bush v. Gore* implications of the Franken–Coleman case. It was, in the view of legal scholars, the first significant interpretation of *Bush v. Gore* in a U.S. court since 2000. The five Minnesota justices noted a key difference on the matter of voter intent. In Florida, when election officials conducted their recount, they were basing voter intent on ballots that were already opened. That is, what did a "dimpled chad" or "a hanging chad" mean? In Florida, there was no statewide standard to direct election officials on how to determine a voter's intent. In Minnesota, voter intent was not in question, but rather, whether an absentee ballot return envelope fulfilled clear state standards. No election official in Minnesota knew what was inside those absentee envelopes. "In summary, we conclude that *Bush v. Gore* is not applicable," the justices wrote.

A reader then came to the fateful words on page thirty-one. "We affirm the decision of the trial court that Al Franken received the highest number of votes legally cast and is entitled under Minn. Stat. § 204C.40 (2008) to receive the certificate of election as United States Senator from the State of Minnesota."

The opinion, as one elections law scholar put it, was "virtually unassailable."[2] Another scholar gushed about the Minnesota Supreme Court's opinion, calling it "one of the most legally significant resolutions of a disputed election in U.S. history . . . [I]t is the first appellate court resolution of a major statewide election after *Bush v. Gore* . . . This unanimous affirmance of the unanimous trial court will stand as a model for how hard-fought battles over the winner of a high-stakes election should be handled."[3]

But what of the politics of it all? Surely the Supreme Court justices discussed the impact of their ruling giving the seat to Franken. Surely they considered handing the U.S. Senate to the Democrats. No, Anderson said. No. He said he received an e-mail from a friend soon after the ruling. "I would love to have been a fly on the wall during your [decisive] conferences because the political discussions must have been fascinating," the correspondent wrote. Anderson said, "I read that and said, 'Boy, there were none.' We never talked politics at all, that's not the way we do it, folks."

Coleman's fight was over. He had prepared for this day, with one statement ready if he somehow won the Court's ruling and another one if he lost. If a split decision came down, there was uncertainty as to how he would respond, but this was no split decision.

Coleman quickly scanned the decision on the screen of his laptop in the living room of his St. Paul home. "Crap," he muttered, saying later, somewhat ruefully, "I thought we had a better case." But someone in the room with him said, "I can tell you that the calm spread across his face" the moment Coleman digested the opinion. A conference call followed with his lawyers, there was even some parsing excerpts of the opinion, searching desperately for anything that might be encouraging, that might keep his options open for an appeal to the U.S. Supreme Court. But, said one of the participants on the call, it felt as if they were "performing CPR on someone for five hours even though you knew he was dead." Coleman would have none of it. "What are you reading, guys?" Coleman asked, the lawyer in him knowing there was no wiggle room.

In another time zone, Stephanie Schriock received a phone call that interrupted a meeting in Helena, Montana, with Governor Brian Schweitzer. David Lillehaug's caller ID number showed. Schweitzer knew what that meant and politely told her she should take the call. She was soon on a conference call with the Franken lawyers, figuring out how to respond to the Supreme Court decision, when an e-mail came through on her Blackberry from Coleman's campaign manager Cullen Sheehan, asking for Franken's phone number. This was the formalized dance of all election endings: the campaign managers communicate, the loser calls the winner.

From his St. Paul home, Coleman telephoned Franken at his Minneapolis townhouse, and these two former New Yorkers who had fought sometimes uncivilly for this very expensive Minnesota Senate seat conducted a civil conversation. "I told him it's the best job that he'll ever have, representing the people of Minnesota in the United States Senate," Coleman reported later. Countered Franken, "I said, 'Norm, it couldn't have been closer.' And I said to him that Franni and I can only imagine what this is like for him and his family." At the end, two men who didn't really like each other were pros. No doubt it was a tougher task for Coleman than Franken.

By 1:47 p.m., Coleman spokesman Tom Erickson announced a news conference in the small backyard of Coleman's house, the first public signal that concession was in the air. At 2:30, as TV camera crews assembled, Erickson threw the UpTake's Noah Kunin out of Coleman's backyard, a final, petty ejection for the news organization most responsible for beaming the recount to the world.

Gray clouds moved through a white sky as Coleman emerged from the back door of his house slightly past 3:00 p.m. His wife, Laurie, who had become a focus of the campaign in its final days, was in Rome, Italy. Coleman was accompanied by his college-age daughter, Sarah. His powder-blue shirt was open at the collar. His khakis were neat, his loafers brown.

"The Supreme Court of Minnesota has spoken. It's time for Minnesota to come together under the leaders it has chosen," Coleman said. "Sure I wanted to win . . . Not just for myself but for my wonderful supporters and the important values I have always fought for. I also thought it was important to stand up for enfranchising thousands of Minnesotans whose votes weren't counted like the others were. After all, issues and politicians come and go, but voting is fundamental. It is the essence of democracy so I knew we needed to do everything we could to get it right."

Then he said, "We have reached the point where further litigation damages the unity of our state, which is also fundamental. In these tough times, we all need to focus on the future. And the future today is we have a new United States senator."

One Franken backer called Coleman "a master manipulator." And, of course, Coleman had a history of wavering with the changing political winds, but on this day, at this moment, he crafted a soft landing to this turbulent ride, and even pivoted to begin repairing an image for, perhaps, a run at yet another office some day. He did not evoke pity—at which he is also skilled—but produced a certain amount of sympathy. A skilled politician, Coleman was pitch-perfect.

"I don't reach this point with any big regrets," he said. "I ran the campaign I wanted. I conducted the legal challenge I wanted. And I have always believed you do the best you can and leave the results up to a higher authority. I'm at peace with that. As to my future plans, that's a subject for another day."

By 4:20 p.m., with curiosity seekers lining both sides of South Tenth Street in the Elliot Park neighborhood near downtown Minneapolis, it was Franken's turn. This was not a good-bye garden affair like Coleman's. This was an energetic urban show, as the senator-elect emerged joyous through the front door of his home, holding hands with Franni. Celebratory balloons were attached to a nearby table of coffee and brownies. As he took his position behind the microphones, Franken, in a blue suit and a multi-colored blue tie, was as senatorial as he could be. For the third time in six months he declared victory: once when the state Canvassing

Board said he had won in January, once when the ThreeJudgePanel declared he had won in April, and now with the ultimate legal stamp of approval.

"I promise to do my best to work hard to stand on principle when I believe I must and, yes, to compromise when I believe that that is in the best interests of the people of Minnesota," said Franken, already sending the message that he was not going to be a comedic left-wing nut, but a sober politician. "We have a lot of work to do in Washington, but that's why I signed up for the job in the first place . . . When you win an election this close, you know that not one bit of effort went to waste . . . I can't wait to get started."

At 5:19 p.m., after Franken ended his victory event, Coleman tweeted at his "SenatorColeman" Twitter site, "the minnesota supreme court has spoken. i congratulated al franken shortly before i spoke to the press. sorry i didn't tweet here earlier!"

At 5:51 p.m., Franken sent an e-mail to his supporters. "As Senator-elect, I intend to take our shared vision of progress to Washington and try to do right by every single Minnesotan . . . That's the good news. Now, the bad news. Even though this process has reached its conclusion, we still very much need contributions to our recount fund." His lawyers' bills and legal fees, nearly six million dollars, were soon due.

At 6:15 p.m., at the Governor's Residence on Summit Avenue, a short stroll from Coleman's house, Tim Pawlenty signed Franken's election certificate. Minutes later, in his State Office Building office, not far from the residence, Secretary of State Mark Ritchie countersigned it.

How Minnesotan could it get? It was a Minnesota-nice transition to the max. In Washington later, Elias surfed the Web. He read reports of Coleman's "gracious tone" at his concession. Elias harrumphed to himself. "Only in Minnesota does a guy get eight months to concede and is considered gracious," he grumbled. Elias celebrated with colleagues at the Perkins Coie offices, but in this complete and total victory, he still couldn't swallow Minnesota's penchant for process and, sometimes faux, civility.

Minnesota's "legal culture," as Justice Paul Anderson called it, was different from Florida's or Washington's. In Minnesota, as Anderson wrote in December during the state Supreme Court's darkest recount hour, "Sometimes, the wheels of justice and due process take time to fully turn . . . I have complete confidence that ultimately the right thing will be done . . ."

CHAPTER FIFTEEN

THUMBS-UP

"I do."

July 7, 2009, broke in Washington as a warm, but not oppressively so, summer day. It fell exactly thirty-five Tuesdays after Election Day 2008. As had been the case since January, Minnesota was represented by one senator, Amy Klobuchar. The U.S. Senate was in session that morning. Various senators speechified about the impending confirmation of a new U.S. Supreme Court justice, Sonia Sotomayor, the revving-up debate over national health care reform, and the sad death of a heroic soldier in Afghanistan. Gradually, the gallery began to fill as young congressional staffers and curious tourists sought to be there when Alan Stuart Franken, fifty-eight, was sworn in as the fortieth U.S. senator from Minnesota, to see the former comedian officially became a serious public servant, and to witness the punctuation mark on the historic recount.

Soon, key characters took their seats in the balcony of the statue-filled chamber, a room that feels so much smaller than it appears on C-SPAN nightly. David Lillehaug was among the first to arrive, and it was particularly eerie and emotional for him. Eighteen years earlier, Lillehaug had sat in the same gallery and watched as another client, Paul Wellstone, was sworn in. Hamilton brought along his college-age son, a Senate intern. For Elias, the lawyer for most of the Democrats in the Senate, it was a day of finality. For Schriock, it was a quick underground train ride from the Hart Senate Office Building to the Capitol. She was back at her "real" job as chief of staff to Senator Jon Tester.[1]

Three miles away, at the law offices of Patton Boggs, Ben Ginsberg picked up his telephone. He wasn't in attendance at the Capitol, of course, and feigned a sort of grumpy disinterest. He was reminded that Franken was soon to be sworn in. His reaction? "I'm glad he has a nice day," and that was all he had to say, this man who normally has so much to say.

Franni Franken took her place in the front row of the Senate gallery, the Franken children to her left. Franni noticed something. To her right, three seats were vacant. How convenient. She thought of three people whom she wanted to fill them. Lillehaug and Hamilton were behind her. Elias was across the aisle. Franni Franken summoned them to sit next to her. It was a maternal move that touched all three men. More than a political move that signaled the importance of good lawyering in tight twenty-first-century U.S. elections, it was a genuine gesture of thanks from a grateful client.

At 12:14 p.m., Senate Majority Leader Harry Reid stood and told Vice President Joseph Biden, the president of the Senate, that the body was in session. A beaming Franken, accompanied by Amy Klobuchar and former Minnesota senator and U.S. vice president Walter Mondale, walked briskly down the blue carpet to meet Biden at his raised dais. Franken took in his left hand a Bible lent to him by Paul Wellstone's family, a link in the chain of Minnesota's liberal legacy and Franken's political philosophy. To get to this moment, Franken campaigned or waited for more than two years. He raised more than thirty million dollars to garner just shy of 1.3 million votes. He paid his recount lawyers about six million dollars.

"Please raise your right hand," Biden ordered.

Franni Franken, with Elias, Hamilton, and Lillehaug at her side, and with Schriock sitting with other Franken campaign advisers across the aisle from her, watched from the gallery. She was looking at Biden, and over Al's shoulder. She was about to relax. She heard Biden ask her husband, "Do you solemnly swear that you will support and defend the Constitution of the United States against all enemies, foreign and domestic; that you will bear true faith and allegiance to the same; that you take this obligation freely, without any mental reservation or purpose of evasion; and that you will well and faithfully discharge the duties of the office on which you are about to enter: So help you God?"

"I do," Franken said. The chamber exploded with applause and cheers. From Biden and Mondale to a flurry of gracious Republicans, such as Lamar Alexander, Mitch McConnell, Orrin Hatch, and George Voinovich, Franken received hearty handshakes. Embraces awaited him from John

Kerry, Dianne Feinstein, and Barbara Boxer. The clapping continued. It seemed to be fading. The show seemed over. Credit Franni Franken for owning impeccable staging skills and for creating a surprising encore.

Tall Elias, thin Hamilton, and white-haired Lillehaug moved from their seats into the aisle, making way for Franni Franken to catch up to her husband downstairs. As the men casually prepared to leave the chamber, something remarkable occurred. Below them, just under the balcony, stood senators Harry Reid, Charles Schumer, and Sheldon White-house. The senators' heads were raised as if they were opera singers acknowledging the far reaches of a theater. They pushed their thumbs up toward the ornate Senate ceiling, thick digits of approval directed at Elias, Hamilton, and Lillehaug. Some of the Senate's most powerful Democrats were offering remote high-fives, honoring the lawyers who, for better or worse, had helped Franken win by 312 votes and give the Democrats a potentially filibuster-proof majority. Most legal cases end when a jury comes back with a verdict, Lillehaug was thinking. This one ended when Al Franken raised his right hand and Reid raised his right thumb.[2]

In St. Paul, the Republican Party chairman Tony Sutton issued a statement on the occasion of Franken's swearing-in, a statement that signaled the start of the 2014 Senate campaign, a mere five years away, and that attempted to undermine Franken's legitimacy. "Al Franken has the opportunity to erase the asterisk by his name by standing up for hard-working Minnesotans against the liberal big spenders in Washington who are leaving future generations with crippling debt," Sutton said. "At a time of great economic anxiety, we hope Al Franken will oppose future tax and spending increases and refuse to march in lockstep with those who continue to push us toward socialism." Even on this day, the political war in Minnesota continued.

(On December 24, 2009, almost six months after Franken replaced Coleman, an Obama-backed national health care reform package passed the Senate by a vote of sixty to forty, with all the no votes coming from Republicans, and with Franken's vote making the difference. The Minnesota Senate recount and election contest directly affected the outcome of that legislation. Franken's critical sixtieth vote evaporated a month later when Massachusetts voters sent Republican Scott Brown to the U.S. Senate, shifting the balance to fifty-nine aligned with the Democrats and forty-one Republicans, erasing the possibility of a filibuster-proof chamber.)[3]

Thumbs-Up

In the Old Senate Chambers, a ceremonial swearing-in was reenacted for Franken's family minutes after the official induction. Reporters shouted questions. Photographers snapped pictures as if at a wedding. Franken kibitzed with Biden and Mondale. Politicians hugged and giggled. Elias watched from behind a gaggle of reporters, photographers, and hangers-on. He wanted to personally walk Franken to his very first Senate Democratic caucus meeting, the regular Tuesday lunch. When all the flashes halted, Franken barged out of the Chambers and toward the Ohio Clock Corridor, crowded with senators, journalists, and security. It was a blur of noise and activity, but, at six foot five, Elias stood above it all. Senator Jack Reed of Rhode Island smiled, "Great job, Marc." Schumer, heading to the same luncheon, waved and smiled. Elias lost Franken as he faded into the throngs ahead and toward his meeting. Elias had another appointment to run to, but was stopped by Senator Christopher Dodd, who grabbed his hand, and said, "Marc, congratulations."

He exited the east side of the Capitol, in his typical hurry, past where Biden's motorcade was parked. Muttering about D.C. traffic, he crossed First Street, and wound up at 122 Maryland Avenue, NE, at his Democratic Senatorial Campaign Committee office. It was the very same place where, on Election Night 2008, he had awaited word of the outcome of the Minnesota U.S. Senate race. Now, in a conference room down a dozen steps from that Election Night war room with its flashing screens and his nervous pacing, the chiefs of staff of U.S. senators were meeting. Those chiefs whose bosses were up for reelection in 2010 were gathered for their monthly election-cycle strategy lunch. The system was cranking up once more, a system that, when all is said and done, worked in Minnesota. Minutes after closing the Franken case file, Elias's political biorhythms were restarting as if on a Senate electoral carousel, which is exactly what it is. His dark sports jacket was off now, his white shirt rumpled, sweat formed on his bald head. He walked through the double doors of the Mott House conference room to face a fawning group of senators' aides. They were eager to congratulate him on his eight-month-long legal, public relations, and political job well done.

The doors closed behind him. Marc Elias had stories to tell.

EPILOGUE

I'm no expert. I'm just a sportswriter who took a hiatus to tell a political and legal tale, but there is much to celebrate and lots to wring our hands over about the 2008–9 Minnesota recount and trial. In June 2009, while Minnesotans waited for their Supreme Court to decide the winner in the U.S. Senate election, there was a disputed election in Iran, a recount, demonstrations in the streets, a crackdown against demonstrators, and lots more questions than those about absentee ballots in Carver County.

"Have you folks been following the Iranian elections?" late-night TV comedian David Letterman asked amid both the Minnesota and Iran recounts. "Well, how about this Mahmoud Ahmadinejad? You know, he has won the election now. And people are angry, and they're demanding a recount. And as a matter of fact, the last unofficial count actually had Al Franken ahead."

Funny, but not really. As Joe Friedberg said during his opening statement back in January, "We're very fortunate that we have this methodology for settling the winner of an election . . . Were we in another country, we would settle it a different way, probably with guns and knives." We should not take our civil society for granted.

On the other hand, to the layperson, there were troubling aspects to the Franken–Coleman recount. The process raised the question, Just how much democracy can we afford? The Pollyannaish answer would be that a fair election is priceless. In this case, that would be wrong. This recount was expensive, and there's something uncomfortable about that. Add the legal fees of the Franken and Coleman campaigns together and the tab runs to about $10 million, about $5.7 million for Franken and about $4.4 million for Coleman, according to Federal Election Commission filings and data provided by both campaigns. That's after both campaigns spent about forty million dollars combined to win the U.S. Senate office by November 4. There's something wrong with that picture.

Let's do some other math. There were 2,921,055 votes cast in Minnesota's U.S. Senate race in 2008. Of those votes, 293,830 were absentee ballots, about 10 percent. Of those, about 11,000 were rejected, roughly 4 percent, and during the Canvassing Board process 1,346 were reconsidered. That means out of 2.9 million votes, about 10,000 citizens were deemed to have screwed up, or 0.004 percent. In most elections it wouldn't make a difference, wouldn't come close. Going back a decade, from Jesse Ventura's gubernatorial victory until 2008, there hadn't been a statewide election closer than 49,000 votes. In most years, this rounding error of 10,000 votes would not have even been noticed. Like hundred-year floods, this was the fifty-year recount. It excuses nothing, but this event was rare.

Candidates learned that if you find yourself ahead by two hundred votes after Election Day, do not declare victory and play defense as Norm Coleman did. In sports, teams that come from behind are among the best. Why the Coleman team, why the Republicans, played this game so poorly in the first days after Election Day remains a mystery to me. How a sitting senator could take the position that not all lawful votes should count—as Coleman's team did in the early stages of Franken's absentee-ballot chase—is another mystery. Coleman should have gone on his own hunt. Or, maybe he knew the votes just weren't there.

As much as I thought Marc Elias was far too antsy in trying to dodge the election contest trial, circumvent Minnesota law, and get Franken to Washington, D.C., too soon, I do believe that Minnesota's law should change. Once the Canvassing Board certified Franken's victory on January 5, 2009, he should have been allowed to be seated provisionally in the Senate while Coleman pursued the election contest. Minnesota should have two senators all the time.

In addition, Minnesota should move to early voting to minimize the number of absentee ballots. For a month or so before the traditional Election Day, voting machines should be set up in city halls and county buildings, in shopping malls and schools, for everyone to begin voting. Many states already do it this way. Why do we have to vote on the Tuesday after the first Monday in November? Bring out the machines on October 1 and let the voting begin. If you're away for the entire month, that's fine, go the absentee route, but there is no way that 293,000 Minnesotans would have voted via tricky absentee ballots if there were more days to vote at the polls.

As the result of reforms backed by Secretary of State Mark Ritchie in the wake of the recount, absentee ballot processing was simplified during the 2010 Minnesota legislative session. Instead of signatures needing to match on a voter's application and ballot, an identification number will now be used in Minnesota. Instead of tired poll workers evaluating the legality of an absentee ballot in a precinct on Election Night, all absentee ballots will now be reviewed by local absentee ballot boards.

But Ritchie and other reformers couldn't get the legislature to change the silly requirement that a witness, who is a registered voter, must certify an absentee ballot for it to be legally cast. That's too bad. To me, the requirement to have a witness is unnecessary.

Absentee voters should self-certify their ballots, just as they do their tax returns. There's no history of fraud in Minnesota's elections, and there's no reason to think it will start now. If it does, there's always jail for the crooks.

I've heard from some Coleman supporters—and it's been written in some "semirespectable" news outlets, such as the *Wall Street Journal*— that "Coleman won the election but lost the recount." The *Journal* wrote in an editorial soon after the Supreme Court ruled:

> The unfortunate lesson is that you don't need to win the vote on Election Day as long as your lawyers are creative enough to have enough new or disqualified ballots counted after the fact...What Mr. Franken understood was that courts would later be loathe to overrule decisions made by the canvassing board, however arbitrary those decisions were. Mr. Coleman didn't lose the election. He lost the fight to stop the state canvassing board from changing the vote-counting rules after the fact...Mr. Franken now goes to the Senate having effectively stolen an election.

The state Canvassing Board became the decisive venue for this election, far more than the election contest court. That is true. It became more than ministerial, that was obvious. When it got into a bind, it sought opinions from the attorney general's office, a political operation, to be sure. But, the last time I looked, the board included two Republican Supreme Court Justices, including the chief justice, who did the Minnesotan right thing: count uncounted votes, not "disqualified ballots."

When Coleman was unhappy, he went where he had a right to go, to the Minnesota Supreme Court, which ginned up a solution that also included counting some previously uncounted ballots. (Hopefully, that Supreme Court order, allowing the candidates to block ballots, will not be considered the law of the land. That was an abomination.)

Were there problems? You betcha, but riddle me this: if Coleman's lawyers would have gotten their way at the trial — after their deathbed conversion — and had a chance to open up all the illegal ballots they wanted to open, would that have changed the results of the election back to the former senator? I would hazard a guess that the answer is no. Indeed, if I were a Coleman supporter, I would have been careful what I wished for. Just look at the results of the opening of absentee ballots by the Canvassing Board on January 3 — ballots his lawyers approved — and then at the trial court on April 7. Coleman got smashed both times. The votes for Mr. Coleman weren't in those envelopes. The votes for Coleman had already been counted.

Good data, strong arguments, passionate public relations, and creative good lawyering all helped, but algorithms and spreadsheets didn't win this election. Votes did. And stolen? If so, it was a theft in plain view of a dozen judges, four of whom sat on the state Canvassing Board, the three-judge trial panel picked by the Supreme Court, and a five-judge Minnesota Supreme Court, with three judges appointed by Republican governors. All thieves, no doubt.

As American politics become more and more polarized, as third-party candidates or challengers to endorsed party candidates increase, it seems to me the likelihood of recounts accelerates, perhaps even more so in primary elections than general elections. Voting machines — at least in Minnesota — are better than 99 percent accurate. They are not the problem. Humans are the problem. Democracy is a human exercise. What we need to do, with early voting, with provisional election certificates, with no-witness absentee voting, with simpler ballots, perhaps with a more-compressed election contest timeline, is work to reduce the sense of chaos.

As for Minnesota's particular flavor of recount, the *Washington Post* put it best:

> Minnesota's . . . election finally has been settled and the candidate with the greatest number of votes, as determined by the canvassing apparatus and the courts . . . now has assumed his office. The delay was embarrassing

to the candidates, to the election machinery, to the canvassing boards, to the courts and to the citizens. Yet, in retrospect, the State of Minnesota has occasion to congratulate itself. The complete canvass of the returns disclosed no evidence of fraud, corruption, ballot stuffing or other deliberate irregularity... Such a close contest could easily provoke chaos in a less settled society. The calm and orderly demeanor of Minnesotans in a difficult and trying situation is a tribute to their political stability and maturity, and to their faith in democratic government.

What's so powerful about that editorial is that it was written in *1962,* following the completion of the Andersen–Rolvaag recount. Punched and sullied, subject to hiccups and verbal attacks, the Minnesota legal and political culture in 2008 and 2009 showed a more-modern demeanor than it did in 1962 and '63, with all the pressures and dollars of Washington peering over Minnesota's shoulders. So, calm? No. Relatively orderly, I think so.

Bush v. Gore and *Coleman v. Franken* will long be mentioned in the same legal breaths by scholars and practitioners, but there was no biased decision by the U.S. Supreme Court in the Minnesota case, there were no attempts by any maverick secretary of state to shut down the recount as in 2000, no intervention by the legislature, no fudging with voter intent, no hard-and-fast deadlines forcing a decision. Statutes, rules, and standards, if not always followed, existed and ballots were reexamined once, twice, thrice. Transparency abounded. Minnesota 2008 was not Florida 2000, not by a long shot.

ACKNOWLEDGMENTS

Many people helped me during the course of reporting and writing this book. Thanks to Todd Orjala, senior editor at the University of Minnesota Press, for his confidence and patience; to reporters Pat Kessler of WCCO-TV, Curt Brown of the *Star Tribune,* Tom Hauser of KSTP-TV, Bill Wareham and Elizabeth Baier at Minnesota Public Radio, and Noah Kunin at the UpTake for supplying me with audio, video, and recollections to aid in my reporting.

Special thanks to key players in the recount: Marc Elias, Kevin Hamilton, David Lillehaug, Charlie Nauen, Chris Sautter, Stephanie Schriock, Jess McIntosh, Andy Barr, J. D. Schlough, Eric Schultz, Will Rava, Ezra Reese, Kate Andrias, Lisa Marshall Manheim, Bob Bauer, Alana Petersen, Jeff Blodgett, Dan Cramer, Andy Bechhoefer, Dusty Trice, Mark Drake, Tom Erickson, Joe Friedberg, Fritz Knaak, James Langdon, Tony Trimble, Matt Haapoja, Cullen Sheehan, John Aiken, Jim Gelbmann, Kate Mohn, Gary Poser, Pat Turgeon, Mark Ritchie, and Chris Channing. Thanks to Franni Franken.

Thanks for guidance from Minnesota Supreme Court experts Fred Grittner, Peter Knapp, John Kostouros, and Robin Wolpert; to election law experts Ned Foley, Joe Mansky, Raleigh Levine, and Rachel Smith, who aided me with thoughts and reviews of technical aspects; and to authors of two key historical books, *Recount* by Ronald F. Stinnett and Charles H. Backstrom and *Too Close to Call* by Jeffrey Toobin.

Thanks to Eric Black, Roger Buoen, and Joel and Laurie Kramer at MinnPost.com, with special appreciation to Don Effenberger and Corey Anderson, the editors who stayed up at all hours to post my stories over the course of eight months during coverage of the recount. Thanks to Garvin Davenport for close reading of early versions of the manuscript and to Bill Glauber for his constant support throughout the project. Thanks to copy editor Pam Price.

Thanks to Judges Edward Cleary, Kathleen Gearin, Elizabeth Hayden, Kurt Marben, and Denise Reilly for their on-the-record cooperation.

Thanks to Sam, Hilda, and Ed Weiner for a lifetime of encouragement, and to John and Kristy Juergens for their kindnesses over the past twenty-five years. Thanks to sons Henry and Nate for your support, and to Waldo T. Weiner for providing vigilant security as I wrote. Immeasurable thanks go to my wife, Ann Juergens, to whom this book is lovingly dedicated.

KEY MOMENTS THAT SHAPED
THE RECOUNT

APRIL 18, 2001 Vice President Dick Cheney calls Minnesota legislator Tim Pawlenty to tell him Norm Coleman is the White House's choice to challenge incumbent Paul Wellstone.

OCTOBER 25, 2002 Paul Wellstone, his wife, his daughter, and five others are killed in plane crash.

OCTOBER 30, 2002 Memorial service for Wellstone. Comedian and writer Al Franken attends. Some conservatives criticize the tone of the event.

NOVEMBER 5, 2002 Norm Coleman wins the U.S. Senate seat, defeating Walter Mondale.

APRIL 13, 2003 Franken writes a *Star Tribune* Op-Ed piece chiding Coleman for claiming he is "a 99 percent improvement over Paul Wellstone."

OCTOBER 14, 2003 Franken attends a publication party in Minnesota for a book about Wellstone, where someone encourages him to run for office. In his book *Lies and the Lying Liars Who Tell Them* he refers to "a suit named Norm Coleman."

SPRING 2005 Franken says he will move back to Minnesota after years in New York and conduct his liberal radio talk show from Minneapolis. Later in the year, he forms a political action group.

2006   Franken campaigns throughout Minnesota for DFL candidates and prepares for his own run.

FEBRUARY 14, 2007   Franken announces his candidacy for Coleman's Senate seat.

JUNE 7, 2008   Franken wins the DFL endorsement.

JUNE 12, 2008   Coleman sets the theme of his campaign against Franken: "It's not good enough just to criticize, not good enough to tear something down."

JULY 16, 2008   Dean Barkley, Independence Party candidate, enters the race.

FALL 2008   The Franken and Coleman campaigns each raise about twenty million dollars. Advertisements from both candidates aggressively attack. Polls fluctuate.

NOVEMBER 4, 2008   Nearly three million Minnesotans go to the polls, giving Barack Obama 54 percent of the presidential vote; Coleman and Franken, about 42 percent each; and Barkley, 16 percent. Once all the results are in, Coleman leads by 215 votes, triggering an automatic statewide hand recount.

NOVEMBER 19, 2008   The recount begins.

DECEMBER 30, 2008   The state Canvassing Board results show Franken wins the recount by forty-nine votes.

JANUARY 3, 2009   Counting additional absentee ballots lifts the Franken lead to 225 votes.

JANUARY 5, 2009   The Canvassing Board certifies Franken's victory.

JANUARY 6, 2009   Coleman files an election contest petition.

JANUARY 26, 2009   The election contest trial begins.

MARCH 13, 2009   The trial ends.

Key Moments

APRIL 7, 2009   Additional votes are counted. Franken's lead grows to 312 votes. Final tally: Franken 1,212,629; Coleman 1,212,317; others 469,109.

APRIL 13, 2009   The ThreeJudgePanel rules that Franken is the winner of the election. Coleman appeals.

JUNE 1, 2009   The Minnesota Supreme Court hears arguments on Coleman's appeal.

JUNE 30, 2009   The state Supreme Court affirms the trial court ruling. Franken wins. Governor Tim Pawlenty and Secretary of State Mark Ritchie sign the election certificate.

JULY 7, 2009   Alan Stuart Franken, fifty-eight, is sworn in as Minnesota's junior U.S. senator.

NOTES

1. EXTRA INNINGS

1. Franken raised a total of $22,502,124 in 2008. Coleman raised $19,298,843, according to Federal Election Commission data. Of all the U.S. Senate candidates in the 2008 cycle, they ranked first and second in spending nationally. They raised additional funds after Election Day 2008 to help pay for the recount and election contest.

2. HUNTING FOR BALLOTS

1. The Florida recount in the 2000 presidential election was en route to being larger than Minnesota's until the U.S. Supreme Court aborted it.

3. NEW SHERIFF IN TOWN

1. Louisiana differs much from Minnesota, but wildly so in seating U.S. senators. In Louisiana, while the election result is contested, the person with the most votes takes her seat in Washington while the contest is underway. Landrieu was a senator while Jenkins fought her victory. In a Minnesota election contest, a U.S. senator isn't sworn in until the Minnesota courts rule that the governor and the secretary of state can sign the formal election certificate. This is a battle Elias would fight during this 2008 recount, and soundly lose.

2. Later, Republican activists would lament that Magnuson and Anderson were two of the most conservative justices on the Supreme Court. By placing them on the Canvassing Board, Ritchie, in some Machiavellian way, effectively removed them from any Supreme Court decisions because, having served on the

Canvassing Board, they would not ethically be able to review their own decisions from the Supreme Court bench. Such a conspiracy theory presumed that (1) Ritchie harangued two Supreme Court justices to volunteer and step into this trap and (2) Ritchie knew in the fall of 2008 that the Franken–Coleman matter would reach the Supreme Court numerous times. The whole theory was groundless and laughable.

4. THE COUNT AT THE TABLE

1. Ronald F. Stinnett and Charles Herbert Backstrom, *Recount* (Washington, D.C.: National Document Publishers, 1964).

2. It should be noted that, once it became known that Lillehaug sent letters to county auditors, the Coleman campaign followed up with their own similar letters and requests.

3. Sometimes election workers don't properly label a duplicate; that's what Coleman's lawyers claimed later in the case. The result is that, during a recount, there's the possibility of counting a voter's original *and* duplicate ballots, or so-called double counting. Coleman's lawyers were never able to prove that, although there was suspicion that double counting occurred in various precincts, perhaps benefiting both candidates, and not enough to alter the election's outcome. There's another possibility, and Franken's lawyers theorized this: Sometimes election workers pulled aside a torn original with the intention of filling out a duplicate, but simply forgot to fill out the duplicate, leaving the original uncounted. These are some of the circumstances that Rule Nine anticipated.

5. WHY ARE WE EVEN HERE?

1. Mark Preston, "Coleman Becomes Big Draw," *Roll Call,* April 7, 2003.

2. Al Franken, "Norm and the Other One Percent," *Star Tribune,* April 13, 2003.

3. Rob Hotakainen, "Franken for Senate?" *Star Tribune,* May 24, 2004, page 9A.

4. *When a Man Loves a Woman,* 1994, and *Stuart Saves His Family,* 1995.

5. Kevin Diaz and Conrad Wilson, "Franken's Porn Story Has Party in a Lather," *Star Tribune,* May 30, 2008, page B1.

6. In exit polls conducted by NBC, women preferred Franken over Coleman, 45 percent to 38 percent, with Barkley scoring higher with women voters than he did with men. But Obama's support among women in Minnesota was 12 percentage points better than Franken's.

Notes

7. Ken Silverstein, "Senator Norm Coleman Gets by with a Little Help From His Friends," Harpers.com, October 6, 2008.

8. Patricia Lopez, "Coleman Withdraws His Negative Ads," *Star Tribune*, October 11, 2008, page B1.

9. Minnesota Public Radio–Humphrey Institute Poll, Center for the Study of Politics and Governance, Lawrence R. Jacobs and Joanne M. Miller, late October 2008.

8. SOLDIERING AHEAD

1. Stinnett and Backstrom, *Recount*. This is the essential, out-of-print, numbers-heavy account of the 1962 recount and election contest.

2. The Minnesota Supreme Court's 2008 decision on the fifth pile, by the way, cited the Andersen case on fixing "obvious errors" when it reopened the matter of wrongly rejected absentee ballots.

3. Relevant Fourteenth Amendment excerpt: "No State shall make or enforce any law which shall abridge the privileges or immunities of citizens of the United States; nor shall any State deprive any person of life, liberty, or property, without due process of law; nor deny to any person within its jurisdiction the equal protection of the laws."

4. Minnesota Statutes § 204C.40, subdivisions 1 and 2.

9. REINFORCEMENTS ARRIVE

1. Under the small-world category, the Ramsey County District Court judge who fined the elder Coleman $128 and twenty-four hours of community service was Canvassing Board member Kathleen Gearin.

2. Dave Orrick, "Coleman Hopes to Tap War Chest for Defense," *Pioneer Press*, December 19, 2008, Main section.

3. Paul Levy, "Friedberg's Law," *Star Tribune*, November 8, 1992.

4. Months after Franken was sworn in, Andrias left Perkins Coie to join Bob Bauer in the White House Counsel's office.

10. PULLING A 180

1. This author was MinnPost's regular man on the scene.

14. THE HUMAN ELEMENT

1. Anderson's comments here are from a series of public forums or speaking presentations, including a meeting with visiting lawyers from Kyrgyzstan, an

237

interview with independent Minnesota broadcaster Curtis Beckmann on December 13, 2009, and a lecture at Duke University Law School on November 23, 2009.

2. Jay Weiner, "Coleman–Franken Senate Race: The Day the Recount Ended and the Fight Turned into Something Really Nice," MinnPost.com, June 30, 2009. www.minnpost.com/stories/2009/06/30/9950/coleman-franken_senate_race_the_day_the_recount_ended_and_the_fight_turned_into_something_really_nice. Comment of William Mitchell College of Law Professor Raleigh Levine.

3. Edward B. Foley, "Impressive Unanimity: The Historical Significance of Coleman v. Franken," Election Law @ Moritz "Free & Fair" blog, June 30, 2009, http://moritzlaw.osu.edu/electionlaw/comments/articles.php?ID=6535.

15. THUMBS-UP

1. By January 2010, Schriock was named president of the women's political advocacy group EMILY's List.

2. The kudos grew more impressive that night at a Franken celebration dinner. Among those in attendance were Mickey Hart and Bob Weir, two members of the legendary rock band the Grateful Dead. When Franken told the guests at the celebration that his legal team was in the room, the crowd erupted into a standing ovation. "I just got a standing ovation from two members of the Grateful Dead," Kevin Hamilton remembered. "That never happened before."

3. When Brown won his election, some Democrats suggested delaying his swearing-in so they could jam a final health care reform bill through the Senate. Franken opposed that, and told Minnesota Public Radio, "This is a substantial enough victory that he should be seated as soon as legally possible. He won by 100,000 votes, which was about 100,000 more votes than I won by."

INDEX

Index

Index

147, 148–49, 176, 214, 227; voting
machines, 98, 226. *See also*
absentee ballots

Wall Street Journal (newspaper),
30–31, 169, 225
Wardheer News (newspaper), 82
Warner, Mark, 5
Washington Post (newspaper), 11, 76,
161, 226–27
WCCO radio, 152, 169
Weinstine, Robert, 83
Wellstone, Paul, 33; Coleman on,
65–66; death, 3, 5, 65, 66–67, 85,
118; and Elias, 36; and Franken, 3,
64, 65; legacy, 46, 55; and Lille-
haug, 50, 55, 218; and Ritchie, 90
Wellstone, Sheila, 67

West Publishing, 163
Whitehouse, Sheldon, 220
Whitford, Bradley, 47
Wicker, Roger, 8
Wilder, Douglas, 51
Winona Daily News (newspaper), 82
Winthrop & Weinstine (law firm), 157
Wolfson, Howard, 76
women voters, 75
Woodword, Bob, 51
Wright, J. Skelly, 178
Wright County (Minn.), 59

Yale Law Journal, 162
Young, Jack: *The Recount Primer,* 9
Young, John Hardin, 48

Zoll, David, 165

JAY WEINER reported on the 2008 U.S. Senate recount and election contest for MinnPost.com, a Minneapolis–St. Paul news Web site. For his coverage, he received Minnesota's prestigious Frank Premack Public Affairs Journalism Award. A longtime Twin Cities sportswriter, he is the author of *Stadium Games: Fifty Years of Big League Greed and Bush League Boondoggles* (Minnesota, 2000). He lives and works in St. Paul.